Writing Winning Proposals

PR Cases

Tom Hagley

University of Oregon

PEARSON

Boston   New York   San Francisco
Mexico City   Montreal   Toronto   London   Madrid   Munich   Paris
Hong Kong   Singapore   Tokyo   Cape Town   Sydney

Series Editor:	Molly Taylor
Series Editorial Assistant:	Suzanne Stradley
Senior Marketing Manager:	Mandee Eckersley
Senior Production Editor:	Karen Mason
Editorial Production Service:	Stratford Publishing Services
Composition Buyer:	Linda Cox
Manufacturing Buyer:	JoAnne Sweeney
Design & Electronic Composition:	Stratford Publishing Services
Cover Administrator:	Joel Gendron

For related titles and support materials, visit our online catalog at www.ablongman.com.

Between the time Web site information is gathered and then published, it is not unusual for some sites to have closed. Also, the transcription of URLs can result in typographical errors. The publisher would appreciate notification where these errors occur so that they may be corrected in subsequent editions.

Many of the designations used by manufacturers and sellers to distinguish their products are claimed as trademarks. Where those designations appear in this book, and Allyn & Bacon was aware of a trademark claim, the designations have been printed in initial caps.

Library of Congress Cataloging-in-Publication Data
Hagley, Tom.
    Writing winning proposals : PR cases / Tom Hagley.—1st ed.
        p. cm.
    Includes index.
    ISBN 0-205-46101-8 (alk. paper)
        1. Public relations. 2. Proposal writing in the social sciences. 3. Communication in organizations. I. Title.

HD59.H214 2006
658.4'53—dc22   2005045949

Printed in the United States of America

10 9 8 7 6 5 4 3   10 09

Dedicated to my students
who enabled me to learn how to teach them
what they must know to succeed in public relations

And to my loving wife Peggy,
whose support through the years
contributed so much to the success of my
professional career, which is the foundation
for this book

Contents

Foreword

*f*inally, thanks to this book, Tom Hagley will be a permanent part of my classroom. I first became acquainted with Tom when I was teaching at the University of Georgia and have been scheming ever since to get him into my classroom whenever possible. He was director of public and investor relations for Alumax, a Fortune 200 company located in Atlanta, when he became a favored guest lecturer and internship mentor in the Grady College of Journalism and Mass Communication. In addition to bringing his considerable experience to the classroom, Tom provided the students with structure, guidance, and an opportunity to grow—the same ingredients that make his new text a must for our classrooms.

When Tom retired from his distinguished career as an executive in corporate and agency public relations—with a stint running his own public relations firm thrown in for good measure—I was teaching at the Missouri School of Journalism. I tried to recruit Tom, knowing that he had spent three decades striving to make the profession better in every way. Tom is committed to embracing innovation as a basis for tempering the metal and sharpening the edge of the profession. Although we competed unsuccessfully with the lures of the Northwest, I now feel that we have finally captured Tom by way of his wonderful textbook. It's not the same thing as having an experienced, compassionate, creative professional in our classroom, but it is the next best thing.

His book is a great piece of work. I say that with respect to its contents, but even more so with respect to the author. *Writing Winning Proposals* comes from a person I always believed was destined to take the "real world" to the classroom. I saw that when Tom spoke to my classes at the University of Georgia and the Missouri School of Journalism. He has a passion for teaching, coaching, and counseling. He listens, recognizes, shares, encourages, tolerates, and even admits his own mistakes to those he mentors. His internship assignments made students stretch far beyond what they thought they ever could do with so little experience.

It is no surprise that in this book he insists on writing by the rules to develop winning proposals. He comes to academe knowing precisely what executive managers want from public relations practitioners. In this book he shows students, as well as seasoned professionals, how to develop winning plans and challenges them to apply the rules in providing solutions to a number of diverse cases requiring public relations action. To add excitement to the challenge he presents each case in a different way, such as role play between hostile parents versus a high school principal, a city contract, a transcription of a private staff meeting, client notes by a practitioner, and more.

Tom packed up 30 years of successful experience, notably including executive positions with Alcoa and Alumax and as a vice president of Hill & Knowlton, Inc., and made a place for himself on the campus of one of the nation's major research universities. After only three years of full-time teaching at the University of Oregon he is bringing to market a text that takes a giant step up to pop the fat balloons of ambiguity in the public relations profession by showing how to propose services for which clients will readily pay and in which employers will readily invest.

I can see by his painstaking use of examples in this text how this challenge was undertaken in classroom instruction. I can also appreciate how painstaking it will be for some seasoned practitioners to break from timeworn methods of proposal writing with hit and miss successes to exercise the discipline necessary to write by the rules to produce winning proposals on a consistent basis. Yet I highly recommend the book to professionals who definitely will find it worth their time. Tom Hagley is reaching out with this book to campuses around the country and to new generations of writers who will learn to practice the profession with a new paradigm of precision that judges of the profession's prestigious competitions will applaud and that clients and employers will welcome with respect.

Glen T. Cameron, Ph.D.
Maxine Wilson Gregory Chair in Journalism Research
Missouri School of Journalism

Introduction

Writing by the rules creates winning proposals. Some of you are reading this book because you want to learn how to write winning proposals. Some of you are experienced in writing public relations plans and are curious about what I have to say about rules for writing winning plans. And some of you would like to see how the techniques presented here apply to writing proposals for related areas of communication designed to influence the behavior of people. This book is designed to benefit plan developers in all areas of the communication profession.

Students of public relations, as well as seasoned practitioners anywhere in the world, will be challenged by this book to achieve a level of clarity and credibility seldom seen even in award-winning public relations plans. The challenge lies in understanding how planning relates to public relations, knowing what is involved in the planning process, and being able to apply specific rules in writing the components of a public relations plan.

What distinguishes this book is that its instruction is presented from the perspective of those who review public relations plans and communication proposals and authorize the resources necessary for their implementation. In short, it tells specifically what reviewers want to see in a plan and how they want the information to be presented.

With this book you can study the basics of developing a plan and apply your skills as an individual or in a team in solving problems, seizing opportunities, or meeting challenges in 10 diverse, real-world case situations, all of which have compelling needs for public relations action. The cases have been classroom tested over seven quarters in university-level instruction and have proved to be effective lessons for a classroom or professional workshop environment. An instructor's manual is available that is a compendium of sample plans and individual assignments written by the rules presented in this book.

Something in your interest brought you to this book, now it's my job to make your effort worthwhile by showing you how to develop plans with the potential for becoming winning proposals.

We would like to thank the reviewers of this text for their helpful suggestions: Signe Cutrone, Tulane University; Lisa Irby, Washington State University; Robert M. Kucharavy, Syracuse University; and Don Stacks, University of Miami.

about the author

An **accomplished instructor** of public relations, Tom Hagley teaches principles, writing, plans, and campaigns courses for the School of Journalism and Communication at the University of Oregon. He has been welcomed as a guest instructor at the University of Georgia, Missouri School of Journalism–Columbia, Linfield College, and the University of Portland. He was inspired to teach by experiences over five years with 21 interns from the Henry W. Grady College of Journalism and Mass Communication at the University of Georgia, where his program was regarded as one of the best the school offered.

Hagley is a **consummate professional** with 30 years of progressive experience as a corporate public and investor relations executive, private consultant, worldwide public relations agency executive, and metropolitan daily newspaper reporter. He managed staffs and annual program budgets of up to $6.5 million, including the title sponsorship of an IndyCar racing team and $10 million in corporate philanthropic contributions. He directed corporate communication in publicizing a company's rapidly rising value from its spin-off as a public entity in November 1993, through a corporate takeover attempt, to the acquisition of Alumax Inc., by Alcoa in 1998 that formed the world's largest aluminum producer with a combined company of 100,000 employees in 250 locations in 30 countries with 1998 revenues of $15.3 billion.

A **published writer**, Hagley is recognized nationally by public relations practitioners and educators as a major contributor to the field. He has published many articles in business and professional journals, including five featured in *The Strategist*, which is published by the Public Relations Society of America. A master of all forms of public relations writing, including plans, congressional testimony, executive speeches, a white paper that the U.S. trade representative selected as a base document in solving an international trade crisis, and persuasive documents, such as a grant requested and received from the federal government totalling $1.25 million for before- and after-school programs for a public school district.

chapter 1

Understanding Why Planning Is Important and How It Relates to Public Relations

Why is it important to learn how to write a public relations plan or program? Here are four reasons:

The first reason is that a plan is the instrument used to propose and obtain approval for executing public relations activities. Executive managers who have responsibility for allocating an organization's resources require various methods, such as a traditional request for authorization, that provide a basis for evaluating expenditures. A public relations plan serves as a proposal to spend a certain amount of an organization's time and money on public relations activities over several weeks, months, a year, or more. The components of a plan provide the information necessary for managers to evaluate proposed public relations activities and approve their execution. Plans are not a fixed blueprint; they must be adaptable to changing conditions and fine-tuned for effectiveness.

Another reason it is important to learn how to write a public relations plan is that a plan provides a mechanism for measuring results of public relations activities. A good plan includes objectives with measurable outcomes. This provides plan reviewers with evidence that a plan is making progress toward achieving the plan's goal. It also provides a sound basis for evaluating the results of a plan and educating reviewers in the power of public relations.

The third reason it is important to learn how to write a public relations plan is that a plan is a product, the quality of which can distinguish its developer as a star among practitioners of all levels of experience. Because the public relations industry in recent years has seen so little in the way of high-quality plans, a well-conceived plan will easily take on a brilliance that wins approvals and adds credibility to the profession.

Communication professionals who serve as judges for the industry's most prestigious Silver Anvil award competition sponsored each year by the Public Relations Society of America review hundreds of public relations plan entries. Judges are outspoken in saying that many industry professionals need to go back and learn the basics of developing successful public relations plans. The criticism is leveled at all but the few plans selected for recognition.

The fourth reason is that a plan often serves as a structure for orchestrating the timing of related activities in marketing or advertising.

So it is important to learn how to write a public relations plan because a plan is the instrument used to propose and obtain approvals, it is a mechanism for monitoring and evaluating, it is a product that distinguishes true public relations professionals, and it is a structure for orchestrating related communication activities. Yet to fully appreciate how planning relates to public relations, it is necessary to know precisely what public relations is and what can be expected of its practice.

What exactly is public relations? I like to challenge people to define public relations in two words. Other professions define themselves in two words—doctors practice medicine, lawyers practice law, accountants keep records. People in these disciplines define their work succinctly, issue invoices, and get paid accordingly for their expertise. Not everyone in public relations can receive compensation so readily for their work because many people—yes, many people—in public relations cannot define what they do. And if you can't define what you do, you can't measure what you do. If you can't measure what you do, you can't evaluate what you do. If you can't evaluate what you do, no one will pay for what you do.

To arrive at a two-word definition of public relations, I looked back over the years, made a list of untold numbers of projects and programs I had completed, and summarized them. I convinced people to support, to vote, to consider, to learn, to champion, to follow, to testify, to read, to buy, to trust, to invest, to listen, to become informed, to join, to leave alone, to contribute, to believe, to participate, to think, to work, to authorize, to accept, to welcome, to compromise, to accommodate, to cooperate, to wait, to attend, to decide, and the list went on and on and on. As I worked on this list, the common denominator, the two-word definition, became perfectly clear. In public relations, we influence behavior.

Whose behavior do we influence? The answer for a public corporation, a private company, or a not-for-profit organization is the same. We influence the behavior of anyone who has or could have an effect—positive or negative—on the organization's ultimate performance. This includes employees, suppliers, customers, shareholders, industry and financial analysts, labor unions, voters, government regulators, special interest groups, individual opinion shapers on the Internet, and many more.

Is this ethical? Of course it's ethical. The ethical principles applied to public relations are no different than those applied to any other profession. Is it ethical to convince someone to replace a heart, a tooth, a roof, or a brake cylinder? Certainly it's ethical if one does, in fact, need to be replaced.

How do we influence behavior? We influence behavior through strategic planning and communication. True expertise in strategic planning and communication is the work of masters. I call it the "magic of the profession" because it requires talent and skills that few public relations practitioners possess and for which fewer still get proper recognition. Strategic communication requires knowledge, skills, and problem-solving experience in the dynamics of persuasion, human interaction, and communication design.

The following characteristics define strategic communication:

1. creative, skillfully planned, managed, and measurable;

2. authoritative;

3. transmitted and received;

4. targeted at individuals or groups;

5. specifically designed to influence behavior.

How do we evaluate the effectiveness of our strategic planning and communication? The answer, simply, is, Did we influence behavior or not? Public relations, then, is the practice of influencing behavior through strategic planning and communication. Planning is the central function in this process.

chapter 2

Meeting the Challenges of the Planning Environment

*P*ublic relations plans are developed in many different environments—publicly owned and privately owned companies, governmental and nongovernmental organizations, not-for-profit organizations, and various other entities. These environments have characteristics that can have a bearing on how plans are developed, whether or not plans are approved, modified, or rejected, and even whether or not plans succeed. So planning cannot be done in a vacuum. Planners must take into account the characteristics of their respective organizations, which will enable them to understand how to meet the challenges of the planning environment. Let's take a look at some major challenges of the planning environment in three areas: organization, leadership, and resources.

ORGANIZATION

A publicly owned corporation can be mission driven or financially driven. Organizations, of course, can and do fall somewhere between these aims, but for our purposes we will look at organizations as if they are on opposite ends of this spectrum.

In a mission-driven organization, employees are considered the key to success. When employees are motivated by meaningful work they invest more than their time in an organization. They work with a purpose that captures their interest and taps their creativity as they reach out to customers with innovative solutions and extraordinary service. By building relationships with customers, an organization grows in sales, profit, market share, and, ultimately, in overall value to its shareholders.

In a financially driven organization, management tends to take employees for granted and simply goes through the motions of showing respect for other stakeholders. The serious interest is in impressing securities analysts and shareholders with short-term performance improvements—quarterly profits. The focus on profits can be so intense that management will do whatever it takes—acquire this, sell that, lay people off, cut back, borrow more—to obtain an attractive stock price.

Developing a public relations plan in a financially driven organization can be a challenge because management in many cases will be inclined to resist plans that

- don't yield an immediate, virtually guaranteed return;

- propose costly benchmarking or other investigative or evaluative research measures;

- require an investment in the long term for building relationships with any of the organization's stakeholders;

- have strategies requiring consistent values, such as telling the whole truth internally and externally versus spooning it out according to the differing tastes of stakeholder groups;

- offer effective solutions but require added costs of using outside services, such as photographers, graphic designers, multimedia studios, and public relation firms.

Financially driven organizations focus narrowly in a specialized area, such as investor relations, leaving other stakeholder groups in the dark.

Developing plans in a mission-driven organization presents a different challenge. The plan developer is in competition for resources with other areas, such as operations, marketing, sales, customer service, and research and development. However, the allocation of resources is evaluated in terms of the organization's mission, rather than short-term financial goals. Management reviews plans for their potential to benefit all stakeholders. The focus is on investing for the long term.

In a mission-driven organization, management is interested in investing in public relations plans that

- motivate and empower employees to provide innovative, superior service to customers;

- win the loyalty of suppliers, partners, and others in sales channels;

- cultivate long-term working relationships with all stakeholders;

- build trust with customers;

- strengthen the bottom line in terms of economic performance, social investment, community involvement, ethics- and values-based performance, and pro-environmental values.

LEADERSHIP

Let's look next at the challenges of the planning environment in the area of leadership. Approval of public relations plans is, in large part, under the control of executives who have no academic education in public relations. This paradox deserves a deeper look.

Next to the ability to manage people and budgets, public relations skill is the most sought-after attribute in top executives by today's corporations, according to private research by a worldwide human resources organization. Yet few executives have any formal education in public relations and slow progress is being made to equip future business leaders with these critical skills.

Schools with MBA programs develop leaders for businesses and governments throughout the world. What these leaders are taught has an influence on the daily lives of millions of people—an enormous responsibility that business schools try to address with the traditional focus on finance, accounting, and marketing.

But examine the dramatic transformation taking place in the role of chief executive officer and one can easily surmise that market demand for formal public relations training is heading toward academe like a high-speed train. Executive leadership today is about building and maintaining trusting relationships with employees, customers, suppliers, investors, analysts, board members, and all major stakeholder groups. It's about influencing the behavior of people through persuasive communication. It's about showing empathy for others. In sum, it's about public relations.

In this post-Enron world, building relationships with compassion and open, candid communication is imperative for the new generation of business leaders. These core values are critical to corporate America's recovery from the traumatic upheavals of an era of acquisitions, mergers, downsizings, and restructurings that has left employees with feelings of instability, insecurity, and uncertainty about their work and personal lives. Business schools are going to have to offer formal public relations training.

It has been said that chief executive officers (CEOs) are hired for their skills and fired for their personalities. CEOs who entered the business world years ago with no formal training in human relations skills are beginning to yield to executives who are learning to lead as compassionate communicators. But it's a slow and, in some cases, painful transition. For example, I returned from a small-ship exploration of Alaska. We traveled through the pristine areas of Prince William

Sound that are still struggling to survive Exxon's corporate arrogance and spilled oil. It was little more than a decade ago that the chairman of Exxon, Lawrence Rawl, at the time head of the nation's third largest corporation in sales, said, "We would have liked to recall the oil off Prince William Sound. We called, but it didn't hear us." While I was there, I picked up a local newspaper and shook my head in disbelief as I read that Exxon was planning to bring its ill-fated Valdez oil tanker back to operate in Alaska where its presence is sure to rekindle memories of great loss and destruction. Exxon still has much to learn about compassion—about being empathetic to public interests, about corporate responsibility.

Public relations textbooks are revised frequently to include updated cases of corporate leaders failing to live up to public expectations of good citizenship. Why is living up to public expectations of corporate behavior a continuing challenge to corporation after corporation? The problem is the absence of formal public relations training among executive managers. Let's consider what can happen, practically speaking, when a chief executive officer has to manage a crisis situation without formal training in public relations. In such a scenario, a CEO has no basis on which to make self-confident decisions and instead must rely heavily on the advice of others.

In a crisis situation, a CEO often turns to corporate counsel for legal advice. However, some attorneys can be so intimidating about liability issues that they paralyze a CEO into a state of inaction. To satisfy lawyers, the CEO often publicly denies culpability even when video recordings make it obvious that the company is to blame. With solid public relations training to balance legal counsel, a CEO might, as one did, say in a crisis situation, "I've been advised by our law department that the company is not responsible, but we are going to act as though we are." Alternatively, a CEO could hire a PR firm with a track record in successful crisis management, but the CEO without PR training could be putting the fate of an entire enterprise into the hands of experts he or she has little or no skills to evaluate or direct. Finally, a CEO could turn to what Warren Buffett calls the "institutional imperative," or the tendency of executives, "to mindlessly imitate the behavior of their peers, no matter how foolish it may be to do so."

We will continue to see major corporations failing to live up to public expectations of corporate citizenship until the top jobs are filled with executives who have the formal training necessary to feel self-confident in directing the public relations function, building trusting relationships through good communication, and leading with compassion. Developers of public relations plans will continue to be challenged to educate senior executives in the practice of public relations. We know that the profession operates on a body of knowledge in the social sciences that has been developed over many years. We practitioners know how to put that experience to work in all areas of public relations. Many executives have yet to learn even the fundamentals of influencing behavior.

Some plan developers are fortunate to have chief executives who are better educated in public relations and the body of knowledge that supports its practice.

These enlightened executives enjoy working with plan developers. A plan developer can show a CEO, for example, that by understanding and participating in the creative process the chief can have visions that trigger in all stakeholder groups convictions to act in support of an organization's mission.

In a *Business Week* article from early 2003, Jeffrey E. Garten, dean of the Yale School of Management, wrote, "Industry can't climb out of its funk just by cutting costs and meeting quarterly goals. CEOs must bet on their vision." Betting on a vision is a risk that many CEOs are hesitant to take. Some prefer to play it safe, managing costs and fine-tuning strategies. Some prefer to mark time, waiting for economic circumstances to improve. Some have promising visions but lack confidence in their ability to carry them out.

Launching a vision is like launching a ship. If you don't know how to score the bottle, you shouldn't swing the champagne. The result could be an embarrassing clunk, instead of a spectacular splash.

Let's consider what it is like to launch a vision with a leader who understands the principles of influencing behavior. First the leader holds someone accountable for developing the vision. The person held responsible is usually a professional communicator, such as the plan developer. Some executives believe that planting a seed with an individual is the same as assigning an individual to the seed's development. It's a safe position for the executive who doesn't want to risk sharing an idea and possibly being challenged, debated, or criticized about its potential or validity. But there's a big difference between sowing a seed and holding someone accountable for the seed's growth and development. Without a process for development and accountability for driving it, a vision will be no more than a pipe dream.

There is no inherent certainty for a leader that what he or she has in mind as a vision, especially in its embryonic state, is clearly right for the organization. The vision should focus on the organization's mission. However, executives must have the courage to engage in constructive debate. Open, ongoing dialogue with others serves to clarify and perfect a vision. A plan developer shows a leader how to share a vision with others, perhaps in a small brainstorming group or among confidants. The developer knows visionary ideas are fragile. They're not complete. They're not perfect.

A plan developer knows how to shepherd delicate ideas through the creative process and how to pursue all of the pathways of human engineering necessary to energize the interest and action of individuals who have a potential stake in the organization's success. A plan developer is quick to point out that a vision is not a directive. It's not a figment of someone's imagination. It must be an achievable condition, an irresistible state of being with the power to turn belief in an idea into a conviction to act on its behalf.

An enlightened leader will work closely with a plan developer, knowing that conveying an idea is difficult and requires a variety of professional communication skills. A leader can turn to a plan developer for the draft of a vision the same way the executive turns to a writer to request a draft of a speech.

The leader and plan developer know the aim of a vision shouldn't be to shoot for the moon. Its aim should be to orchestrate readily available resources to achieve results that move an organization to a higher level of innovation, competitive strength, market position, and profitability. An experienced public relations plan developer has the position and skills to move freely throughout an organization to gather insights from sources such as industry analysts and to expose an idea to a broad spectrum of expertise in sales, marketing, law, finance, and research and development and to meld ideas into a vision with universal appeal.

The leader and plan developer know that a vision must contain appeals to all stakeholders—employees, existing and potential investors, industry analysts, bankers, journalists. Enlightened executives know that to have the power to trigger convictions to act, a vision must have ownership by all of its stakeholders. It is not a one-sided opportunity. It must be a multifaceted, irresistible opportunity for stakeholders within and outside the organization. No one in an organization has a better grasp of the diverse views of stakeholder groups than an organization's experienced public relations professional. Research is a cornerstone of the profession and public relations professionals who perform the function in developing annual reports, establishing Web sites, preparing news announcements, drafting speeches, position papers, and other forms of corporate communication are well equipped with the skills to research and develop the basis for a vision.

An astute leader knows that once crafted, a vision must be delivered, not by a "town crier," but by the whole company. It's not an edict. It's a vision. It's the seed of an idea. It needs time to unleash its power in the imaginations of the people it captivates. It needs time to be considered, studied, and evaluated.

As a vision is pursued by the chief executive and plan developer and evidence of its potential develops and is shared with its stakeholders, a vision gains validity. It is assimilated and communicated in one voice with the personal conviction of all of its stakeholders. Results of the vision continue to validate its potential and trigger in the minds of its stakeholders convictions to act in support of the vision. As the process unfolds it energizes employees to produce, customers to buy, investors to invest, bankers to lend, analysts to recommend, journalists to write, suppliers to support. For public relations plan developers who are fortunate to have chief executives who are enlightened and willing to explore what can be accomplished by leveraging the credibility of public relations in a vision, the challenge of planning can be an exciting experience.

RESOURCES

Finally, let's look at the challenges of the planning environment in the area of resources. The plan developer might have a choice of using resources within the organization or outsourcing work to various service firms. Or the plan developer might have to rely entirely on the organization's resources.

The advantages of using the organization's resources are

- people involved have a vested interest in the organization's mission and are likely to have a personal commitment to contributing to its success;

- control of the plan is internal among the people involved with its implementation;

- expenses are minimized by enlisting the involvement of existing personnel and obtaining support from existing budgets.

The plan developer may find it advantageous to call on an outside resource, such as a public relations firm, to help develop and/or implement a plan. PR firms generally have the ability to be objective, to provide specialized expertise, to facilitate connections with a wide range of people of influence, and to obtain points of view from different constituencies. However, the planning challenge increases when the plan developer must outsource work. A plan developer might not have a choice but to outsource work to a firm already retained by the organization. Whether the developer must use a designated source or select a source, careful management of the source's performance is essential, whether the work is assigned to a photography studio, graphic design firm, multimedia production house, or public relations firm. To illustrate, let's consider what is involved in managing the outsourcing of work to a public relations firm.

Generally speaking, public relations firms are service driven. However, some PR firms are cost driven. Unless one is prepared to lose one's shirt, it's best to select a service-driven firm. By selecting a service-driven firm, a plan developer is far more likely to develop and execute a winning plan.

So what distinguishes a service-driven PR firm from a cost-driven PR firm?

- A service-driven firm uses time to provide service. A cost-driven firm uses time to cover costs at the expense of client service. Firms become cost driven when the cost of operating—office rent, auto and electronic equipment leases, salaries, and other overhead—is so high that meeting those expenses drives the business.

- A service-driven firm provides a plan developer with an experienced account representative. A cost-driven firm provides an experienced account representative initially, but then might switch to a less experienced representative at the same high billable rate.

- A service-driven firm provides a plan developer with the full depth of the firm's expertise. A cost-driven firm limits client service to the experience of the account representative to allow others in the firm to concentrate on more lucrative business.

- A service-driven firm is willing to absorb the cost of "getting up to speed" on a client and its PR needs. A cost-driven firm seeks to be paid for orienting itself to a client's business.

- A service-driven firm provides a plan developer with high-quality resources for graphic design, photography, video production, and whatever is needed. A cost-driven firm attempts to use its own, often mediocre, resources to keep profits in-house.

- A service-driven firm drives the plan developer's assignment to completion. A cost-driven firm is less responsive, causing the client to do the account representative's work of staying on schedule and on budget, which enables the account representative, instead, to handle more accounts.

- A service-driven firm is willing to tailor its services to a plan developer's own performance criteria. A cost-driven firm insists on its own way of providing service and resists client attempts to manage and evaluate the firm's performance.

- A service-driven firm knows how and is willing to serve as an extension of a plan developer's staff. A cost-driven firm is inflexible and insists on doing things its own money-making way.

- A service-driven firm keeps working until the work meets the plan developer's expectations. A cost-driven firm offers excuses for substandard work and sometimes tries to get the client to accept and pay for the PR firm's mistakes, inability to follow directions, poor writing, careless editing, and other unprofessional practices.

- A service-driven firm charges a predetermined fee, often a retainer, and within that fee does whatever additional work is necessary to satisfy a client. A cost-driven firm charges an hourly rate for all the time it takes to do the job.

To manage a plan that will involve the services of an outside firm, a plan developer must understand the challenges involved in outsourcing and directing various forms of services. A plan cannot be developed or implemented in a vacuum. The environment in which a plan is developed can present substantial challenges in the areas of organization, leadership, and resources.

THE PLAN DEVELOPER

There is one more factor to consider before studying the public relations plan and its component parts and that is you—the plan developer. Acceptance of plans that you propose will depend, in large part, on plan reviewers' confidence in your ability to deliver what you propose. Such confidence comes from how reviewers see you as a public relations practitioner. So let's consider the matter of professional image.

The traditional characterization of public relations practitioners suggests they fall somewhere on a continuum ranging from lower-paid technicians to higher-paid consultants and that the ultimate career position is membership in the dominant coalition or leadership of an organization. This characterization implies that practitioners have a choice to make between being a technician or a consultant and that if an individual chooses to be a technician, such as a newsletter editor, the individual will not have the esteem of a consultant in the eyes of senior executives.

I would like to offer a different view. Having worked with colleagues in all aspects of public relations for more than 30 years and with more than 400 young men and women studying to enter the profession, I would characterize practitioners as having unique combinations of technical communication and consulting talents and skills. I believe practitioners, through their academic training and education and professional experience, develop a professional capability comprising both technical and consulting skills.

Practitioners have the ability to confer on situations, from simple to complex, and recommend ways to influence people—even millions of people—to behave one way or another in response to meaningful communication activities. A skilled practitioner, for example, has the consulting skills to recommend public communication and all of the technical skills to develop a news announcement, guide it through the review process, reconcile reviewers' differences, disseminate the announcement worldwide, handle resulting inquiries from reporters, and provide more information or correct erroneous reporting errors.

The combination of consulting and technical skills is a great strength. However, I do caution young men and women to be conscious of the image they project—someone who scurries around with a pencil behind one ear, clutching a clipboard, and dangling a camera from a neckstrap is going to have a difficult time being regarded as a counselor, rather than a technician. So, if you don't want to be seen as a mechanic, don't carry a big wrench. Young men and women entering the profession should take delight in acquiring a combination of technical and consulting skills and enjoy developing that unique professional capability to the fullest extent possible.

chapter 3

Writing and Leading with Integrity

*O*ne of my students at the University of Oregon was asked in a job interview to identify weaknesses in the PR profession. Unable to think of any, she turned to the interviewer who admitted that she couldn't think of any either. Understandably, we don't dwell on our weaknesses. However, public relations, as a relatively young and developing profession, does have vulnerabilities. As practitioners and particularly as plan developers, we have a responsibility to be aware of them and to help ensure that public relations continues to grow in practice and in character.

What can we do as plan developers to strengthen the profession? One thing we can do is market and deliver what we do best. We are strategic communicators. A review of Silver Anvil winners in the category of PR tactics showcases the tremendous talent we have in communication. Because public relations is not clearly defined—it has hundreds of definitions—expectations of results can be wide-ranging. The temptation exists to pursue hot markets, like high-tech, health care, and corporate governance, with loosely formed but firmly hyped expertise. This tendency oftentimes sets up great expectations, only to be dashed by disappointing results and invoices that make boards of directors resistant to return to the profession for services. It is better to market our core competencies in communication than to promise more than we can deliver.

Another thing we can do—as we do in the classroom and in this book—is strive to bring public relations planning into sharper focus. Because there is limited textbook instruction in developing public relations plans, practitioners have almost as many different definitions of goals, objectives, strategies, and activities as we have for defining the profession itself. A public relations plan that puts its audience into a state of confusion and rejection over terms and form brings great injury to the profession's reputation. Public relations is not an exact science, so we cannot

13

guarantee the outcomes of plans. However, we can show how we draw on bodies of knowledge in the social sciences and methodically and strategically formulate plans to increase our effectiveness in achieving objectives.

We can strengthen the profession by establishing PR firms with cost structures that enable competitive billing and by ensuring that our practice of public relations is always service-driven. Examples exist of public relations firms whose overhead costs for expensive office space, leased cars, furniture and office equipment—instead of quality service—drive the practice, demanding more and more billable hours any way a firm can get them. There are examples of individual practitioners whose work is driven by personal ambitions at any cost rather than by a genuine desire to provide quality service. The profession's reputation cannot afford these excursions any more than today's corporations can afford the liberties many have taken with accounting practices.

Being rock solid in upholding the principles of the profession, as enumerated in the Public Relations Society of America's Code of Ethics, is especially important at a time when public relations is heavily engaged in counseling others about reputation management. Public relations has yet to be fully accepted as a true profession. There are no standardized educational requirements. There is no mandatory licensing or certification. There is no effective self-regulation.

When we market our core competencies in strategic communication, when we bring public relations planning into sharper focus, when we ensure that our practice of public relations is service-driven, we are leading with integrity. We are demonstrating a passion for principles that commands respect and develops mutual trust. By leading and writing with integrity we enable the profession to grow in practice and in stature.

chapter 4

Beginning the Planning Process with Accountability

*i*t is easy to get caught up in the excitement of developing a public relations plan, especially if its creative elements are likely to delight or impress reviewers. However, focusing mainly on creative strategies could be a serious miscalculation on the part of a plan developer. That's because a plan, regardless of its degree of creativity, must be backed by accountability for cost, completeness, effectiveness, and measurability.

A plan reviewer could be expected to ask, How do you justify this plan in terms of cost, benefits, and need? In other words, will the benefits you expect to derive from the plan be worth the time, money, and energy that have to be put into the plan to accomplish its goal? A question of equal importance that a reviewer must contemplate is, How does the need for this action rank among all of the other pressing needs of the organization?

A plan must establish a clear need for public relations action and must propose a cost-effective orchestration of communication activities that is within the sponsoring organization's budget. A public relations plan could require from $500 to well over $300,000 to implement. A request for such an expenditure, assuming that it is an expense over the existing budget, must compete on its merits with all other special requests for an authorization of funds. So the plan's costs, benefits, and necessity must be made absolutely clear to a reviewer. A plan also must be affordable to the organization receiving the proposal. That's not to suggest cutting corners or lowering standards to suit an organization. If a public relations action can't be done right it shouldn't be attempted. Fortunately, in public relations, there are many different ways to accomplish communication objectives cost-effectively.

A plan reviewer also could be expected to ask, What's the basis for this plan? With this question, the reviewer is holding the plan developer accountable for completeness. The reviewer wants to see that you have all of the information necessary for the reviewer to make a thorough assessment of the plan to decide whether or not to approve it. To be thorough the plan developer must include 10 components in the public relations plan (discussed in Chapter 5): (1) problem, challenge, or opportunity statement, (2) situation analysis, (3) goal, (4) primary focus, (5) objective, (6) strategy, (7) activity, (8) evaluation/measurement, (9) execution timeline, and (10) budget. As you develop a plan, ask yourself if you are presenting all the information a reviewer would require in each area to make an assessment and reach for a pen to approve your plan.

A reviewer also could be expected to ask, How do you know this plan will be effective? With this question, the reviewer, who likely will have no formal education in public relations, is looking for assurances that what is proposed in the plan is what will be necessary to obtain some reasonable measure of success in achieving the plan's goal. It is incumbent on the plan developer to convince the reviewer that public relations plans are based on proven principles of communication and persuasion. This is best achieved when the plan itself calls on the body of knowledge in the social sciences that has been acquired by the profession over several decades.

Another important way to assure effectiveness is with research. The use of research, despite its immense value, has yet to become fully established in the profession. The term *research*, by its own definition—connoting formal, costly, time-consuming study, documented investigation, examination of a condition in one past moment or period of time—retards its use. Heads of organizations who have ultimate control of public relations spending historically have resisted spending money on research.

Measuring effectiveness doesn't always require formal research. The fact is there are many forms of research that are not costly and time-consuming. In the broadest terms, everyone conducts research. We all gather information to find solutions to problems. It is an important function in our daily lives, but we typically do not have a formal process we follow. Research is vitally important in the development of PR plans and should not be summarily dismissed.

A plan reviewer could be expected to ask, What indications will you have to show that your public relations plan is, in fact, proceeding effectively toward accomplishing its goal? With this question, the reviewer is holding the plan developer accountable for measurement. Assuming the plan is being implemented, how can its effectiveness be measured? The answer should be that the plan's objectives—all of them—are measurable. Every one of a plan's objectives should be written, as will be explained later, to include a desired behavioral outcome and the resulting behavior should be measurable in qualitative or quantitative terms.

PLANNING PROCESS OVERVIEW

So far we understand how planning relates to public relations, the challenges of the planning environment, and the importance of leading with integrity and planning with accountability. Now let's take a broad look at the planning process.

We said earlier that public relations is the practice of influencing behavior. Well, planning is the method by which behavior is to be influenced. A plan focuses on a problem, challenge, or opportunity that would significantly benefit its sponsoring individual or organization. The subject of a plan could be the result of an organization's initiative or could arise as a result of circumstances beyond the organization's control. In either case, a plan is required to deal with the subject and derive benefits for its sponsor.

Planning begins with gathering information, first to understand the problem, challenge, or opportunity, second to develop ways to accomplish the plan's goal, and third to track and measure effectiveness in achieving the plan's goal. Planning efforts are likely to fail if you approach the task as a lone star. Effective planning requires information gathering to achieve a depth of knowledge and this, in turn, requires gaining the cooperation of many different sources.

One source of information, of course, is yourself and the knowledge you have acquired from your professional experience. Depending on the subject of your plan, you also will look within your organization to draw on the knowledge and background of other individuals. They can provide on-site expertise in law, marketing, product development, finance, sales, human resources, engineering, technology, and other professional disciplines.

You will look to information sources outside your organization, such as customers, suppliers, distributors, sales agents, industry trade associations, government agencies, nongovernmental organizations, and professional and service organizations, and you will tap other sources around the globe through the World Wide Web. Gaps in information will have to be filled and assumptions validated through informal (qualitative) or formal (quantitative) research recommended in the plan or conducted for development of the plan.

The information you gather must be assessed and funneled into development of the plan's *situation analysis*. (See Figure 4.1 on page 18.) From the analysis you should be able to

- write a *statement* summarizing the problem, challenge or opportunity;

- establish a *goal* with compelling reasons for taking public relations actions to achieve it;

- decide what must be done to accomplish the goal, which is the role of *objectives*;

- determine the *primary focus* of the plan—people whose behaviors must be influenced to accomplish the plan's objectives;

- develop *strategies* with detailed *activities* to show how the plan's objectives are to be achieved.

The process of strategically influencing the behavior of individuals or groups of individuals must take into account all dimensions of communication as shown in Figure 4.2 on page 19. The process requires careful development of what is to be communicated, selection of channels through which messages are to be conveyed, consideration for how the communication might become obstructed and/or filtered, and regard for how messages will be received by the intended audience, depending on its disposition toward the message and its source. A plan developer must decide how much of this process can be based on professional experience and intuition and how much should be based on formal or informal research.

Another important part of the planning process is providing methods of *evaluation* for tracking and gauging the plan's progress as it is implemented and for measuring its ultimate effectiveness in achieving the plan's goal. The planning process includes development of an *execution timeline* that provides an at-a-glance view of major preparatory steps and milestones leading to achievement of the plan's goal. Finally, a plan provides an estimated *budget* for its implementation.

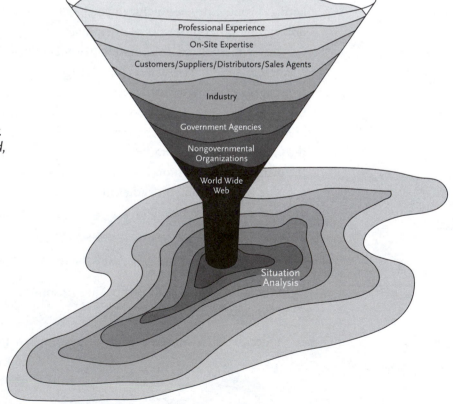

FIGURE 4.1 *The Data Collector. Information is gathered, studied, and funneled into a situation analysis.*

FIGURE 4.2   *Factors to Consider in Communicating Strategically to Influence Behavior*

Influencing behavior through strategic communication requires that a message be received, noticed, understood, believed, remembered, and acted on. The sender of a message must focus on message development, source and channel selection, exposure, and navigation around obstacles and through cognitive filters. The following factors should be considered in planning strategic communication.

FACTOR	DESCRIPTION	AT-A-GLANCE
Source	The source of the communication should be someone who is familiar to the intended audience or public, who is trusted, who is considered knowledgeable and credible, and who normally is looked to for information.	Familiar Trustworthy Knowledgable Credible
Message	In developing a message, a sender should know what's on the intended target's mind and should try to align the message with existing attitudes. The sender should know what the intended audience or public talks and thinks about and how the receiver converses with peers so that the message can be written in familiar language as part of the receiver's natural routine. Content of the message must be clear, appropriate, meaningful, memorable, understandable, and believable. The message should get the receiver involved using triggers—reasons or incentives for the receiver to act on the message—in other words, telling what's in it for the intended audience if it responds as requested. The behavior requested must be within the intended audience's ability to perform or its ability to learn to perform.	Aligned Language Clear Appropriate Meaningful Understandable Memorable Believable Appealing Beneficial Triggers Ability
Channels	The message should be sent through one or more channels that are familiar to and relied on for information by the target audience or public. Selection of channels must be accurate. The channels must be adequate to convey the message completely and accurately. Redundant use of channels may be necessary to penetrate or circumvent communication barriers.	Familiar Adequate Redundant Accurate
Exposure	Day of week, time of day, and frequency with which the message is communicated are important factors in determining message exposure.	Timing Frequency
Obstacles	To be effective, communication of the message must overcome obstacles, such as noise, clutter, and competition.	Clutter Noise Competition
Cognitive filters	Communication of the message must penetrate a receiver's thinking process, passing through cognitive filters of attitude, culture, experience, affiliations, and needs.	Attitude Culture Experience Affiliations Needs
Target	The intended receiver could be an individual, group of individuals, or a larger audience or public. To be effective, strategic communication must be noticed, understood, believed, accepted, remembered, and acted on.	Noticed Understood Believed Accepted Remembered Acted Upon
Behavioral outcome	When the message reaches the intended receiver its strategic value will be seen in the behavioral response of the audience or public. The response could be inaction, predisposition to act, or the action desired. If the outcome is other than what was desired, it will be necessary to make adjustments and initiate the strategic communication process once again until the desired behavioral outcome is achieved.	Inaction Predisposition to Act Desired Action

chapter 5

Defining Components of Public Relations Plans and Rules for Writing Them

*P*ublic relations plans are presented formally or informally, verbally or as a written proposal. Writing the plan in a conversational style is appropriate for all forms of presentation. In the industry, you will find that plans and their parts vary from organization to organization and from public relations agency to agency. It's not the lack of standardized form, but rather the lack of definition that does a great disservice to the profession. The plan format presented here has 10 clearly defined components. They are: the problem, challenge, or opportunity statement; situation analysis; goal; primary focus; objective; strategy; activity; evaluation; execution timeline; and budget. We will look at each one from the perspective of the plan reviewer, the person responsible for authorizing funds to implement a plan.

1. PROBLEM, CHALLENGE, OR OPPORTUNITY STATEMENT

The plan begins with a statement describing a problem, challenge, or opportunity, which, when addressed with public relations activity, would in some significant way benefit the organization you work for or that you have as a client. This part of the plan should be headed Problem, Challenge, or Opportunity. It's important to plan reviewers because it tells in capsule form what the situation is and why public relations actions should be seriously considered. The statement should be written after information has been gathered and the situation has been analyzed.

A public relations plan is aimed at influencing behavior, so the statement must focus on communicating with people. It should show clearly that a situation exists that warrants public relations action and an expenditure of resources. The statement is a call to action. To test your statement, ask yourself if a reviewer of your plan would easily recognize the significance of a situation and understand why taking public relations action would benefit the organization.

Rules for Writing a Problem, Challenge, or Opportunity Statement

1. Label the statement as a problem, challenge, or opportunity without including the word *statement*.

2. Write the statement in a conversational style summarizing the situation analysis the way you would describe it to reviewers of your plan.

3. Begin the statement by identifying the nature of the situation, for example, "There is a problem . . . , We have a challenge . . . , or XYZ has an opportunity . . . ."

4. Present the statement in a storytelling format briefly describing how the situation developed and reached a point requiring public relations action.

5. The statement must lead up to providing a compelling argument for public relations action, but must stop short of suggesting a solution or course of action.

6. The statement must be complete and accurate, but must not be judgmental or place blame.

Following is an example of a problem statement, headed simply "Problem."

Problem

Industrial Products, Inc., started planning a plant expansion and discovered that a large lagoon on the construction site contained hazardous material. The lagoon has to be cleaned out and closed before plant expansion work can begin. Closing the lagoon will be in the public eye and will raise questions, especially about people seen working in hazardous materials safety suits. If everyone who sees the activity—news media, community residents, employees, local government representatives, and others—is left to speculate about what they see, the community could become unnecessarily alarmed.

Media reports could exaggerate health risks and call the company's reputation into question. The general public could pressure government for information and public meetings about the project. Local government officials could delay issuing permits for expansion. Employees could become outraged about earlier potential exposure of their families to health risks.

We don't want anyone to become alarmed unnecessarily. We don't want expansion plans to be delayed because needed modernization is already costing the company money and inadequate capacity is causing the company to lose market share. This is clearly a potential public relations problem with serious consequences that must be addressed.

exercise 1

Using the rules for developing a problem, challenge, or opportunity statement, write a problem statement using only the information provided in the following case summary.

Tropicana Tries to Trumpet Nutrition

It used to be that food processors could market products for their good taste. Today it is evident that people are more interested than ever before in their health and fitness. When they shop, they want to know what products will do to them, and more importantly, what they will do for them. Health claims on products have an influence on buying decisions. Tropicana figured that when you have a product that is not only great tasting, but also naturally nutritious, it makes sense to promote the natural health benefits. The company wanted to put a health claim on its Pure Premium orange juice. It wanted to spotlight the fact that its Pure Premium orange juice contains potassium. The mineral potassium is found in orange juice. The company wanted to point out that in clinical trials potassium has been shown to reduce the risk of both high blood pressure and stroke. Tropicana Products petitioned the Food and Drug Administration (FDA) to carry the health claim about potassium on its Pure Premium orange juice label. The company spent 18 months researching and writing the petition and working with FDA employees on drafting the claim's language. The petition was accepted. Now Tropicana can market the potassium health benefit claim, but so can any other juice producer. Banana suppliers can do the same with their product. Tropicana wants to use the health claim, but has to keep other orange juice producers, as well as banana suppliers, at bay.

2. SITUATION ANALYSIS

The second component of a public relations plan is the situation analysis. Why is this component of the plan important to plan reviewers? The analysis is important to reviewers because it assures them that you have a complete and accurate understanding of the situation from which to develop a plan. The manner in which the analysis is written gives reviewers evidence of your depth of knowledge, the breadth of your experience, your level of professionalism, your understanding of the organization and its needs, the seriousness of your commitment to addressing the situation, and your overall understanding of public relations.

In developing a situation analysis, it is important to consider all aspects of the situation and to gather and record information necessary to provide an in-depth understanding of the problem, challenge, or opportunity, as illustrated with the Data Collector in Figure 4.1 on page 18. The analysis should be a focused investigation of internal and external factors necessary to achieve a level of understanding that will identify areas requiring further study and possible research and that will support effective strategic planning.

Be judicious in preparing the analysis. Collecting and assembling everything that could possibly relate to a situation—including volumes of peripheral information that might be useful for other purposes and conducting broad-based communication audits that might or might not contribute to addressing a situation—could be seen by reviewers as a costly, overindulgent, unnecessary use of resources.

For the analysis to be a useful component of a public relations plan, it should organize and convey information in a familiar, easy-to-understand manner. What better way could there be to describe a situation than to do what comes naturally, that is, tell a story?

In this context, the story will describe a series of happenings that, when related or connected, enables others to grasp the significance of a problem, challenge, or opportunity. It is up to you in your storytelling to enable others to sift through events, understand how and why they occurred, and understand what part they played in creating the situation under study.

Storytelling allows you to describe the development of a situation from its origin to its current state based on a thoughtful review of explicit, as well as tacit, information. In other words, an analysis will involve hard evidence as well as unseen influences and factors difficult to evaluate. It will be necessary to decide to what extent you can rely on intuition to form an analysis and to what extent it will be necessary to conduct and/or recommend primary or secondary research to help validate your "story" of how the problem, challenge, or opportunity surfaced. Research to be recommended and/or conducted could be, for example, in the form of in-depth interviews, focus groups, field observation, tabulating telephone calls, postal mail and electronic mail surveys, or content analysis.

Rules for Writing a Situation Analysis

1. The situation analysis is more than a report of known facts, it is your analysis of the situation. Present the information you have as you understand it and include recommendations for further investigation (informal or qualitative research/formal or quantitative research) into areas that you believe require clarification or verification.

2. Write the analysis in a conversational style as though you are explaining your assessment of the situation to your client or employer.

3. Present your analysis in a storytelling format—begin at the beginning and tell how the situation developed and reached a point requiring public relations action.

4. Include media history and current media coverage.

5. The analysis should provide a compelling argument for taking action.

6. The analysis should be forthright about problems, weaknesses, and mistakes, but must not be judgmental or place blame.

7. The analysis must not include solutions or suggestions for dealing with the situation; however, it should provide a strong argument for public relations action.

Based on the rules for developing a situation analysis, read the following case overview and describe what additional information you would want to have to do a thorough analysis of the situation. Include in your critique recommended informal or formal research that you think should be conducted to verify certain information or suppositions or to shed more light on the situation.

Community Shelter Board Works to End Homelessness

At one time, homeless individuals (mostly men) lived and searched for food on land along the riverbank in downtown Columbus, Ohio. However, in 1998 the area came under rapid change with the development of expensive homes, a science museum, and an arena. The Scioto Peninsula Relocation Task Force was formed by the Community Shelter Board (CSB), a leader in providing homeless services, to help homeless men who were threatened with being displaced from the riverfront property.

The task force studied the situation and conducted public meetings. It came up with a five-year plan proposing to locate 800 apartments for homeless men throughout the county, build a shelter in an inner-city neighborhood, and a facility for alcoholic homeless men. The idea was to reduce homelessness and have the permanent housing and support services replace a variety of emergency shelters.

The plan faced significant challenges. Affordable housing hasn't been popular anywhere in the country, not even Franklin County, which is more tolerant than many other counties. NIMBYism (Not In My Back Yard—opposition by nearby residents to a proposed building project, especially a public one) is common. People are not inclined to want to live next door to formerly homeless men, many of whom have mental illness and addictions. CSB doesn't know what to do to win acceptance of the plan or how to successfully raise money for an unpopular effort.

3. GOAL

The next component of a plan is the goal. The goal is a condition or state of being described as if it has already been achieved. It is distinguished by the use of the infinitive phrase *to be* and answers the question, What do you want the ultimate condition to be as a result of having executed your public relations plan? Goal examples: For XYZ to be respected as an industry leader; for the medical center to be serving 50 additional patients; for the student chapter to be operating with 15 new members; for XYZ to be merged with ZYX with the support of all stakeholders.

Why is a goal important to plan reviewers? It is important because the goal in a public relations plan provides four key functions.

One function is to provide a vision of a desired position or condition. A plan should have one ultimate aim: All of a plan's objectives should be directed toward achieving the plan's goal. The goal can be specific to the public relations task—for example, for XYZ to be trusted by the community for its safe use of chemicals. Or it can relate to broader organizational aims that require plans from other functions, such as human resources, marketing, and finance—for example, for XYZ to be merged with ZYX with the support and understanding of all stakeholders.

Another function of a goal is to provide a target on which to organize resources. A goal gives followers of a plan a point of reference on which to center their efforts. It enables them to set their sights on what is to be the overall result of the combined efforts of all contributors to the plan. A goal should use the infinitive phrase *to be* to distinguish this targeting function. What follows *to be* should be stated as though the position or condition has been achieved—for example, the goal for XYZ is to be a recognized leader in its field. This goal clearly rallies an organization's resources around making it a recognized leader in its field.

Another function of a goal is to provide verification that the plan is focused correctly. By stating the goal, plan developers can demonstrate to plan reviewers that the plan focuses on the correct priority. For example, if the client's goal is for XYZ to be viewed as an essential, unique, and authoritative resource for diversity education on the university campus and in the greater community, the goal would not be focused correctly if it were stated, For XYZ to be a well-funded campus organization. Directly stated, when a client's goal calls for everyone to be eating Big Macs, plan developers had better not be writing about Chicken McNuggets. That may sound exaggerated, but sometimes client or employer instructions are not followed explicitly or are overlooked entirely and the experience for them is exasperating because they are putting up major resources to accomplish a specific job that is important to them.

Another function of a goal is to provide a measurement of success. When a desired condition or position is evident as stated in the goal, a plan's objectives have been met. In other words, the fact that a certain condition or position now exists is evidence that the plan's objectives have been achieved successfully. Let's say, for example, the goal is for a hospital to be serving 50 more children. When the hospital is, in fact, serving 50 more children, that is proof or evidence that the plan's objective (e.g., to raise $20 million for hospital expansion) has been successfully achieved. So the goal of a public relations plan has four functions—it provides a vision, a target, verification, and measurement. (See Figure 5.1 for examples of goals.)

FIGURE 5.1   *Examples of Goals*

1. For X *to be* recognized nationally for its expertise in nubyonics.

2. For employees *to be* accepting greater financial responsibility for their health benefits.

3. For customers *to be* relying on X for its technical expertise and creative solutions.

4. For X *to be* merged with Y and the new organization vigorously pursuing a common mission.

5. For X *to be* relocated with a minimal amount of confusion.

6. For (person) *to be* a sought-after expert in launching new ventures.

7. For X *to be* recognized by the community as a leader in economic development.

8. For employees *to be* satisfied with the measures taken to ensure their safety relative to the new hazardous materials operation.

9. For X *to be* serving fifty more patients.

10. For (country) *to be* supportive of adding a new industry to its economy.

11. For the community *to be* satisfied with the level of public participation afforded by X on the proposed energy project.

12. For X *to be* expanding its operation with the support of local and state governments.

13. For X *to be* regarded by subscribers as the authority on health issues.

14. For X *to be* seen by potential employers and experts in public relations planning.

15. For X *to be* increasing membership at a rate of 10 percent a year.

16. For X *to be* approaching strike issues with open communication with Y.

17. For members of X *to be* making appearances on TV shows around the world.

18. For all students of X *to be* supported by individual sponsorships.

19. For X *to be* the most popular Web site for information about Y.

20. For consumers of X *to be* the preferred customers of Y.

21. For wind surfers throughout the world *to be* aware of Hood River on the Columbia River as one of the most popular locations for the sport.

22. For X *to be* regarded as the most popular wine-tasting festival in the Pacific Northwest.

FIGURE 5.1 *(continued)*

23. For artisans of the Columbia River Gorge *to be* discovered by and publicized internationally for their unique creations.

24. In the acquisition of X by Y, for all employees *to be* fully supportive of the merger.

25. For the new comet-like logo *to be* seen by employees as a more progressive representation of the organization's identity than the old logo that was fondly referred to as the "flying meatball."

Rules for Writing a Goal

1. Focus the goal on a single aim.

2. State the goal in a single sentence and avoid the temptation of telling what must be done to achieve it. That is the role of objectives. (Acceptable: For XYZ to be a trusted member of the community with its use of hazardous chemicals. Unacceptable: For XYZ to be a trusted member of the community with its use of hazardous chemicals *by communicating its safety record*.)

3. Describe the ultimate condition or state of being desired as though it has already been achieved. Example: For the medical center to be serving 50 additional patients.

4. Distinguish the statement as a goal by using the infinitive phrase *to be*, answering the question, What do you want the ultimate condition to be as a result of having executed the public relations plan successfully? (Acceptable: For XYZ *to be* operating as a recognized leader in its field. This is written as though the company has arrived at a new level of esteem—a new state of being. Unacceptable: For XYZ to become a recognized leader in its field. This leaves XYZ in its current unrecognized position or state of being—trying to become a recognized leader.)

5. Avoid using an objective for a goal. (Unacceptable: For XYZ to raise $15 million to expand the hospital. This is an objective describing what must be done to accomplish the ultimate goal—*to be* serving 50 more patients in a new addition to the hospital. The goal should be evidence that a plan's objectives have been successfully completed.

Goal Examples

Unacceptable: To provide eligible families with a smooth transition from Island Health Offspring to Children's Health Insurance Program.

Reason: It does not center on the infinitive phrase *to be* followed by an ultimate vision, state of being, or desired condition.

Acceptable: For eligible families *to be* receiving increased benefits from the Children's Health Insurance Program, having made a smooth transition from Island Health Offspring.

Unacceptable: The goal of the Clean Teeth campaign is to heighten awareness about the importance of tooth brushing.

Reasons: It does not center on the infinitive phrase *to be*, which the rules reserve for forming a goal—a desired condition or state of being.

Acceptable: For people around the world *to be* more aware of the importance of brushing teeth.

Unacceptable: To have the public adopt natural garden care by changing certain gardening behaviors.

Reasons: It does not center on the infinitive phrase *to be*, which the rules reserve for forming a goal—a desired condition, state of being, or ultimate vision. The phrase "to have the public adopt natural garden care" tells *what* must be done, which is the role of an objective. The phrase "by changing certain gardening behaviors" tells *how* something must be done, which is the role of a strategy.

Acceptable: For male homeowners, ages 25 to 54 in the Garden Gateway area, *to be* using natural gardening practices.

Unacceptable: For ABC Company to become accepted as an economic partner in the community by participating in local service clubs.

Reasons: It is not centered on the infinitive phrase *to be*, which is necessary to introduce a desired condition, state of being, or ultimate vision. "To become accepted" tells *what* must be done, which is the role of an objective. And "by participating in local service clubs" tells *how* to do something, which is the role of a strategy.

Acceptable: For ABC Company *to be* operating in the community as a full-fledged economic partner.

Unacceptable: For Children's Hospital to raise $100,000.

Reasons: Raising $100,000 is not the vision, the desired state of being, or condition. Raising $100,000 is *what* must be done to achieve the vision, which, according to the rules, is the role of an objective. The vision or goal is for the hospital *to be* serving more patients.

Acceptable: For Children's Hospital *to be* serving 25 more patients in a new wing of the hospital.

Unacceptable: For XYZ, Inc., to be closing one assembly plant.

Reasons: Closing one assembly plant is not the ultimate vision, goal, or state of being. It is *what* must be done to achieve the goal or vision, which, according to the rules, is the role of an objective.

Acceptable: For XYZ, Inc., *to be* operating more competitively having closed one assembly plant.

---

exercise 3

Explain why the goals in the following article would not be acceptable according to the rules, and write one goal for the museum that would be acceptable.

The Cleveland Museum of Natural History

Museums have to work hard to attract interest and visitors. The Cleveland Museum of Natural History is no exception. However, it decided to break out of the low-attendance crowd by adding a planetarium. It was a $6.9 million project. The museum launched a PR campaign. It had two goals: generate publicity that would position the museum as a world-class institution, and boost revenue through increased attendance.

The museum set up an Awareness Committee of PR professionals and representatives from local TV and radio stations and newspapers. It used its member resources to help publicize the grand opening of the Shafran Planetarium. A media teaser campaign was also launched that used puzzles and direct mail postcards to visually convey the planetarium's design. Media events for the planetarium were sold out. The campaign was a complete success with all attendance goals exceeded, planetarium shows sold out for the first three months, and the museum positioned as a learning center.

---

4. PRIMARY FOCUS

The primary focus of a public relations plan, without exception, should always be on people because public relations is the practice of influencing human behavior. The primary focus of a plan could be on an individual, on individuals comprising an organization or segment of an organization, on individuals comprising an audience, or individuals comprising an entire public. For example, the focus of a plan could be on a labor leader, on the management of a labor union, or on members of the nation's trade unions. To illustrate further, the focus of a plan could be on a business, community, activist, or student or government leader. It could be on the management of a public, private, non-profit, or government agency, or a non-governmental organization. It could be on employees or members of organizations. It could be on community residents, journalists, industry analysts, or potential investors. The focus could be on individuals in any combination of these configurations.

Rules for Writing the Primary Focus Component of a Plan

1. Make the primary focus of the plan people: an individual, a management staff, a target audience, or target public.

2. Describe the entities who are the primary focus of the plan.

3. Explain why each entity is a focus of the plan.

4. Tell what each entity knows about the subject of the plan.

5. Describe the disposition of each entity toward the subject of the plan.

6. Describe the disposition of each entity toward the organization developing the plan.

7. Provide demographics of each entity that are particularly relevant to the plan.

8. Write about each entity separately; do not combine entities.

9. Make the primary focus of a plan on target audiences (receivers of information), or on target publics (people with a vested interest in the organization originating the plan).

10. If part of a plan centers on a client, for example, for training and counseling, refer to the client as a primary focus, rather than a target of the plan.

The following is an example description of a target audience written by a student team.

Parents of Apple Elementary School Children

Parents of students at the neighboring Apple Elementary School are among the most concerned audiences about the use of chemicals at WaferMaker, Inc. Parents are concerned for the safety of their children and want to be assured that the wafer plant operation near the school is not a risk to their children's health or safety. Many of these parents are already highly emotional about the situation and want their questions answered immediately. Parents regard WaferMaker as a good corporate citizen and up until this time were unaware of the company's use of many hazardous chemicals. They are members of the local community and it is important to make sure that they trust and continue to be supportive of WaferMaker, Inc.

exercise 4

Based on the rules for developing an entry for a target public or audience, explain how the following entry could be improved.

The ABC Transport System
Key Target Audiences:

- Landowners
- Local elected officials
- Community leaders
- Media
- State elected officials, regulatory/admin staff
- U. S. Senators, Reps & staff from 6 states
- Fed regulators
- Rural /farm groups

5. OBJECTIVE

Objectives tell plan reviewers *what* actions must be taken to achieve a plan's goal. Usually more than one objective is needed to achieve a goal. An objective stops short of telling *how* something must be done. That is the role of a strategy. So a writer must resist the temptation to include in an objective a phrase, such as "by holding a news conference" that tells *how*, for example, an objective would be accomplished.

An objective has three parts. It tells (1) what must be done; (2) with whom; (3) and why such action is necessary for achieving a plan's goal. Let's examine the three parts of an objective.

Part I: Tells what action is to be taken. The action must be stated and preceded by the word *to*, used in the sense of producing or causing a result, to form an infinitive phrase. Example: The objective is *to provide* complete information.

Part II: Tells with whom the action is to be taken. An objective always includes a target audience because nothing can be accomplished without some form of human involvement. Example: The objective is to provide complete information to journalists. The target audience is *journalists*.

Part III: Tells why taking an action with a particular target audience is necessary toward achieving the plan's goal. In other words, it tells the purpose of the objective. Example: The objective is to provide complete information to journalists *so they are able to write articles based on accurate facts and figures.* The purpose of the objective is expressed as a measurable outcome telling reviewers what behavior is expected of the target audience as a result of the action to be taken. Completing the third part of the objective—stating its purpose—enables measurement. Did journalists publish articles? How many? What was the quality of their content? Complete objective: *The objective is to provide complete information to journalists so they are able to write articles based on accurate facts and figures.*

OBJECTIVE EXAMPLE

Action	To provide complete information
Target	Journalists
Purpose	So journalists write articles based on accurate facts and figures
OBJECTIVE	To provide complete information to journalists so they are able to write articles based on accurate facts and figures.
Measure	Did journalists publish articles? How many? What was the quality of their content?

It is the third part of an objective that most often is omitted, which is a crucial error because it is this component that makes an objective measurable. The previous objective might have been written, *To provide journalists with complete information.* This is not measurable because it does not tell why journalists are being provided information. It does not tell what journalists are expected to do—a desired behavioral outcome—as a result of being provided information.

INCOMPLETE OBJECTIVE

Action	To provide complete information
Target	Journalists
Purpose	???

The reason for providing journalists with information cannot be taken for granted. It must be stated. Reviewers who are paying the bill for a plan to be implemented want to know what outcomes to expect from every objective. Reviewers would be expected to ask, Why are we spending money to provide journalists with information? To answer the question, an objective must tell why journalists should be provided information.

OBJECTIVE EXAMPLE

Action	To inform about the company's skyrocketing payments for medical insurance
Target	Employees
Purpose	So employees accept an increased share of the cost
OBJECTIVE	To inform employees about the company's skyrocketing payments for medical insurance so they accept an increased share of the cost.
Measure	Did employees accept an increased share of the cost of medical insurance provided by the company?

Rules for Writing an Objective

1. An objective must have three parts. It should tell (1) what must be done, (2) with whom, (3) and why such action is necessary to achieve a plan's goal.

Part I: Tells what action is to be taken. The action must be stated and preceded by the word *to*, used in the sense of producing or causing a result, to form an infinitive phrase. Example: *To provide*.

Part II: Tells with whom the action is to be taken. An objective always includes a target audience because nothing can be accomplished without some form of human involvement.

Part III: Tells why taking an action with a particular target audience is necessary for achieving the plan's goal. In other words, it tells the purpose of the objective. Example: The purpose of the objective is expressed as a measurable outcome telling reviewers what behavior is expected of the target audience as a result of being provided complete information. Completing the third part of the objective—stating its purpose—enables measurement.

2. An objective must be measurable; it must include a desired outcome that can be measured.

3. An objective must be achievable; it must aim at a result that is possible to obtain cost effectively.

4. An objective may include a target date or deadline; however, that information is easier to review and assess when presented in the plan's timeline.

5. An objective should include only targets over which the plan's developer has complete control. Do not include items such as goals for sales, return on investment, and employee productivity, which involve factors that are the responsibility of other management areas and over which public relations has no control.

Figure 5.2 provides a table of examples of the three main components of an objective: (1) what action must be taken; (2) with what audience or public; (3) for what reason or purpose?

Objective Examples

Unacceptable: Work on many levels of the problem simultaneously to deliver a "cannon shot" impact that is deep and long lasting.

Reasons: This is gobbledygook; it contains no information that would be meaningful to plan reviewers.

Unacceptable: Generate publicity that strongly links Box of Snaps with baseball and highlights new "prize inside" series.

Reasons: An objective must focus on an audience and it must start with the word *to*. In this case there is no target audience, nor is there any indication of what the writer of the plan wants the implied audience to do as a result of the publicity. Also, plans should take advantage of lessons learned from research on persuasion, shown in Figure 5.4, pages 37–39. A reviewer of this objective might ask, Have you taken into account that research has shown that messages, especially those presented through the public media, are quickly forgotten if they are not at least moderately reinforced by repetition and that repetition is useful for keeping ideas in the public mind?

Acceptable: *To generate* publicity that in the minds of Major League Baseball fans strongly links Box of Snaps with baseball and raises an interest in the new "prize inside" series so that more fans buy Box of Snaps.

FIGURE 5.2   *Objectives Have Three Components*

1. **One action** that must be taken with a target audience or public in order for an objective to contribute toward the achievement of a plan's goal.	2. **Target audience or public,** whose participation is necessary to accomplish the objective.	3. **Purpose** for the action to be taken with the target audience or public.
To accommodate	analysts	accept
To address	backpackers	apply
To advise	bankers	approve
To alleviate	chamber of commerce	assemble
To apprise	college students	attend
To assure	commissioners	believe
To attract attention	community leaders	buy
To change	council members	capitulate
To communicate	customers	contact
To compile	development council	contribute
To convey	educators	demand
To describe	employees	demonstrate
To diffuse emotion	environmental activists	donate
To educate	executives of nonprofits	e-mail
To enlighten	farmers	empathize
To explain	fashion editors	enroll
To focus	government regulators	experience
To forecast	government representatives	help
To generate interest	high school students	insist
To heighten interest	homeowners	invest
To honor	investors	investigate
To improve	landowners	join
To increase knowledge	lawyers	keep
To inform	local elected officials	lead
To instill	local news media	leave alone
To mobilize	news media	march
To negotiate	parents	participate
To offer	pet owners	petition
To organize	physicians	play
To orient	product partners	promote
To pique	professional organizations	publicize
To placate	program directors	question
To present	prospects	recommend
To prove	residents	reconsider
To provide opportunities	seniors	reject
To raise awareness	service clubs	report accurately
To recognize	service providers	seek
To reconcile	shareholders	sell
To recruit	special interest groups	sing
To reduce anxiety	suppliers	start
To restore confidence	talk show hosts	stop
To reveal	teachers	support
To sensitize	trade press	sympathize
To share	U.S. representatives	travel
To show	U.S. senators	trust
To simplify	veterans	try
To stimulate interest	voters	

Unacceptable: Promote each member of Smith's family of digital audio players through individually tailored campaigns to maintain market share of at least 30 percent.

Reasons: This objective does not begin with an infinitive phrase formed with the word *to*. It has no target audience. "Through individually tailored campaigns" tells *how* the objective is to be accomplished, which is the role of a strategy. Most importantly, public relations is a staff function and has no direct control over marketing—certainly not over all of the many factors necessary to promise a market share of 30, or any, percent.

Unacceptable: Collect $5 million in contributions by conducting a capital fund drive.

Reasons: The statement does not begin with an infinitive phrase formed with the word *to*. No audience is specified. The phrase, "by conducting a capital fund drive" tells *how* something is to be accomplished, which is the role of a strategy.

Acceptable: *To convince* targeted donors to pledge by Dec. 1, 20XX, a total of $5 million for expansion of the XYZ Medical Center.

Unacceptable: To fully inform the news media about the incident.

Reason: The objective has no stated purpose. What is expected of journalists if they are fully informed of the incident? In other words, what are journalists to do as a result of being fully informed?

Acceptable: *To fully inform* the news media about the incident to help ensure that their news reports are complete and accurate.

---

exercise 5

Study the objectives in the following article. Explain how the objectives would be written according to the rules.

Procter & Gamble—Charmin Ultra

To help promote Charmin Ultra, P & G conducted a traveling road show. An 18-wheel semi was converted into a "commode on the road" with 27 private bathrooms. The facilities had hardwood floors, sinks with running water, uniformed attendants, and Charmin Ultra toilet paper.

Teaser promotions were sent to local media in advance of each appearance of the Potty Palooza. They included T-shirts with "Potty

Palooza 2002 . . . It's Loo-La-La" on the front; on the back was a U.S. map and stars marking each stop on the tour. The shirts were compressed and shrink-wrapped into the shape of an 18-wheel trailer. Press releases were sent to local media two days before each festival or fair's opening day. A media alert invited the press to visit the Potty Palooza. The main objectives were to get at least 30 million media impressions, secure at least 30 aired segments on TV news, and to drive sales of Charmin Ultra. The objectives were surpassed, with more than 62 million media impressions, more than 45 video news hits, three national news stories plus print and TV coverage in all local market stops. Also, research showed a 14 percent increase in Charmin sales among consumers who used the Potty Palooza. The budget for the program was $300,000 and the agency was Manning, Selvage & Lee.

6. STRATEGY

The next component of the plan is the strategy. Why are strategies important to plan reviewers? They are important because strategies describe *how* you will achieve your plan objectives. Reviewers want to assess your methods for achieving objectives, the creativity behind your methods, the feasibility and practicality of your methods, and your knowledge of applying the fundamentals of persuasion in influencing behavior.

Every objective must have a strategy that describes how, in concept, the objective is to be achieved. More than one strategy might be necessary to accomplish an objective. A strategy must be realistic; it must take into account the amount of time, energy, personnel, expertise, and financial resources available for its accomplishment. A strategy can state key themes or messages to be reiterated throughout a campaign.

A strategy must be mapped according to the dynamics of communication shown in Figure 4.2 on page 19. Strategies must be adaptable to changing circumstances and must lend themselves to fine-tuning. A strategy should be developed in building blocks that lead to milestones indicating progress in how the strategy's objective is being achieved. Milestones should be shown in a plan's execution timeline.

The strategy component provides the plan developer with an opportunity to educate plan reviewers on communication and persuasion. A model of how the seed of an idea develops into a conviction to act is shown in Figure 5.3.

When developing a strategy, you will strengthen what you propose by basing it, where possible, on lessons learned by public relations practitioners. You will find a sampling of commonly known facts about persuasion in Figure 5.4. There are lessons relating to message sources, message structure, message content, media, and target audiences. It is wise to review each of your strategies and ensure

FIGURE 5.3 *Model of How the Seed of an Idea Becomes a Conviction to Act*

Seed of an idea is planted.

Example: A report is published in a financial journal about a manufacturing company with promising profit potential because of its exceptionally low operating costs—a possible investment opportunity.

Receiver takes an interest in the idea.

A securities analyst takes an interest in the company because of its low-cost operation and promising profit potential.

Receiver learns more about the idea.

The analyst begins taking an interest in the company by paying attention to the company's announcements (new releases), speeches by executives, articles in the trade press, and other available information about the company.

Receiver begins to develop ownership in the idea.

The analyst begins to talk about the company as if he or she made the discovery of this low-cost operation with promising profit potential.

Receiver becomes passionate about the idea and is ready to act on the idea.

The analyst strongly believes that the company would be a good investment and is on the edge of recommending it.

Something triggers within the receiver a conviction to act on the idea.

The analyst accepts an invitation to tour the company's manufacturing operation. Seeing the highly computerized, efficiently operated facility validates all that the analyst wanted to believe about the company and triggers within the analyst a decision to recommend the company as a good investment.

Belief in an idea becomes a conviction to act on the idea.

The analyst features the company and its low-cost operation in his or her next published report with a "buy recommendation."

FIGURE 5.4 *Commonly Known Facts about Persuasion*

Sources	1. People are strongly and quickly influenced by people they feel they can trust and believe.
	2. People give even more credence to someone whose opinions are repeated by others who are looked up to in the community.
	3. People don't take seriously what they hear from people they don't trust, but over time they recall what was said and forget who said it.
Message structure	4. It's usually best to make your argument first, refute opposing arguments, and restate your own position.

FIGURE 5.4 (continued)

5. The last word is the one most likely to be remembered, especially with less-educated people.

6. It's more effective to give both sides of an argument than to give one side, especially with educated audiences.

7. A one-sided argument might change attitudes initially, but the effect may fade when another side is heard.

8. People who hear both sides of an argument are likely to maintain a position even when other arguments are heard later.

9. It's more persuasive to state a conclusion than to expect people to draw their own.

10. Repetition keeps issues in the public eye. Messages, especially in the media, are quickly forgotten if they're not reinforced.

Message Content

11. People listen to what they like and ignore what they dislike.

12. People pay attention to messages that favor what they believe and ignore those that don't.

13. People interpret things the way they think; they see what they want to see.

14. People remember what they consider to be relevant and forget the rest.

15. People remember things that support what they believe.

16. Facts and emotional appeals are more effective than either one alone.

17. Messages aimed at the interest of a target audience are likely to get attention.

18. Trying to incite fear, guilt, or other negative emotions, or to issue threats will most likely turn people away.

19. The use of fear is more effective when combined with suggestions for avoiding it.

20. Fear can affect how people think, but not necessarily how they act.

21. Humor can win the hearts of an audience and alienate people if it seems manipulative.

The Media

22. Face-to-face communication is more effective in changing minds than communication through various types of media.

23. Verbal communication conveys less but is more readily accepted than written communication.

24. Public media are more useful in reinforcing existing attitudes than in changing attitudes.

FIGURE 5.4 (*continued*)

25. Print media produce more comprehension, especially with complex issues, than broadcast media.

26. Broadcast media are more attention-getting than print media.

Audience   27. People with low self-esteem are more influenced by unsupported messages and fear appeals than people with higher self-esteem.

28. People with high self-esteem are more likely to be persuaded by well-substantiated messages.

29. People who make a commitment are likely to resist changing their minds afterward.

30. People who actively participate in making decisions are likely to retain changes in attitude over the long term.

that they are in line with the lessons learned. As mentioned earlier, this is your opportunity to educate plan reviewers; therefore, where applicable, include a reference in your strategy, such as "experience in the profession has shown that. . . ." Do not refer to a particular experience unless it is totally appropriate to the situation. And be sure not to propose a strategy that is contrary to professional lessons learned unless you can provide a solid rationale for the recommendation.

Rules for Writing a Strategy

1. A strategy should describe how, in concept, an objective is to be accomplished. More than one strategy might be required to accomplish a single objective.

2. A strategy may include an explanation about the use of persuasive techniques based on lessons learned through research; however, research findings should not be included unless they apply specifically to the situation.

3. A strategy may include a discussion of messages or themes.

4. A strategy is the place in a plan for creativity—a platform for presenting ideas that plan reviewers have not considered.

5. Details of a strategy are presented as activities or tactics.

To understand the relationship between an objective and strategy, let's divide an objective into its three component parts and include a strategy in the diagram. To illustrate, our objective is: To present effectively to community residents plans for expanding the airport so they support the project.

OBJECTIVE'S ACTION	To present plans effectively for expanding the airport
OBJECTIVE'S TARGET	Community residents
OBJECTIVE'S PURPOSE	So community residents support the project
STRATEGY	So how can we present the plans in a way that will compel community residents to support the project? One strategy we propose is making a public announcement through a news conference because it will be big news to the community, it will be difficult to keep secret, and there is considerable information to impart that will require an open dialogue with the media. Further, if we want to shape perceptions, we have to be first to make the announcement and we must provide a complete picture of the project. We don't want to be put in a position of having to reshape an impression made for us by someone else. Because the airport commission's executives will be major participants in making the announcement, we are providing the following details that will be of particular interest.
(ACTIVITY)	• We should schedule the conference for a Tuesday, Wednesday, or Thursday. Those are the best days for holding a news conference; on the other days newsrooms are short-staffed. The best time is mid-morning. That gives reporters time to do some additional research and for broadcast journalists to prepare their reports for the evening news. We should allow about 40 minutes for the conference, including questions.
(ACTIVITY)	• Our key theme for the announcement should focus on the town's need for economic development. We will work that into remarks for the executive participants. This will be more than informative; it will be a persuasive presentation with a compelling argument for total community support. The theme will be repeated and elaborated on in all of the printed materials we will develop for an information kit. The same information will be posted on the commission's Web site the day of the announcement. We also suggest announcing a hotline that will take questions from community residents.
(ACTIVITY)	• We propose holding the conference at the airport. The Davenport lounge is large enough to accommodate our scale model of the project and the media's needs for Internet connections, phones and power for equipment. We can display a large reproduction of the commission's emblem on the wall behind the podium and place a smaller one on the front of the podium.
(ACTIVITY)	• We suggest having Arnold Applebutter be moderator for the conference. He will introduce each of the three airport commissioners. Following 10 minutes of remarks and a brief overview of the project will be a Q&A. We will provide some executive training on this and schedule a rehearsal for the participants.
(ACTIVITY)	• After the conference we will expedite delivery of a video of the conference, B-roll of airport scenes and the project model to media no-shows.

Notice how responsive the strategy is in describing how the objective is to be achieved. The first sentence of the strategy is written to show how this could be one of several strategies for this objective, in which case it would be labeled Strategy A. Notice also that the strategy and activity details are presented in a coherent discussion of how to achieve the objective and that the entries are presented as suggestions or recommendations because the plan usually is a proposal requiring authorization. As you will see later, it is not necessary to label the activities, but simply to present them as bulleted items.

Strategy Examples

Unacceptable: The campaign strategy is a simple message for the campaign that could be conveyed through all mediums: "When it comes to keeping your water features clear, count on Barley Bob." Bob is an honest country boy who chews on barley and is spokesperson for the campaign.

Reasons: The strategy, according of the rules, must explain how an objective is to be accomplished. In this statement, the explanation is vague. A strategy may contain and explain the use of a particular message and may include the description of a character to deliver the message. However, this strategy falls short of explaining the strategic use of the message and the campaign character. According to the rules, a strategy must explain how an objective is to be accomplished and should include details in the form of a bulleted list of activities. A strategy should take into account lessons learned by public relations professionals. A plan reviewer might ask, for example, Have you taken into account experience that has shown that humor sometimes can generate a liking for the message source, but can backfire if the audience thinks the use of humor is a manipulative device?

Acceptable: We will accomplish [Objective #1] by communicating through a variety of media a message for people to "Count on Barley Bob to keep water features clear." The message promoting the use of barley to keep ponds and other water features free of algae the natural way will come from Barley Bob, the campaign's spokesperson. Research has shown that humor can be effective if it seems natural and not contrived. Bob is a friendly and believable character who delivers the natural care message with a hint of humor. The message from Bob will be conveyed to the region's homeowners through six different activities.

Unacceptable: Develop key messages and create benefit-focused materials that set a celebratory tone.

Reasons: This is gobbledygook; it contains no information that would be meaningful to plan reviewers.

Unacceptable: Invite parents to an informational meeting.

Reasons: There is nothing strategic about this action. There is not sufficient detail to instill confidence that this strategy will accomplish its objective. There is no attempt to use this opportunity to educate plan reviewers on the techniques of persuasion or communication methods or to elaborate with a message theme or other details.

Acceptable: Contact parents by phone and provide compelling reasons why it is important for them to attend an informational meeting on Jan. 1, 20XX. Enlist volunteer parents to make the phone calls to give credibility to the communication.

Have parent callers make note of feedback from the calls and have them try to confirm attendance of parents they contact to get an estimate of the total number likely to attend the meeting. Have callers stress that "No cases of this health problem have been detected and that the purpose of the meeting is to inform parents how to protect their children from becoming susceptible to the problem."

exercise 6

Based on the rules write a strategy for the case that follows. Use only the information provided in the case summary and stop short of listing the details (activities) of how the strategy is to be carried out.

W. P. Carey & Co. LLC with Oxford University

Off-balance-sheet financing is what got Enron in trouble. So you can appreciate how any company that provides off-balance-sheet financing could easily be associated with such scandalous behavior. W. P. Carey & Co. is a leading provider of net-lease financing, a traditional form of off-balance-sheet financing. The company worried when the Enron scandal hit that all forms of off-balance-sheet financing would be discredited and considered invalid. The company decided to go on the offensive by launching a media campaign designed to differentiate the company's net-lease financing from Enron's use of special-purpose entities. W. P. Carey wanted to capitalize on the high media interest by educating investors and corporate executives about the advantages of net-lease financing and promoting the company as the best firm to provide such financing.

W. P. Carey, together with Pricewaterhouse Coopers, arranged a luncheon with journalists from the *Wall Street Journal, Fortune*, Dow Jones, Bloomberg, and others. The company created advertisements that highlighted its financial capabilities and aimed at executives whose companies held leases whose value could be increased through net-lease financing. The company also produced an acquisitions brochure that was distributed to senior-level corporate executives. As a result of these efforts, W. P. Carey was able to complete more than $1 billion in net-lease transactions in 2002, a new record for the company and more than double its 2001 results.

7. ACTIVITY

An activity or tactic is what puts a strategy into action. Why is the activity component of importance to plan reviewers? It's important because activities provide the details of a strategy and reviewers want to assure themselves that they concur with the ways in which strategies are to be carried out.

One or more activities are usually required to implement a strategy. Typically, activities include the use of communication tools, such as brochures and news releases, along with various actions and events. (See examples of communication tools in Figure 5.5.) However, a plan developer must resist the temptation of throwing out a list of communication tools to solve a problem, meet a challenge, or take advantage of an opportunity (e.g., "We can solve this problem with two brochures, a poster, and a fact sheet").

FIGURE 5.5 *Communication Tools*

Actuality	Fax, on demand	Presentation
Annual meeting	Feature, business	Print publication
Annual report	Feature, educational	Printcast
Archive video	Feature, personality	Product profile
Archived Webcast	Feature, trend	Product review
A-roll	Infographics	Public Service Announcement— radio
Background video	Information kit	
Backgrounder	Insert and enclosure	Public Service Announcement— TV
Biographical sketch	Instant messaging	
Booklet	Interview—print media	Publicity event
Briefing paper	Interview—radio	Publicity photo
Broadcast news release	Interview—TV	Q & A
Brochure	Intranet	Quarterly earnings statement
B-roll	Leak	Questionnaire
Bumper sticker	Letter	Report
Buzz	Letter pitch	Rolling one-on-one
Byliner	Letter to editor	Safety meeting
Card stacking	Media advisory	Satellite media tour
Case history	Media alert	Social responsibility report
Circular	Media interview	Speakers' bureau
Closed circuit TV	Media tour	Speech
Collateral publication	Memento	Spokesperson tour
Commentary	Memo	Streaming video
Communication audit	Message board	Syndicated service
Communication meeting	Mission statement	Talk show
Contingency statement	NetBriefing	Testimonial
Corporate profile	News briefing	Testimony
Cover letter	News kit	Tip sheet
Demonstration	News release	Tours
Direct mail	Newsgroup seeding	Town hall meeting
Door hanger	Newsgroups	Trend story
Editorial	Newsletter	TV standup interview
Editorial board briefing	Newswire	Video news release
E-mail alert service	Online newsroom	Video teleconferencing
E-mail campaign	Op-ed commentary	Virtual conference
E-mail pitch	Opinion actuality	VO-BITE
E-mail survey	Organization profile	Voice mail
E-newsletter	Personality profile	VO-SOTs
Episodic framing	Phone pitch	Web conference
E-tour	Photo caption	Web monitoring
Event	Photo news release	Web news conference
Exclusive story	Pitch for radio talk show	Webcast—audio presentation
Expert news source	Pitch for TV coverage	Webcast—full feature
Fact sheet	Pocket points	Webcast—video presentation
Factoid	Position paper	White paper
FAQ	Poster	
Fax, broadcast	Prepared statement	

Avoid beginning activities with communication tools. It is always better to emphasize a strategic step rather than the vehicle that will be used to implement it. This is illustrated in the following table.

Strategy Emphasized	Communication Tool Emphasized
Generate interest and excitement about the sponsorship among reporters with a message from Bobby Apple and views of him racing in past competitions by sending them a short, specially produced communication on videotape or CD.	*Send a backgrounder* video to all targeted media outlets to generate excitement about the sponsorship with a message from Bobby Apple and scenes of him racing.
Entice the media to interview Bobby Apple and photograph the show car at the Los Angeles Convention Center during the annual car show by sending them a media advisory loaded with photo op ideas.	*Send a media advisory* that entices the media to interview Bobby Apple and see the team's show car at the Los Angeles Convention Center during the annual car show.
Announce XYZ's sponsorship of the Indy race car team with attention-grabbing quotes from driver Bobby Apply in print and video news releases.	*Send a print and video news release* announcing XYZ's sponsorship of the Indy race car team with attention-grabbing comments from driver Bobby Apple.

Every tool must be used correctly by itself and in conjunction with other activities. It would be incorrect, for example, to use a news release in place of a media alert to announce a news conference. A plan developer must realize that plan reviewers at the senior level, for the most part, are not professional public relations practitioners. It is likely, for example, that they would not know a white paper from a position paper, a tip sheet from a fact sheet, or a news conference from a news briefing. So when an activity calls for the use of a communication tool, you must describe what the device is as well as its purpose.

Activities should not be a list of routine logistical chores, such as "picking up donuts for the meeting," "copying and mailing letters," "renting a car," and so on. Plan reviewers are interested in strategic details.

Activities should be comprehensive so that the plan developer does not unwittingly shift the job of development to the reviewer. For example, when an activity is described simply as, "Hold a meeting of faculty members who teach courses related to diversity," it raises questions, such as Hold a meeting where? When? How many faculty members? How would they be identified? What courses do they teach? How would the meeting be conducted? By whom? For what purpose? Providing answers to these questions is the job of the plan developer. In summary, activities should provide reviewers with a detailed strategic sequence of moves necessary to carry out a strategy.

Following is an example of a list of activities written by a student team:

- The company will provide a phone number for employees to call to receive information and ask questions about the company's downsizing activities. The phone number will be activated on Sept. 18, 20XX, and will be deactivated Dec. 31, 20XX.

- Managers and supervisors will establish, or in most cases reaffirm, their open-door policy so employees will be more inclined to approach management with questions about the company's downsizing activities. The open-door policy will be implemented Sept. 20, 20XX, and will continue indefinitely.

- The company will provide the most current downsizing information in monthly employee newsletters or memos. To increase employee confidence, the newsletters and memos will include success stories of laid-off workers who have found new jobs outside the company. The first newsletter or memo will be sent to employees Oct. 31, 20XX, and will be published monthly through Jan. 31, 20XX.

- Managers and supervisors will recognize and reward employees for both their accomplishments and their efforts in this time of transition. Employees want to work for an organization and in a department that is successful, and they need something back in return. They need to know how they are doing: Are they succeeding or failing? Are they average or exemplary? What can they do to improve when improvement is needed? Receiving awards helps employees know that their work is appreciated. Awards will be given on a case-by-case basis to recognize individual and sometimes group effort. There will be no starting or ending dates. Recognition will be publicized in the aforementioned newsletters or memos.

Rules for Writing Activities or Tactics

1. Activities are detailed steps to be taken to carry out a strategy.

2. Activities should not be a to-do list of logistical chores (e.g., reserve a meeting room, order coffee, bring name tags, etc.).

3. Activities should not be a skeleton list of communication tools (e.g., brochure, news release, backgrounder, etc.); each communication tool must have a stated strategic purpose and must be employed in the correct manner.

4. Activities should be described as a series of strategic moves.

5. Activities should provide complete information; they should not burden plan reviewers with unanswered questions.

Activity Examples

Unacceptable:

- arrange a phone bank for parent callers

- assemble callers

- provide refreshments

Reasons: These activities are simply logistical chores. Activities should be an elaboration of the strategy in specific detail.

Acceptable:

- Recruit parent volunteers to help plan the informational meeting, announce it, and assist with hosting the event so that the event has credibility as a parent-based activity.

- Recruit parent volunteers to work the phone bank to notify all parents of the meeting.

- Provide and train callers with a script with compelling reasons for parents to attend the meeting.

- Establish a small resource group of medical experts to assist parent callers with technical questions they might be asked by other parents.

exercise 7

Explain without rewriting the entries how the following tactics (activities) should be written according to the rules.

Tactics

- Develop tag line: "Glasses that see skin dangers," and key messages about Skin Scanners.

- Press kit: new product release; compiled list of safety milestones that highlights the evolution of diagnostic innovations including Skin Scanner; backgrounder on Glasses, Inc.; bios on a Glasses, Inc., medical consultant and Skin Scanner inventor; visuals and captions. (Material distributed to wire services, trade books, newspapers, consumer magazines, online services, and radio stations.)

- Follow-up pitch calls to target media.

- Video news release distributed via satellite.

- Follow-up calls to TV stations nationwide.

- Press kit posted to 6,000 dot com news sites, and registered journalists were notified online about the story. Journalists could download images and VNR.

- Web site developed. Journalists could access site and download information and images.

- Timing: Press materials and Web site were launched on Jan. 2, 20XX; early release to WSJ.

__8. EVALUATION/MEASUREMENT__

The evaluation component of a plan must have a short-term monitoring function to track and manage progress toward achieving each objective and a longer-term assessment of outcomes. Plan reviewers require that a plan will be managed and results assessed by measurable objectives. This is especially important when you consider that the decision maker who approves your plan is accountable for authorizing the expenditure, for overseeing its implementation, and for its results. So plan reviewers have a vested interest in the management of a plan as well as in its ultimate results.

Let's consider how the areas of management and results are served by measurable objectives.

Measurable objectives enable reviewers to gauge the success of a plan through an assessment of outcomes or results. Every objective, according to the rules, must tell what is expected of an intended audience as a result of being subjected to strategic communication activities. That is the desired behavioral outcome. Determining to what extent the desired behavior was achieved determines the success of a particular objective or determines what modifications must be made prior to relaunching the plan or initiating a new plan.

Measurable objectives also enable reviewers to gage incremental progress in the plan's implementation by providing benchmark opportunities for determining to what extent strategic activities are achieving a particular objective. The assessment either will confirm the effectiveness of the activities or provide an opportunity to make timely adjustments.

For example, incremental progress can be determined toward achieving the following objective: To educate students about the benefits of participating in student government so that enough candidates will apply for all available student government positions for the coming term. By using an appropriate form of formal or informal research, such as personal interview spot checks, one can determine whether or not students are understanding the benefits of office. By checking applications, one can determine whether or not applications for student government positions are being submitted. If progress toward achieving this objective is not satisfactory, it may be necessary to adjust the strategy, for example, by intensifying the education process to communicate the benefits of holding office or creating an event to publicize opportunities available in student government. This is an example of managing the implementation of a plan by measurable objectives.

A plan reviewer wants a regular means of assurance that a plan is being implemented the way it was proposed—every strategic step executed on schedule, on target, and on budget. The plan reviewer knows that the implementer of a plan cannot guarantee results, but can be and should be held accountable for performance. Public relations is not an exact science and results can range from being totally successful to disappointing because of unexpected circumstances beyond the plan developer's control. Plan developers and implementers must be careful to establish with reviewers realistic expectations of a plan and promise only what implementers can totally control and perform themselves.

Plan developers and implementers can provide reviewers with means to monitor progress and performance in the execution of a plan with a Weekly Progress Tracking Report. The report can provide an at-a-glance visual check to see that activities of the plan are on schedule, on target, and on budget, and whether or not they have been completed. The rules for writing the evaluation require a progress tracking report for each objective. These reports can be consolidated into one report. Once a template is formed the report can be updated easily each week and submitted to reviewers on paper or electronically as a PDF file. Where the tracking reports and the overall evaluation belong in the plan and how they are to be written are subjects discussed in the rules that follow.

Rules for Writing an Evaluation

1. The evaluation component of a plan must have a short-term monitoring/managing function to track progress toward achieving each objective and a longer-term assessment of outcomes.

2. There must be one Progress Tracking Report for every objective following the description of strategies and activities. The entry must show how progress toward achievement of the objective is to be monitored. Tracking monitors performance—that is, it shows plan reviewers that strategic activities for each objective are being carried out on schedule, on target, and on budget.

   In the report example that follows, the strategic activities are a hotline, information kit, town meeting, and site sign. If these activities are on schedule, on target (effective in achieving their purpose), and on budget, the cells in the second column across from the activities would be yellow. If one of these activities was behind schedule, off target (not achieving its purpose), or over budget, the cell in the second column across from the activity would be red. When an activity is completed, the cell across from the activity in the third column is green. A red cell in any report signals a plan reviewer that the activity to which the red cell relates requires prompt attention and probable adjustment. A tracking report would be issued weekly.

PROGRESS TRACKING REPORT FOR OBJECTIVE #1—TARGET AUDIENCE: COMMUNITY RESIDENTS

Activity	On schedule On target On budget (yellow)	Behind schedule Off target Over budget (red)	Completed (green)
Hotline			
Information Kit			
Town Meeting			
Site Sign			

3. There must be a section titled "Evaluation" following the plan's objectives, strategies, activities, and progress tracking. This entry must provide a longer-term assessment of outcomes. Begin the evaluation section with the following paragraphs:

> Evaluation of this plan is provided for in two ways: (1) short-term progress tracking—a weekly report included with every objective that shows how progress toward achievement of each objective is to be monitored; and (2) a longer-term assessment of outcomes that explains how the desired outcome for each objective is to be assessed or measured.

> Progress tracking is shown in the plan under each objective. Assessment or measurement of outcomes is described in this section following a restatement of each objective.

Restate each objective and follow each one with an entry that begins with the label "Assessment:" and explain how the desired outcome of the objective is to be assessed or measured.

Assessment (example)

> Success in achieving this objective will be determined, informally, based on feedback supervisors receive from employees indicating employee understanding and support of the need for a change in procedure.

The evaluation section should close with the following statement:

> By achieving the desired outcome for each of the plan's objectives we will accomplish the goal: (State the goal.)

Based on the rules for developing an evaluation explain how the following entry could be improved.

Evaluation

The public forum on February 29 was well attended (300 people). Initial questions regarding the problem shifted to broader questions regarding health policy and were directed to the present officials. The center was not the main focus as before. Media coverage on February 30 and March 2 reported on the forum as well as the court findings of no wrongdoing. And for the first time in months, things got quiet. The hotline recorded 10 phone calls—many from customers wanting reassurance that their warranties remained unchanged. Employees who had borne the brunt of angry customers were acknowledged with a series of appreciation events, including a pancake breakfast served by the president. Further positive anecdotal feedback from community leaders and the quick resolution of negative media coverage were great indicators of initial success. The topic, which held the attention of the media and community for nearly four months, has dissipated entirely.

9. EXECUTION TIMELINE

The execution timeline is a schedule of activities and their implementation. Success of a plan depends on the meticulous scheduling and disciplined execution of timeline activities. The timeline is important to reviewers because it provides a visual—at-a-glance—sequence of actions with dates and an overall time frame for the plan. The timeline is especially important to the plan developer because it provides an opportunity to show reviewers how much preparation time is necessary for each step of the plan. It is unlikely that a plan reviewer would know how much time is necessary to research a speech, produce a trade shoe display, write, review, and clear a news release, or produce a four-color brochure. See Figure 5.6 for a sample timeline.

FIGURE 5.6   *Sample Execution Timeline*

July 8	• Conduct plant closure planning meeting—review business rationale and approve Q & A
July 12	• Notify manager of Cyber plant closure
July 15	• Meet with Cyber plant manager to discuss business issues relative to closure
July 17–19	• Conduct three-day work session with human resources director and Cyber plant manager (review operational shut-down plan and time table; identify core staff; develop retention plan; approve communication plan; discuss government regulations; approve news releases; review employment information; develop employment assistance; finalize security arrangements; approve contingency plan)
July 26	• Notify all plant managers by phone of Cyber plant closure
	• Notify all functional managers of Cyber of closure
	• Have customer mailings ready
	• Deliver by courier information kits to division managers
July 27	• Have information kits ready for sales representatives, sales managers, and service center managers
July 28	• Follow up with Cyber functional managers
	• Notify district sales managers by phone
	• Review news media procedures with human resources director
July 29	**Plant Closure Announcement**
	• Inform service center managers

FIGURE 5.6 *(continued)*

- Inform Cyber supervisors

- Conduct meetings with Cyber employees

- Inform community (hand-deliver news release to local media)

- Inform sales representatives by phone

- Inform Cyber customer service reps in face-to-face meeting

- Notify employees of relocation opportunities

- Distribute news release to corporate personnel

- Transmit news release to state wires via BusinessWire

- Distribute letter from CEO to all employees

- Call community opinion leaders

- Call or fax local and state officials

- Notify key suppliers by phone

- Fax news release to trade press

- Mail letter and news release to customers

- Mail letters and news release to suppliers

- **Period following announcement**

- Follow up on all communication to ensure complete and accurate understanding by all audiences

Rules for Writing an Execution Timeline

1. Include in the timeline all major preparatory steps in the plan with dates and/or date ranges.

2. Show execution dates for all major plan activities (e.g., make public announcement).

3. Maintain a parallel structure—begin every entry with a verb.

4. Use a two-column format (this is simply prepared using the table function in a word processor program)—place dates in the first column and activities in the second column.

5. Arrange table by days, weeks, months, or quarters; however, execution dates must be specific.

6. A third column may be added to show who is responsible for executing each activity.

10. BUDGET

The budget is of paramount interest to reviewers. One of the quickest ways to have a plan rejected is by proposing a budget that is out of line with the organization's resources. An experienced plan developer will gather the information necessary to present a budget appropriate to the organization. It is much better to present a budget that is on target than to present one that is out of the ballpark and will require major modifications, even elimination of some creative strategies, to be acceptable. With public relations, communication objectives can be accomplished in many different ways at different levels of expense. Developing a plan within a particular budget is one of the responsibilities of the plan developer.

A proposed budget should be developed from one of two positions. One position is that you represent a public relations firm or agency and your plan is for a client. The other position is that you are an employee of an organization with responsibility for public relations and your plan is for your employer. You must use a budget format that is appropriate for your position.

Let's look first at a budget format for a plan developed by a public relations agency. The budget should have two parts: (1) time billing for agency personnel and (2) billing for out-of-pocket expenses. For time billing, you must estimate the amount of time required by agency personnel to carry out the work of your plan. Most of the work on an agency account will be done by an account executive—the lead person—and an account coordinator, account assistant, or assistant account executive. A certain amount of administrative/secretarial work is also usually required. Time for personnel more senior to the account executive might be included for their particular expertise or experienced counsel. For a highly complex plan time might be budgeted for an account supervisor who would be responsible for managing the use of additional expertise and services, such as opinion research or advertising.

Following are public relations agency hourly billing rates to use in developing a budget for the case exercises in this book.

PUBLIC RELATIONS FIRM OR AGENCY HOURLY BILLING RATES

President, General Manager, PR Director	$220
Vice President	$175
Account Supervisor	$150
Senior Account Executive	$125
Account Executive	$110
Assistant Account Executive	$95
Account Coordinator, Account Assistant	$85
Secretary	$60

Next your budget should show out-of-pocket expenses. These are expenses the agency would incur or contract for on behalf of the client, such as photography, graphic design, opinion research, media monitoring, long-distance phone charges, photocopies, printing, and so on. See a suggested format below for a budget that includes both personnel billing and out-of-pocket expenses.

ESTIMATED BUDGET				
Personnel Billing				
Agency Staff	Rate/Hour	Estimated Hours/Day	Estimated Days	
Account Exec.	110.00	2	12	2,640.00
Assistant AE	95.00	3	12	3,420.00
			Subtotal	6,060.00
Out-of-Pocket Expenses				
Photography (one day)				2,000.00
Brochure (layout and design, 12 pages, color)				4,000.00
			Subtotal	6,000.00
TOTAL ESTIMATED BUDGET				12,060.00

Next let's look at a budget format for a plan that you, as the person responsible for public relations, would develop for your employer. One major difference between this budget and one developed by a public relations firm is that time for work done by you and various staff members is already accounted for in your salary and some of the expenses shown in the plan, such as photography, might already be covered in your organization's annual public relations budget. So, in this position, the budget should show only items or services that require additional funding for which you must obtain authorization. Following is a suggested format for a budget plan developed by company public relations personnel.

ESTIMATED BUDGET		
Expenses		
Photography (one day)		1,000.00
Brochure (design, layout, color, 12 pages)		3,000.00
	Subtotal	4,000.00
TOTAL ESTIMATED BUDGET		4,000.00

Rules for Writing a Budget

1. A proposed budget from a public relations firm must show billing for personnel and for out-of-pocket expenses.

2. An estimated budget for a public relations function within an organization must show only extraordinary expenses—those not covered in an annual department budget.

3. Budgets should be presented in a spreadsheet format (see the examples shown on page 53)

and can be easily prepared with the table function in your word processor.

4. Proposed budgets should be affordable to an organization.

5. Budget items should be self-explanatory.

6. Budget figures must be aligned on a decimal point.

See Figures 5.7 and 5.8 for model student public relations plans.

FIGURE 5.7   *A Student-Initiated Public Relations Plan Proposed to The Center on Diversity and Community at the University of Oregon[1]*

Problem   The Center on Diversity and Community strives to promote racial, ethnic, and cultural diversity on the University of Oregon campus and in its surrounding communities. The center currently lacks sufficient resources to increase its visibility among faculty, students, potential university and corporate donors and surrounding communities about the universal benefits of diversity issues education.

Currently, some marketing challenges that the center faces include: limited financial resources, advertising and communication that is insufficiently tailored to multiple and specific audiences.

The center's executive committee recognizes the pressing need for a strategic public relations plan in its efforts to position the organization to fulfill its mission. Without the success that a plan could provide, which includes a financial development facet, the center could be seriously restricted in its ability to achieve its goals. The center is requesting assistance with these serious public relations problems.

Situation Analysis   In spring of 1999, a student publicly made a racially insensitive remark in a large University of Oregon classroom. A heated exchange ensued between the student and others attending the course, which spilled outside the class through violent threats and e-mails. The incident brought to light concerns of diversity and equity in classroom environments and throughout the University of Oregon campus. The incident led to an approximate 95-person sit-in at Johnson Hall. Students, faculty and staff demanded the administration address diversity issues on campus in a formal setting.

---

[1] Reprinted by permission of The Center on Diversity and Community at the University of Oregon.

FIGURE 5.7 (continued)

In the summer of 1999, the President's Office created an action staff to produce a Diversity Internship Program Report, a document describing how the University of Oregon could proactively address and promote diversity throughout the institution. Based on the report's findings, a research team was established.

The team developed a proposal for the Center on Diversity and Community, an interdisciplinary research center. Created in October 2001, the center promotes inquiry, dialogue, and understanding on issues of racial, ethnic and cultural diversity. The center considers cultural diversity to include such identity factors as socioeconomic status, sexual preference, nationality and language.

CoDaC offers competitive research grants and awards, diversity dialogue and facilitation training programs, public events and workshops, resource guides, and student internships. Its governing body is the executive committee that is composed of faculty, administrators, and student leaders. Executive committee meetings are held twice a term along with additional subcommittee meetings. CoDaC reports to the Office of the Vice President for Research and Graduate Studies and the Office of the Vice Provost for Institutional Equity and Diversity.

Currently, the center is funded by a one-time allocation from the Associated Students of the University of Oregon plus funds from the University of Oregon administration. Its marketing strategies use its Web site, e-mail lists, three-times-a-year newsletter, posters and flyers, campus announcements, UO media relations, announcements through local news outlets and Web sites, and display ads in the *Eugene Weekly, Oregon Daily Emerald* and *The Register-Guard.*

Goal

For the Center on Diversity and Community to be fully institutionalized as an essential, unique and authoritative resource for diversity education on the University of Oregon campus, and to be making greater regional and national impact.

Primary Focus

Graduate Students

Many graduate programs require a research project. The grants offered by the center provide a financial resource for graduate students to complete such research. The completed research acknowledges the center as the funding source and serves as a promotion tool. These students participate in an annual Graduate Research Conference organized by the center.

Potential Corporate Sponsors

The center seeks to receive funding from corporations, specifically Northwest-based and progressive-thinking national companies that value diversity and cultural competency. In an effort to continue the center's operations, the executive committee is seeking corporate or foundation sponsors. This target audience is important both because of its potential for funding the center and because many companies seek to increase diversity and cultural competency in the workforce. It is also the most time-consuming audience to research because, to be effective, contact must be made with senior management, one

FIGURE 5.7 *(continued)*

organization at a time, and any such relationship must relate closely both to the center's and the company's mission and values.

Undergraduate Students

The center is seeking greater visibility with undergraduate students. This audience comprises the majority of the university's population and can be viewed as the most impressionable of all target audiences. Some undergraduates could be experiencing their first meaningful encounter in a culturally diverse environment. The center strives to educate these students on diversity and cultural competency issues to encourage a positive college experience.

Faculty and Staff

The center seeks to improve its visibility with faculty as a resource for promoting and supporting their diversity-related research activities. The center also works with staff on increasing individual and organizational cultural competency.

Community

Despite successful public events and articles in the local press, many Eugene-area residents are not currently aware of the center's efforts, but could benefit from its programs and research. Greater knowledge and awareness of the center throughout the community would give more public emphasis to the program and would lead to more opportunities for obtaining sponsorships.

Potential/Current University Funding Sources

This audience is also important because it has a direct bearing on future funding of the center. The center provides its reporting offices with formal annual reports and informal reports on its activities and successes. Greater awareness of these results and reports may produce greater university funding sources, both current and potential.

A critical prerequisite to the recommendations contained in this plan is a suggestion to modify the organization's name. Currently, the center does not wish to change its name due to the recognition that it has accrued to date on campus and in the community, but it may consider doing so in the future if its mission were to undergo significant change. Potential funders and others unfamiliar with the organization might confuse "CODAC" with the Kodak brand. In order to clarify what the acronym signifies and to distinguish itself, the center has contemplated a change in printed appearance and logo from "CODAC" to "CoDaC." No name modifications or changes are suggested in this proposal.

Objective #1   To attract the interest of corporations and/or professional and business organizations that would like to raise their public profiles in the area of diversity so they become active participants in and financial supporters of the Center on Diversity and Community.

FIGURE 5.7 *(continued)*

Strategy

The center could better engage potential financial supporters through presentations to professional, business and civic organizations in the Eugene community and through personal contact with Oregon graduates who are employed by potential sponsors. We recommend implementing this strategy according the following:

1. Obtain from the Oregon Alumni Foundation the names of graduates who are employed currently by companies that the center has selected as potential financial supporters. Use graduates as "rainmakers" in helping the center establish relationships with the graduates' respective organizations and ultimately requesting financial support.

2. Call on selected graduates for assistance in arranging and possibly making a presentation to their respective companies.

3. For soliciting financial support from these organizations, develop a brochure of irresistible funding opportunities. The brochure would describe various ways to support the center in a range of marketable packages of opportunities with clearly defined forms of public recognition for the sponsors.

    a. For example, one important area of funding would be for the design, production and special packaging of 1,000 cast bronze mementos to be known as the center's Diversity Medallion, a gesture of recognition to be earned by individuals and organizations by volunteering time, talent and energy to embrace diversity. The medallion could have on one side a graphic symbol of the center and a slogan, such as a phrase borrowed with permission from the song, "Shed a Little Light,"—"We are bound together by the task that stands before us." On the other side could be the center's mission, "Men and women dedicated to promoting inquiry, dialogue and understanding on issues of racial, ethnic and cultural diversity." The role of the medallion will become clear as this plan unfolds. The sponsor that provides funds for the medallion could receive public recognition in the form of a credit line on each medallion, such as "Provided by The (Name) Foundation."

    b. A range of funding opportunities from $100 to $100,000, each in an irresistible marketing package like the medallion with clearly defined public recognition of sponsors would be described in the center's brochure.

4. Expand the center's executive committee membership, or create a community advisory board, to include organizational memberships for professional, business and civic organizations in the Eugene community that would like to embrace diversity more openly.

    a. Present each organization that joins the board with a membership plaque with the center's Diversity Medallion. The plaque could have a heading borrowed

FIGURE 5.7 (continued)

with permission from the song, "Shed a Little Light," that says, "There are ties between us, all men and women living on the earth, ties of hope and love."

i. Board membership would require board member representatives of these organizations to host an annual presentation of the center to their respective organizations.

ii. The presentations would be scheduled to be held during the week of the city "Diversity Walk," an annual commemorative event established by the Eugene City Council, which is described later in the plan.

iii. The presentation would honor organizations for their support of diversity activities and would announce volunteer opportunities that would especially benefit from the joint participation of community and campus leaders.

iv. Community leader participants could earn the center's Diversity Medallion for their efforts and involvement.

v. The center's fund-raising brochure would be included in all presentations.

WEEKLY PROGRESS TRACKING REPORT				
Objective/Audience	*Activity*	*On schedule On target On budget (Cells color-coded yellow)*	*Behind schedule Off target Over budget (Cells color-coded red)*	*Completed (Cells color-coded green)*
Objective #1 Donors	Names			
	Rainmakers			
	Brochure			
	Memberships			

Objective #2 To increase graduate student awareness of competitive research grants and conference opportunity available through the center so that more students participate in research on issues of diversity.

Strategy

We recommend that the center strengthen its appeal to graduate students through graduate-to-graduate briefings and through a special event. This strategy could be implemented as follows:

Organize current graduate student grant recipients to undertake a series of graduate-to-graduate student briefings about the center and its research-funding opportunities. Make

FIGURE 5.7 *(continued)*

this outreach responsibility a requirement for every student who receives a grant in the future. It would be the responsibility of each grant recipient to inform through informal briefings all graduate students in the recipient's particular school of center activities throughout the grant recipient's period of center-sponsored research. As part of their participation in the Graduate Research Program, grant recipients would be given a certificate entitling each to receive a Diversity Medallion upon completion of their research.

<table>
<tr><td colspan="5" align="center">WEEKLY PROGRESS TRACKING REPORT</td></tr>
<tr>
<td>*Objective/Audience*</td>
<td>*Activity*</td>
<td align="center">*On schedule
On target
On budget
(Cells color-coded yellow)*</td>
<td align="center">*Behind schedule
Off target
Over budget
(Cells color-coded red)*</td>
<td align="center">*Completed
(Cells color-coded green)*</td>
</tr>
<tr>
<td>Objective #2
Graduate students</td>
<td>Briefings</td>
<td></td>
<td></td>
<td></td>
</tr>
</table>

Objective #3 To heighten interest among students in the center's undergraduate-focused programs and resources, so that more individuals participate in the organization.

Strategy

We recommend that the center heighten interest among undergraduates by communicating the benefits of participating in the organization frequently through multiple and familiar channels. Activities to consider are the following:

1. Publicize and fill openings for one or more credit-based internships in specific areas, such as public relations, Web site development, campus outreach, community outreach, faculty staff liaison, student group liaison, ASUO liaison and graduate student liaison and use this cadre of talent to produce promotional materials, such as brochures, newsletters and flyers. Each student that completes an internship would earn one of the center's Diversity Medallions.

2. Recruit, train and dispatch a dozen student volunteers who would like to develop their presentation skills as the center's ambassadors spreading word of the center's mission and events before large lecture classes in business, ethics, sociology, management—all areas of study, and before professional student organizations, such as the Society of Professional Journalists, American Marketing Association and Business Honors Society. Students who make a certain number of presentations on behalf of the center would earn Diversity Medallions.

3. Develop a conspicuous presence for the center during the fall student orientation programs, perhaps in the form of a short workshop on conflict resolution or other

FIGURE 5.7 (continued)

skill-building activity related to diversity to educate students on diversity issues to encourage a positive college experience.

4. Partner with the appropriate organization for publicizing the upcoming dedication of the $1.5 million Longhouse being built on campus to represent student members of Native Americans throughout the Pacific Northwest. At an appropriate ceremony, present the leadership of the Longhouse with a piece of Native American art with the Diversity Medallion embedded in its design and publicize the presentation with a photo news release to all area media.

		WEEKLY PROGRESS TRACKING REPORT		
Objective/Audience	*Activity*	*On schedule On target On budget (Cells color-coded yellow)*	*Behind schedule Off target Over budget (Cells color-coded red)*	*Completed (Cells color-coded green)*
Objective #3 Undergraduate students	Internships			
	Ambassadors			
	Workshop			
	Longhouse			

Objective #4 To raise the Eugene community's awareness of the center, its role and activities in the community and on campus, so community members get involved and participate in the center and its diversity-related events.

Strategy A

This objective could be accomplished by having the city establish an annual "Diversity Walk" for the greater Eugene area with proceeds contributed to the center for managing the event. This would require:

1. Making an informal inquiry of Councilman David Kelly, who represents the university area, to gage the interest in a possible council action to designate an annual "Diversity Walk."

2. If the inquiry receives a positive response, the center would work with Councilman Kelly to draft a council resolution establishing the annual event to promote diversity.

3. Council would pass the resolution and the day following the council meeting the mayor would announce the declaration at a special ceremony at city hall.

FIGURE 5.7 *(continued)*

4. The center would manage the event for the city and receive some or part of the entry fees collected.

5. The center would be identified with the city on Diversity Walk tee-shirts that would be worn by all participants.

Strategy B

Another strategy for achieving this objective would be for the city of Eugene each year to honor an individual who deserves special recognition for promoting diversity in the community. This could be accomplished in the following manner:

1. The mayor and council would select and announce the "Citizen of the Year for Exemplary Efforts in Promoting Diversity."

2. The mayor would decorate the individual with a Diversity Medallion suspended from a ribbon and placed on the honoree in the manner of an Olympic medal presentation. (Some medallions would be produced with an eye through which a ribbon could be passed.)

3. This would be an award made jointly by the center and the city.

4. The honoree would become a special ambassador to the center, would be featured in the center's annual report, and would have a portrait photo displayed at the center.

WEEKLY PROGRESS TRACKING REPORT				
Objective/Audience	*Activity*	*On schedule On target On budget (Cells color-coded yellow)*	*Behind schedule Off target Over budget (Cells color-coded red)*	*Completed (Cells color-coded green)*
Objective #4 Community residents	Inquiry			
	Positive response			
	Resolution			
	Event			
	Tee-shirts			
	Citizen award			
	Ceremony			
	Center/City			
	Honoree			

FIGURE 5.7 *(continued)*

Objective #5 To motivate university faculty and staff so they take an interest in and actively support the center and its mission on campus and in the community.

Strategy

One way to accomplish this objective would be to enlist the cooperation of the U.S. Ambassador to the United Nations to personally encourage University of Oregon faculty and staff to advance the cause of diversity among all people for the benefit of world peace. The letter would be sent to all faculty and staff members with a cover letter from the university president that would endorse the ambassador's message and urge individuals to advance diversity on campus by participating in the center's activities and earning a Diversity Medallion. Prior to this communication the university president would be awarded a Diversity Medallion in a publicized ceremony. This strategy would require the following:

1. Discuss the proposal with the university president.

2. Discuss the president's endorsement and proposal with the ambassador's staff.

3. Draft a letter for the ambassador's review, approval and signature addressed to University of Oregon faculty and staff.

4. Draft a cover letter for the university president.

5. Follow distribution of the ambassador's letter one week later with a letter from the center referring faculty and staff to the center's new Web site with a link to a screen with specific ways in which faculty and staff could support the center and earn a Diversity Medallion for their contribution.

WEEKLY PROGRESS TRACKING REPORT				
Objective/Audience	*Activity*	*On schedule* *On target* *On budget* *(Cells color-coded yellow)*	*Behind schedule* *Off target* *Over budget* *(Cells color-coded red)*	*Completed* *(Cells color-coded green)*
Objective #5 University faculty and staff	President			
	Ambassador			
	Letter Ambassador			
	Letter President			
	Web site			

FIGURE 5.7 *(continued)*

Objective #6 To better communicate to potential and current university funding sources the achievements the center has made toward its goal so that donors will see progress and be motivated to provide or continue to provide financial support.

Strategy

This objective would be accomplished through an annual survey with results published in an annual report to be distributed to potential and current university funding sources. The strategy would require:

1. An on-line campus climate survey developed and conducted by the center. The survey would be publicized and participation would be encouraged by enabling students who answer several questions to qualify for a drawing in which the winner would receive textbooks free for one quarter.

   a. Survey findings would be published by the center in a news release.

   b. The center's intern cadre would prepare a by-lined op-ed piece for the director discussing the campus climate survey results and its implications to be submitted in two different versions, one to the *Oregon Daily Emerald* and the other to *The Register-Guard*.

2. The survey results would be included in an annual report published by the center and delivered and discussed in one-on-one visits with the center's current and potential university funding sources.

		WEEKLY PROGRESS TRACKING REPORT		
Objective/Audience	*Activity*	*On schedule* *On target* *On budget* *(Cells color-coded yellow)*	*Behind schedule* *Off target* *Over budget* *(Cells color-coded red)*	*Completed* *(Cells color-coded green)*
Objective # 6 Donors	Survey			
	Annual report			

Evaluation Evaluation of this plan is provided for in two ways: (1) short-term progress tracking, a weekly report included with every objective that shows how progress toward achievement each objective is to be monitored; and (2) a longer-term assessment of outcomes that explains how the desired outcome for each objective is to be assessed or measured. Progress tracking is shown in the plan under each objective. Assessment or measurement of outcomes is described in this section following a restatement of each objective.

FIGURE 5.7 *(continued)*

Objective #1 To attract the interest of corporations and/or professional and business organizations that would like to form a symbiotic relationship so they become active participants in and financial supporters of the Center on Diversity and Community.
Assessment: Success in achieving this objective will be based on total contributions received one year from the time the plan is launched.

Objective #2 To increase graduate student awareness of competitive research grants and conference opportunity available through the center so more students participate in research on issues of diversity.
Assessment: Success in achieving this objective will be determined by the external support of the Graduate Student Research Award program, and by increased community attendance at the annual Graduate Research Conference.

Objective #3 To heighten interest among students in the center's programs and resources among undergraduate students so that more individuals participate in the organization.
Assessment: Success in achieving this objective will be determined by the following:

1. internship positions have been filled;

2. major events are regularly and successfully co-sponsored with other university organizations, as measured by attendance, event quality, and other factors;

3. student volunteers made an acceptable number of large class presentations on behalf of the center;

4. a center workshop has been established as part of the student fall orientation;

5. the center participated in the dedication of the Longhouse.

Objective #4 To raise the Eugene community's awareness of the center, its role and activities in the community and on campus, so community members get involved and participate in the center and its diversity-related events.
Assessment: Success in achieving this objective will be based on completing preparations for the events, conducting the actual events and assessing by sign-ups and field observation participation of community residents in the center's activities.

Objective #5 To motivate university faculty and staff so they actively support the center's activities on campus and in the community.
Assessment: Success in achieving this objective will be based on distribution of the ambassador's letter and sign-ups by faculty and staff in the center's activities for earning Diversity Medallions.

FIGURE 5.7 *(continued)*

Objective #6 To better communicate to potential and current university funding sources the achievements the center has made toward its goal so that donors will see progress and be motivated to provide or continue to provide financial support.

Assessment: Success in achieving this objective will be determined by completing the survey and annual report, communicating the center's accomplishments to potential and current university funding sources and spot-checking feedback from these sources through informal conversations.

By achieving these and other desired outcomes for each of the plan's objectives we will advance a crucial goal: for the Center on Diversity and Community to be an increasingly institutionalized and more visible resource, recognized on campus, throughout the region, and on the national level as an essential contributor to inquiry, dialogue and understanding on diversity and cultural competency issues.

EXECUTION TIMELINE

ACTIVITIES *(major preparatory steps)*	Target Execution Date
Research name change or modification	
Prepare publicity materials	
ANNOUNCE NEW OR MODIFIED NAME	Martin Luther King Jr. Week 2004
Develop internships and student executive board positions	
Prepare publicity materials	
SELECT INTERNS	Martin Luther King Jr. Week 2004
Identify UO alumni rainmakers employed by potential financial supporters	
Develop fund-raising brochure	
Identify potential title sponsor to finance production of Diversity Medallions	
LAUNCH FUND-RAISING CAMPAIGN	March 2004
Organize meeting of grant recipients	
BEGIN SCHEDULE OF GRADUATE-TO-GRADUATE BRIEFINGS	March 2004
Train cadre of ambassadors to make presentations to student classes	
BEGIN SCHEDULE OF AMBASSADOR PRESENTATIONS	March 2004
Enlist cooperation of U.S. Ambassador to the United Nations	
Coordinate with university president's staff	
Send ambassador letter with president's cover letter to faculty	
SEND FOLLOW-UP LETTER TO FACULTY	March 2004
Plan workshop on conflict resolution for student orientation	
CONDUCT WORKSHOP DURING STUDENT ORIENTATION	Orientation Week 2004
Research opportunity to partner in Native American Longhouse dedication	
PARTICIPATE IN LONGHOUSE DEDICATION	TBA
Plan meeting with Eugene mayor to discuss possible "Diversity Walk"	
Obtain city resolution for "Diversity Walk"	
MANAGE "DIVERSITY WALK" FOR CITY OF EUGENE	Martin Luther King Jr. Week 2005
Develop online campus climate survey	
CONDUCT CAMPUS CLIMATE SURVEY	Martin Luther King Jr. Week 2005
Plan and produce annual report	
PUBLISH ANNUAL REPORT	Martin Luther King Jr. Week 2005
Coordinate with university president's staff	
Send Ambassador letter with president's cover letter to faculty	

ESTIMATED BUDGET

For the 10-week period January 5 to March 12, 2004

Staff	Hours	Rate	
Account executive	30	75.00	2,250.00
Account coordinator	30	65.00	1,950.00
Secretary	40	50.00	2,000.00
General manager	5	150.00	750.00
Subtotals	**105**		**6,950.00**
Out-of-Pocket Expenses			
Publicity materials			600.00
Production of fund-raising brochures			1,000.00
Production of presentations materials			450.00
Production of workshop materials			300.00
Subtotal			**2,350.00**
TOTAL			**9,300.00**

WEEKLY PROGRESS TRACKING REPORT (INCLUDES ALL OBJECTIVES)

Objective/Audience	Activity	On schedule On target On budget (Cells color-coded yellow)	Behind schedule Off target Over budget (Cells color-coded red)	Completed (Cells color-coded green)
Objective #1 Donors	Names			
	Rainmakers			
	Brochure			
	Memberships			
Objective #2 Graduate students	Briefings			
Objective #3 Undergraduate students	Internships			
	Ambassadors			
	Workshop			
	Longhouse			
Objective #4 Community residents	Inquiry			
	Positive response			
	Resolution			
	Event			
	Tee-shirts			
	Citizen award			
	Ceremony			
	Center/City			
	Honoree			
Objective #5 University faculty and staff	President			
	Ambassador			
	Letter Ambassador			
	Letter President			
	Web site			
Objective #6 Donors	Survey			
	Annual report			

FIGURE 5.8 *A Sample Public Relations Plan Written by University of Oregon Students*

Problem	There is a problem at South County High School (SCHS) because recent incidents and rumors have painted the high school as an unsafe environment with unclear policies concerning free speech, cultural responsiveness and school security.

Parents are concerned that their students are no longer safe at school and want concrete answers to their questions. Without support from parents, school programs and funding could suffer. Media reports could damage the school's reputation in the community if journalists are excluded from school meetings and can only report on rumors and second-hand information. School faculty could lose confidence in the administration if their ability to teach and work is compromised by poor attendance and in-class disruptions. Community members could become outraged and question the ability of the school administration to react to difficult situations.

We do not want parents, staff, community members or the media to lose confidence in the school administration's ability to provide a safe and culturally aware environment for the students. This is a public relations problem with serious consequences that need to be addressed immediately. |
| **Situation Analysis** | SCHS recently experienced a situation that sparked concern among parents, faculty, administrators and students about safety and diversity.

Last week a boy, who is not a student, came to the school to see a girl during lunch. While there he tried to hand out Ku Klux Klan patches, but was immediately apprehended and escorted off campus. After this happened students began to talk about the incident along with other issues like freedom of speech and race.

The following day the school was subject to random acts of vandalism. In the wood shop 60 birdhouses were glued to the workbench. A refrigerator door was cemented shut in the home economics room, and some pushing and shoving broke out in the band room.

That weekend SCHS Principal Howard Burdick called for an emergency parent meeting in the high school auditorium. Burdick wanted to explain the situation that unfolded earlier that week, but was unexpectedly confronted with streams of questions and concerns from angry and irritated parents. With emotions on high throughout the meeting, neither Burdick nor the parents were able to leave feeling they had accomplished something.

In addition, a journalist came to the meeting uninvited. The journalist was unhappy that Burdick would not answer his questions and assured him that an article would be run the next day.

Later that day another emergency meeting was held at the high school with Burdick, the district superintendent, a student body president, faculty and staff representatives, the president of the Parent Teacher Association, and a member of the local law enforcement office. The group developed a four-point, short-term emergency action plan that includes: security, a leadership team, and a school initiative in cultural awareness and a community enrichment symposium. SCHS will implement the four-point action plan immediately. |

FIGURE 5.8 *(continued)*

South County High needs public relations help to inform community members about the situation, to relieve parents and staff of their safety concerns, to smooth things over with the journalist, to give students a voice and to educate the principal.

Goal

For South County High School to be operating as a safe environment that embraces diversity.

Primary Focus

Faculty and Staff

Educators are an important focus of our public relations plan. They know about the events that happened last week at SCHS and are now concerned for their own safety as well as their students' safety. Educators do not know about the public relations plan, but are closely linked to its success.

Parents

Parents of SCHS students are an essential target audience because they support the school and its programs. Many parents are very emotional because they feel school administrators have not been forthcoming with information concerning rumors of fights, weapons and vandalism at the school. These parents are concerned about the safety of their children and want their questions answered immediately. The school can't be successful without the confidence, financial investments and moral support of parents.

Howard Burdick

As the principal, Howard Burdick is the figurehead of SCHS. Whether something good or bad happens, everyone looks to him for answers and steady leadership. Burdick must interact with students, parents, staff, media and the community regarding day-to-day matters and in times of crisis. He welcomes training and input because he understands the need for public relations planning and wants to successfully implement the four-point plan.

Media

SCHS administrators have a strained relationship with local media. We need to develop a good, working relationship with the media in order to receive fair and accurate coverage. If administrators are not honest, local media will feel free to report inaccurate and unfair information about the high school.

Community Members

The community members of South County are an important audience because it is their tax dollars that support the school. They have a right to be informed about the school

FIGURE 5.8 *(continued)*

and any situation that may arise that would impact the community. The community has not received any information from the school. So far, anything they know has come from the media.

Students

Students are an important audience because the four-point plan directly affects their daily lives. We should not restrict their input in the four-point plan just because they are not adults. Students are an important resource for information about keeping diversity in the school and violence out of the school.

Objective #1 [faculty and staff]

To train faculty and staff in diversity and violence in schools so they are prepared to handle any incidents that might occur.

Strategy

We will accomplish objective #1 by teaching faculty and staff how to respond in emergency situations and how to encourage diversity. Faculty and staff will need to be informed about the new four-point action plan that has been established. We recommend this strategy be implemented as follows:

1. Inform faculty and staff about the new four-point action plan so they will understand the changes made at SCHS. A memo from Burdick will be given to every educator and staff member that will outline each of the four points, emphasizing the heightened security, which is a big concern for them.

2. Members of the local law enforcement will conduct a seminar on how to handle school violence in order to train faculty and staff in emergency response practices. The seminar will be offered to everyone at SCHS and will cover topics such as warning signs of violence, how to intervene and when to get help.

3. Provide faculty and staff with an emergency response information packet so they will understand procedures and guidelines. The packet will not only outline ideas from the seminar, but also provide information about the official school procedures for dealing with emergencies.

4. Offer a variety of weekend courses on diversity topics to inform faculty and staff about the growing need for sensitivity toward diversity. The courses will be held on the first Saturday of each month and will have a different topic each time. Members of local cultural organizations and college professors will teach the weekend courses.

FIGURE 5.8 *(continued)*

PROGRESS TRACKING REPORT FOR OBJECTIVE #1—TARGET AUDIENCE: FACULTY AND STAFF

Activity	On schedule On target On budget	Behind schedule Off target or Over budget	Completed
Memo			
Seminar			
Information packet			
Diversity courses			

Objective #2 [parents] To inform parents about SCHS's new diversity and campus safety plans so they feel they can allow their children to return to school.

Strategy

We will accomplish objective #2 by informing parents of our four-point plan to make the school safer and more culturally aware. The school's purpose is to educate students while providing them with a safe learning environment. Parents expect this and will demand change if their children's needs are not being met. We want the parents to feel informed about the changes being made to enhance the safety and diversity of the school. We recommend this strategy be implemented as follows:

1. Distribute a special-edition newsletter that will specifically address parental concerns that came up during the first parent meeting at the school.

2. Include a feedback form with the newsletter so parents can ask questions and make comments about anything involving the school's current status. Parents will have the option of returning the feedback form via the school's Web site, regular mail or by calling the school's main office.

3. Plan a well-organized public meeting that will focus on school safety and diversity issues; plans for growth and increased security at the school; and questions and comments provided by parents via the aforementioned feedback form.

PROGRESS TRACKING REPORT FOR OBJECTIVE #2—TARGET AUDIENCE: PARENTS

Activity	On schedule On target On budget	Behind schedule Off target or Over budget	Completed
Special-edition newsletter			
Feedback form			
Public meeting			

FIGURE 5.8 (continued)

Objective #3 [Howard Burdick]	To educate Howard Burdick about media relations, community relations and crisis management so he can better communicate with parents, staff, students, media and the community.

Strategy

We will accomplish objective #3 by helping Burdick implement the short-term emergency plan and providing him with long-term solutions that will equip him with the necessary tools to effectively interact with these groups. We recommend this strategy be implemented as follows:

1. Increase relationships with local law enforcement by inviting them to periodically visit the campus.

2. Have the central office task force review with Burdick the district policies relating to cultural diversity and the zero tolerance rule for harassment and violence. Burdick needs to know the policies, have the adequate tools and training to implement them, and understand the ramifications of not employing them.

3. Have the central office task force review with Burdick the district sanctioned methods and procedures of effective communication with parents, media, students, faculty and the community. With a better understanding of communication, Burdick will be better equipped when dealing with minor issues that can easily balloon into crisis situations.

4. Use media training to provide Burdick with an understanding of how the media work and how he should interact with them.

5. Help Burdick initiate a series of student-led groups relating to diversity and safety issues, so students feel like they have a say and stake in the success of their school.

PROGRESS TRACKING REPORT FOR OBJECTIVE #3—TARGET AUDIENCE: HOWARD BURDICK

Activity	On schedule On target On budget	Behind schedule Off target or Over budget	Completed
Media training			
Law enforcement relations			
Diversity and zero tolerance training			
Student groups			
Communication policy training			

FIGURE 5.8 *(continued)*

Objective #4 [media]   To establish a good working relationship with the media so they will not publish unbalanced information.

Strategy

We will accomplish objective #4 through a variety of activities aimed at building a relationship with the media. We want to offer information to the media that is factual and show that the administration is not trying to be secretive. SCHS wants to facilitate a relationship with the media that is based on truth and objectivity. We recommend this strategy be implemented as follows:

1. Burdick will invite the media to the school for a press briefing on the incident and the four-point action plan.

2. Prepare a media kit for journalists that are unable to attend the press briefing. The kit will include a news release about the incident and implementation of the four-point plan, a tip sheet on how parents can prevent their children from becoming involved in violence, fact sheets on violence in schools and the four-point plan.

3. Administration will have a Q & A sheet on hand so they can answer phone calls from media correctly.

4. Track media coverage to see if they are reporting fairly and accurately.

5. Keep track of inquiries from media with a chart acknowledging who has been called back, who needs to be called back and what question they need answered.

6. Designate administrators who will be returning phone calls and train them to answer questions.

7. Burdick should invite Clark Cantwell to the school for a personal interview and photography opportunities.

PROGRESS TRACKING REPORT FOR OBJECTIVE #4—TARGET AUDIENCE: MEDIA

Activity	On schedule On target On budget	Behind schedule Off target or Over budget	Completed
Press briefing			
Media kit			
Q & A			
Train administrators			
Call-back chart			
Track coverage			
Interview			

FIGURE 5.8 *(continued)*

Objective #5 [community members] To inform community members that the high school is a safe and diverse environment so they regain confidence in the school administration.

Strategy

After they hear about the situation at the high school, the community will need reassurance that the school is a safe environment that openly embraces diversity. Our strategy addresses point four of Superintendent Maxine Gradeletter's four-point plan. We recommend this strategy be implemented as follows:

1. Conduct a broad-based community enrichment symposium. The purpose of the symposium is to determine sustainable ways to recognize the strength of our increasing ethnicities in our high school and community with a sense of pride. This will become an annual event held in the high school auditorium. The leadership team, as well as the student body council, will be in charge of directing the event. The community will be invited to attend and have input in the symposium.

2. Before the symposium, an announcement about the symposium will be sent out via direct mail. Attached to the announcement will be a survey for community members to fill out. Questions about their ideas about community diversity and how they think the school and community in general have handled issues of diversity. The responses from the surveys will be presented at the symposium.

3. A feedback and evaluation form will be handed out to the community members after the symposium. They will be able to evaluate the symposium, give their feedback, ask questions that may not have been addressed and sign up for future diversity activities.

PROGRESS TRACKING REPORT FOR OBJECTIVE #5 — TARGET AUDIENCE: COMMUNITY MEMBERS

Activity	On schedule On target On budget	Behind schedule Off target or Over budget	Completed
Enrichment symposium			
Pre-symposium survey			
Post-symposium feedback			

FIGURE 5.8 *(continued)*

Objective #6
[students]
To include students in the planning and implementation of diversity and security plans so they continue to feel safe in their school.

Strategy

Students are the audience that will be directly affected by issues concerning diversity and violence. We should use ideas generated by students to initiate certain parts of the four-point plan. Student groups should immediately start implementing the four-point plan. We want each student to feel they have a voice and to feel confident that their ideas will be seriously considered. We recommend this strategy be implemented as follows:

1. Point one in the four-point plan concerns the security issues at the school. We want the students to be included in this part because their security is at the core of the issue. Students will implement this part of the four-point plan through student groups initiated by Principal Howard Burdick as follows:

    a. The new security guards at school should be introduced to all student leadership groups.

    b. There should be a mandatory assembly for the new security guidelines to be introduced to students and introductions of the new security guards. The students will also learn the facts about the incidents that occurred at the school.

    c. The student newspaper will run a story on new security measures.

    d. Burdick will initiate a new student group called Secure Students. Students in the group will develop new ideas about how to keep students safe and feeling secure. This program will be run by students with an advising teacher present.

    e. Burdick will also develop Student Court for less serious student infractions. Student Court will also decide on punishments for student infractions with supervision from teachers, administration and volunteers from law enforcement.

    f. A survey will be handed out in every classroom to every student. The survey will ask questions regarding how students feel about safety and diversity. Another survey will be handed out at the end of the year.

2. Point two in the four-point plan is the initiation of leadership teams. While some parents feel that students should not be involved in the diversity program planning process, we feel that not including them is discriminatory. Students will help implement this part of the four-point plan as follows:

    a. Burdick and student body President Mitch Rivers will develop a new student group called Diversity First. This group will develop a new student diversity mission statement outlining school policies on discrimination and consequences

FIGURE 5.8 *(continued)*

for failing to follow those rules. This program will be run by students with an advising teacher present.

b. Diversity First will develop a peer counseling program for students who feel discriminated against. This will be a confidential program where students can anonymously give information about other students who are not following discrimination policies.

c. Students who run Diversity First will track how many students seek help from the peer counseling program.

d. Two students will be on the central office Leadership Team with Burdick to be spokespeople for the students. These students will bring information back to the Diversity First group that will then give that information to student publications for dissemination to the rest of the student body.

3. Point three in the four-point plan is to develop cultural awareness at the school. This part of the strategy will be implemented as follows:

a. Student body President Mitch Rivers is in charge of contacting a flag vendor about donating a flag for each country represented at SCHS.

b. In each issue of the student newspaper there should be a profile of a student from a different country.

c. In each mandatory assembly held during the school year will be a performance by a student from a different culture. The first will be a performance by the Native American student group.

d. There will be a day designated Diversity Day at the end of the year when students are encouraged to come to school dressed in a costume celebrating a part of their culture.

4. Point four will engage the students and community in understanding diversity and cultural awareness through the planning and involvement in an event. This part of the strategy will be implemented as follows:

a. Student groups will develop an event on the weekend after Diversity Day that parents and other community members will be invited to. This event will be designed to show the community how the school is a safe, diverse learning environment.

b. Student groups will ask local restaurants to donate food from different cultures for the event.

c. There will be showcases set up around the school with visual aids for community members to walk around and learn about the different cultures represented in the school. Students will create a map for people to follow around the school.

FIGURE 5.8 *(continued)*

    d. A news release will be sent to local media about the event.

    e. Thank you letters will be sent from student groups to all businesses that sponsor the event.

PROGRESS TRACKING REPORT FOR
OBJECTIVE #6—TARGET AUDIENCE: STUDENTS

Activity	On schedule On target On budget	Behind schedule Off target or Over budget	Completed
Assembly			
Newspaper story			
Secure students group			
Student court			
Survey #1			
Diversity First group			
Peer counseling			
Contact flag vendor			
Student profiles			
Student performance #1			
Diversity Day planning			
Donated food			
Culture showcases			
Map			
News release			
Thank-you letters			
End-of-year survey			

Evalution   Evaluation of this plan is provided for in two ways: (1) short-term progress tracking, a weekly report included with every objective that shows how progress toward achievement of each objective is monitored; and (2) a long-term assessment of outcomes that explains how the desired outcome for each objective is to be assessed or measured.

    Progress tracking is shown in the plan under each objective. Assessment or measurement of outcomes is described in this section following a restatement of each objective.

FIGURE 5.8 (continued)

Objective #1 To train faculty and staff in diversity and violence in schools so they are prepared to handle any incidents that might occur.

Assessment: Success in achieving this objective will be determined by the faculty and staffs' knowledge of how to handle incidents at the school and their increased awareness of diversity.

Objective #2 To inform parents about SCHS's new diversity and campus safety plans so they feel they can allow their children to return to school.

Assessment: Success in achieving this objective will be determined by the attendance of parents at the public meeting, as well as the quality of the feedback they give back to the school.

Objective #3 To educate Howard Burdick about media relations, community relations and crisis management so he can better communicate with parents, staff, students, media and the community.

Assessment: Success in achieving this objective will be determined by Burdick's ability to effectively communicate with these groups.

Objective #4 To establish a good working relationship with the media so they will not publish unbalanced information.

Assessment: Success in achieving this objective will be based on the accuracy of articles in local newspapers.

Objective #5 To inform community members that the high school is a safe and diverse environment so they regain confidence in the school administration.

Assessment: Success in achieving this objective will be based on the feedback we receive from the community members after the community enrichment symposium.

Objective #6 To include students in the planning and implementation of diversity and security plans so they continue to feel safe in their school.

Assessment: Success in achieving this objective will be based on a survey handed out at the beginning of the school year that will be compared to another survey handed out at the end of the school year. Success will be achieved when there is a decline in students seeking counseling from the Diversity First student group and a decline in students saying they have been harassed.

By achieving the desired outcome for each of the plan's objectives we will accomplish a critical goal: for SCHS to be operating as a safe environment that embraces diversity.

FIGURE 5.8 (continued)

WEEKLY PROGRESS TRACKING REPORT (CONSOLIDATED)

Objective/ Audience	Activity	On schedule On target On budget	Behind schedule Off target or Over budget	Completed
Objective #1 Faculty and staff	Information packet			
	Seminar			
	Memo			
	Diversity courses			
Objective #2 Parents	Special-edition newsletter			
	Feedback form			
	Public meeting			
Objective #3 Howard Burdick	Law enforcement relations			
	Media training			
	Diversity and zero tolerance training			
	Student groups			
	Communication policy training			
Objective #4 Media	Train administrators			
	Media kit			
	Q & A			
	Press briefing			
	Call-back chart			
	Track coverage			
	Interview			
Objective #5 Community Members	Enrichment symposium			
	Pre-symposium survey			
	Post-symposium feedback			

FIGURE 5.8 (continued)

Objective #6 Students	Assembly			
	Newspaper story			
	Secure students group			
	Student court			
	Survey #1			
	Diversity First group			
	Peer counseling			
	Contact flag vendor			
	Student profiles			
	Student performance #1			
	Diversity Day planning			
	Donated food			
	Culture showcases			
	Map			
	News release			
	Thank-you letters			
	End-of-year survey			

TIMELINE

Monday, May 2	Invite media to press briefing scheduled for 11 A.M. Wednesday Prepare and distribute memo about four-point plan to faculty and staff Create tip sheet, Q & A, fact sheets, news release, call-back chart, and feedback and tracking forms Train Burdick on the district's communication, diversity and zero tolerance policies Announce security guidelines and facts about recent events at student assembly Clarify recent events, four-point plan and security measures to parents in special-edition newsletter Provide administration with Q & A to field media calls
Tuesday, May 3	Train Burdick to work effectively with the media Invite local police to periodically patrol campus and conduct a safety seminar for faculty and staff Distribute backgrounder, fact sheet and news release, if requested, to media Prepare information packet about safety for faculty and staff Announce public meeting about school safety scheduled for Friday night
Wednesday, May 4	Announce specifies of recent events and four-point plan at press briefing Invite media to interview Burdick Distribute information packets to faculty and staff Generate article about safety in student paper Create student survey form about safety and diversity
Thursday, May 5	Schedule community enrichment symposium for June 18 Create survey and feedback form for symposium Conduct student survey about safety and diversity
Friday, May 6	Lead public meeting about safety and diversity
Monday, May 9	Train teachers to deal with safety issues through police seminar Initiate student diversity programs Schedule Diversity Day for June 17
Monday, May 16	Monitor student requests for business donations to community symposium Generate showcase displays for symposium
Friday, June 3	Prepare news release and map for symposium Invite community to attend symposium by sending a piece of direct mail
Monday, June 13	Announce symposium through news release
Friday, June 17	Conduct Diversity Day
Saturday, June 18	Educate community about diversity through community symposium
Ongoing	Track media coverage and call-backs Compile parent feedback forms Conduct student diversity programs Facilitate student newspaper articles about diverse student population Educate faculty about diversity during monthly Saturday seminars

Provide support to student body president for flag project Organize yearly diversity assembly and Diversity Day Organize weekend diversity courses for faculty and staff

ESTIMATED BUDGET		
Expenses		
Press materials	25.00	
Thank you notes	25.00	
Newsletter	750.00	
Direct mail	1,500.00	
Survey and feedback materials	100.00	
Information packet	100.00	
Diversity Day	50.00	
Community symposium	500.00	
Saturday seminars	150.00	
Subtotal	3,200.00	
Total		3,200.00

University of Oregon Students (from left) Amanda Ginther, Jenna Kangiser, Josh Alder, Beth Reniff and Kelsea Michael

chapter 6

Public Relations Cases: Problems, Opportunities, Challenges

*t*his section of the book features 10 real-world cases—situations with compelling needs for public relations action. Each case is presented in a different manner, such as a role play of a meeting, a contract for services, a transcript of private meetings, or field notes by an account executive. Each case includes a team assignment to develop a public relations plan and individual team member assignments to provide written elements in support of a plan, such as a news release, briefing notes for a TV show, or pocket point cards. There are no solutions offered for the cases because, realistically, in public relations, there are different ways to address situations effectively. However, there is an instructor's manual with example plans and individual plan elements for each case.

Research is fundamental to the planning process. Each case provides a wealth of information with which to write a comprehensive analysis of the situation, objectives, and creative strategies to achieve them. Additional information that applies to more than one case can be found in the index.

It has been shown that student teams (ideally comprising five or six people) can do a case a week with individual assignments. It is recommended that plans and individual assignments be critiqued and participants given an opportunity to revise their work as would be the case in an actual work environment. The cases are as instructive in a professional workshop as they are in a classroom.

CASES

COMMUNITY RELATIONS
Contaminated Lagoon

This is a case of a contaminated lagoon. Plans were being made for the expansion of Industrial Products, Inc., in Douglas, U.S.A., when management discovers that a lagoon on plant property is contaminated with hazardous chemicals. The hazard must be removed before plant expansion work can begin. Industrial Products decides that it does not have the expertise necessary to handle public communication regarding the hazardous waste site cleanup and calls on the public relations staff of corporate headquarters for assistance. A staff member is dispatched to meet with the management of the subsidiary operations.

Details of the case unfold in a dialogue between the headquarters public relations staff person, Kelly O'Connel, and management staff at Douglas. The conversation, presented in the form of a classroom/professional workshop role play, begins on page 87. More detail is available in Kelly O'Connel's handwritten field notes that follow the script. The article, "Community Relations Can Facilitate Corporate Growth," on page 96, provides a broad perspective on the value of good community relations.

Team Assignment

Your team assignment is to develop a public relations plan for closing the contaminated lagoon. You and your team are staff members of the headquarters public relations department of Rockover, Inc., owner of subsidiary operations, Industrial Products, Inc., located in Douglas, U.S.A. The goal of your plan, stated by the operations manager, is for Industrial Products, Inc., to be expanding its facilities with minimal delays from the lagoon closure.

INDIVIDUAL TEAM MEMBER ASSIGNMENTS

Each team member is to complete a different one of the following items that might or might not be included in the design of your plan. (See Chapter 7: Samples of Effective Public Relations Writing.)

1. Statement to the news media to be used proactively, or reactively—only if reporters inquire about the project.

2. Memo from the manager of human resources to employees about their possible health and safety concerns with regard to the project.

3. Q & A for management personnel to use in discussing the cleanup project with people within or outside the company.

4. Letter to government representatives (David Hall, mayor, or Randy Don, county commissioner) apprising them of the project so they are prepared to answer questions from their constituents.

5. Fact sheet on the cleanup project with construction scheduling information. (See field notes on page 92.)

6. A one-page backgrounder exclusively on the subject of PCBs. Provide information that would be useful to journalists, not chemical engineers.

7. A pocket point card for management (all levels through supervisor) with information on both sides with talking points about the lagoon project.

FACT-GATHERING SESSION AT INDUSTRIAL PRODUCTS, INC.

Cast

Kelly O'Connel: PR Assistant
Bob Elwood: PR Director

Sam Seaberg: Operations Manager
AJ Detweiler: Production Manager
Jordan Slagel: Environmental Engineer
Terry Troubaugh: Safety Manager
Sharon Duncan: Administrative Assistant
Casey Dilena: Manager, Human Resources
Narrator

PUBLIC RELATIONS DEPARTMENT
ROCKOVER, INC., CORPORATE HEADQUARTERS

(Public Relations Assistant approaches Public Relations Director for assignment.)

KELLY (PR Assistant): Good morning.

BOB (PR Director): Hi Kelly. Ready to work?

KELLY (PR Assistant): (Not knowing what to expect) I'm ready!

BOB (PR Director): That's good. I'd like you to make a plane reservation to Douglas, U.S.A. They're expecting you for a meeting tomorrow morning.

KELLY (PR Assistant): (Clearly caught off guard . . .) Douglas! Who's expecting me?

BOB (PR Director): (Privately amused by her reaction, but totally confident that she can handle the job) I would have handled this myself, but I've got a speech to write for the chairman.

KELLY (PR Assistant): So who's the meeting with?

BOB (PR Director): The manager of Douglas Operations and members of his staff.

KELLY (PR Assistant): What's it about?

BOB (PR Director): A lagoon. They have to deal with it before they can proceed with their expansion plans.

KELLY (PR Assistant): (Half joking) Why does a lagoon need public relations?

BOB (PR Director): You need to hear the whole story firsthand. The lagoon is contaminated.

KELLY (PR Assistant): Are they worried about publicity?

BOB (PR Director): That's part of it.

KELLY (PR Assistant): What else are they worried about?

BOB (PR Director): Employees. Sorry, I've got to see the chairman.

KELLY (PR Assistant): I'll make the reservations.

NARRATOR: At an altitude of 37,000 feet heading for Douglas

KELLY (PR Assistant): (Musing to herself) I can't believe this . . . My first assignment . . . A polluted lagoon . . . That's all right. I can do this.

NARRATOR: Conference Room, Douglas Operations

(Kelly has been introduced; meeting is under way.)

SAM (Operations Manager): Thanks for coming Kelly. We were making plans to expand our operations. In the process we discovered that we have a polluted lagoon. We need to be undertaking the expansion with minimal delays from the lagoon closure. That's our goal.

JORDAN (Environmental Engineer): (Interjecting) We tested sediment in the bottom of the lagoon and found a significant concentration of PCBs. PCBs are . . . (pause)

KELLY (PR Assistant): (Interrupting) I know. Polychlorinated biphenyls (by-fee'-nals). Not very friendly to people. I did some quick research before I left headquarters. So how did the PCBs get into the lagoon?

AJ (Production Manager): We think it happened years ago with the old forming operation. They mixed water from the lagoon with a petroleum-based lubricant for cooling. The water was recycled back into the lagoon. PCBs probably floated to the bottom and settled into the sediment.

KELLY (PR Assistant): (Mentally starting to shape a message) So, we can say that the pollution isn't the result of any of our current operations, but that we're taking full responsibility for cleaning it up.

SAM (Operations Manager): Yes. And it will be closed. The lagoon will be closed as part of our overall plant expansion plan.

KELLY (PR Assistant): What do you mean, closed?

JORDAN (Environmental Engineer): It will be lined and used as a storm water retention basin.

KELLY (PR Assistant): How big is this lagoon?

JORDAN (Environmental Engineer): Surface size of the lagoon is about 37,000 square feet.

KELLY (PR Assistant): That's a small lake!

SHARON (Administrative Assistant): (Abruptly interjecting in a tattletale tone of voice) It used to be a picnic area for employees. With tables . . . And benches, and . . .

KELLY (PR Assistant): (A dreaded thought occurred. Were employees exposed? She interrupts Sharon.) Don't tell me . . . A place where families could play in the water? Are employees at risk?

CASEY (Manager, Human Resources): No. Fortunately, the lagoon has always been fenced off. We're confident that no one is at risk. But employees might not be easily convinced of that.

JORDAN (Environmental Engineer): PCBs are heavy. They don't float. They're in the sediment, not the water.

KELLY (PR Assistant): (Thinking to herself: I wonder how assured I would feel as an employee who worked for ten years or more around a hazardous waste site.) Where is the lagoon?

SHARON (Administrative Assistant): (She exclaims in her tattletale tone of voice) That's easy! Don't ya know? It's in plain sight of the whole world!

CASEY (Manager, Human Resources): Get a grip, Sharon. (pause) It's behind the finishing and forming operations. Unfortunately drivers coming into town in the morning look directly at it from City Expressway. You could read a billboard in the time it takes to pass by.

TERRY (Safety Manager): The lagoon will be designated a hazardous materials area and workers will be wearing hazardous materials suits.

KELLY (PR Assistant): You mean . . . moon suits?

TERRY (Safety Manager): They do look like space suits.

KELLY (PR Assistant): (Thinking to herself: We've got a lot of communicating to do.) Who knows about this situation?

SAM (Operations Manager): The state Department of Environmental Resources.

KELLY (PR Assistant): The media?

SAM (Operations Manager): No, not yet.

KELLY (PR Assistant): What about employees?

SAM (Operations Manager): No. When they do, the long-time veterans are going to be concerned. They'll remember the picnic grounds.

SHARON (Administrative Assistant): (Admonishing the company) You bet they will! They'll remember all right!!

KELLY (PR Assistant): I would think so. Not the best place to eat hot dogs.

SHARON (Administrative Assistant): (Emotionally charged, she exclaims) Listen, Kelly. Just the mention of toxic chemicals and some people will go into orbit! Know what I mean? Do you know what I mean!!

KELLY (PR Assistant): What about government? City and county officials? Do they know?

SAM (Operations Manager): No. And there's a potential problem. We don't have the best working relationship with local and county government. It's not bad. It's just that . . . Well, we just don't have one and we need their support to get construction permits.

KELLY (PR Assistant): When is work supposed to start on the lagoon?

JORDAN (Environmental Engineer): May 15th.

KELLY (PR Assistant): Today is May 1st. We have precious little time to do a lot of communicating.

AJ (Production Manager): (Grumbling about headquarters involvement) What's the big deal? It's not like we're into a meltdown. Why do we need public relations? The facts will speak for themselves. Alls we need to do is get the contractor in here and get the job done.

SAM (Operations Manager): Not so fast, AJ. Let's think about this. Douglas is about to discover that it has toxic waste on the edge of town. Rush hour drivers coming into town are going to see workers in moon suits. Veteran employees are going to be fearful of possible health hazards to themselves and their families. Local and county officials could get flooded with phone calls from residents wanting to know what's going on. And who knows how the media is going to play this.

AJ (Production Manager): (Grousing to himself about getting PR involved and unable to keep to himself) Come on, Sam. We've been a good company to work for, for years. I don't know why people have to meddle in our affairs.

SAM (Operations Manager): (Realizing that some people are more sensitive about public relations than others, Sam ignores AJ's comment and turns to Kelly.) Kelly, we obviously need some help from the PR department.

KELLY (PR Assistant): I'm here to help, Sam. Could we take a few minutes to go over the plan so I have an idea of what's ahead?

SAM (Operations Manager): Sure. We hired BBEO Remediation and Construction Company to close the lagoon.

AJ (Production Manager): (Straightening up and trying to be a constructive participant) It's a Jersey company. They have experience in cleaning up hazardous waste.

JORDAN (Environmental Engineer): The state Department of Environmental Resources is overseeing the cleanup.

AJ (Production Manager): Our engineers and BBEO staff have a detailed closure plan. First the water will be pumped out of the lagoon.

JORDAN (Environmental Engineer): It will be treated, tested, and discharged into a connecting stream. The sediment will be excavated from the bottom of the lagoon. It will be pressed through a filter to get rid of excess water. Then it will be tested and stored in sealed containers.

KELLY (PR Assistant): What happens to the containers?

JORDAN (Environmental Engineer): They'll be loaded on a train and taken to a regulated disposal site. We'll cover the area with a liner and it will be used as a storm water retention basin.

TERRY (Safety Manager): The entire work area will be fenced in. Only authorized workers will be allowed access to the site. There will be strict safety rules. Workers will have to wear protective gear that will be cleaned and properly disposed of daily throughout the process.

KELLY (PR Assistant): (Testing the accuracy of what she thought she heard) So we can say the water will be pumped out, tested, and discharged into a connecting stream. The polluted sediment will be excavated, stored in leak-proof containers, and shipped by rail to a regulated disposal site. The area will be lined and used as a storm water retention basin.

SAM (Operations Manager): That's correct Kelly. The project will take about six to eight weeks. After BBEO brings in its heavy equipment, the area will be closed. No company equipment will be used. Workers will wear protective suits, gloves, boots, and respirators that will be cleaned or disposed of each time they leave the site.

KELLY (PR Assistant): Is there any health risk to people around the site?

JORDAN (Environmental Engineer): The chemicals are in the sediment, not in the water. PCBs are not airborne, so there's no chance of contact with employees or plant visitors or area residents.

KELLY (PR Assistant): (Thinking to herself: Employees will wonder, if there's no risk, why do workers have to wear moon suits? I need to know more about PCBs, like what are the effects of PCBs on people? She thumbs through her notes. Sam hands her a project schedule.) Sam, how will closing the lagoon affect your expansion plans?

SAM (Operations Manager): The project might delay our plant expansion work. But it's essential that we clean things up properly, and safely.

NARRATOR: The meeting adjourns. Kelly returns to headquarters to draw up a PR plan.

WORK SCHEDULE KELLY RECEIVED FROM SAM

The work schedule has three phases:

1. Mobilization and site preparation; BBEO brings and sets up equipment; start date May 15, finish date May 24.

2. Site remediation activities; lagoon dewatering starts May 25, finishes June 16; sediment removal starts June 1 and finishes Aug. 9; belt press dewatering starts Aug. 8 and finishes Aug. 23; post-removal sampling starts Aug. 24 and finishes Aug. 30; preparation for structural backfill starts Aug. 31 and finishes Sept. 4.

3. Demobilization and closeout activities; removal of temporary facilities and controls starts Sept. 5 and finishes Sept. 11; demobilization starts Sept. 12 and finishes Sept. 13; closeout meeting Sept. 20.

Kelly's Initial Research Notes

PCBs or polychlorinated biphenyls are a class of compounds consisting of two benzene rings joined together at one carbon on each ring . . . the rings are then substituted with one to ten chlorine atoms . . . developed in 1929 they have been used as electrical insulating fluids, fire-resistant heat transfer, and hydraulic fluids, lubricants, and as components in elastomers, adhesives, paints, pigments, and waxes . . . PCBs were very attractive in industrial use because they are nonvolatile, nonflammable, chemically stable, and are good electrical insulators. Because PCBs are very stable, they do not break down in the environment; therefore they are environmentally unsuitable . . . in 1976 Congress enacted the Toxic Substance Control Act (TSCA), which required the Environmental Protection Agency (EPA) to establish rules regarding PCBs . . . production ceased in 1977 . . . in 1979 the EPA published the PCB ban rule, which prohibits the manufacturing, processing, distribution in commerce, and use of PCBs except in a totally enclosed manner. Concentrations of PCBs 50 parts per billion or over fall under EPA regulations and must be disposed of under EPA guidelines . . . PCBs can affect the body if inhaled or swallowed or if there is contact with the eyes or skin . . . they may cause irritation of the eyes, nose, and throat and an acne-like skin rash . . . they may also cause liver disorders, which would result in effects such as fatigue, dark urine, and yellow jaundice . . . studies on laboratory animals showed the chemicals caused liver, reproductive, and gastric disorders, skin lesions, and tumors.

 Kelly's notes from fact-gathering meeting with Operations Manager Sam Seaberg and staff, Industrial Products, Inc., Douglas, U.S.A. subsidiary of Rockover, Inc.

May 1

What is the situation at Douglas?

We were in the process of planning plant expansions

Discovered that a small lagoon on our property was polluted

How small?

A lagoon approximately 37,114 square feet in surface size

Where?

Located behind the finishing and forming operations

What kind of pollution?

Tested sediment in the bottom of the lagoon; found a significant concentration of PCBs (polychlorinated biphenyls).

The PCBs likely entered the lagoon as a result of the old forming operation . . . the water was mixed with a petroleum-based lubricant for cooling . . . the water was then recycled back into the lagoon . . . PCBs likely floated to the bottom and settled into the sediment.

The lagoon will be closed as part of the overall plant expansion plan. It will be lined and used as a storm water retention basin.

Did the company dump PCBs in the lagoon?

The PCBs are not a result of any of our current operations.

We're taking responsibility for cleaning and closing the lagoon

Possible quote: "The pollution is not a result of any of our current operations at the plant. But we will take full responsibility for cleaning it up."

Is this a health hazard to employees? Or to area residents?

The chemicals are settled in the sediment.

They're not in the lagoon water.

There's no possibility of contamination to any plant employees or visitors, according to plant staff members.

The PCBs are not airborne; there's no chance of contact.

The situation poses no danger to plant employees or residents.

Possible quote: "Although we are dealing with hazardous waste, we want to assure the public there is no danger to residents, plant employees, or to the surrounding environment. Our primary concern is to have this project done in the safest manner possible."

What are the best ways to communicate with employees?

The plant operates three shifts: (1) 7 A.M. to 3 P.M.; (2) 3 P.M. to 11 P.M.; and (3) 11 P.M. to 7 A.M. On each shift employees are given a twenty-minute lunch break. Supervisors conduct safety meetings every day at the beginning of each shift. Supervisors also conduct communication meetings once each month. The plant manager talks to employees quarterly by shift. The most effective ways to communicate with employees are (1) through supervisors; (2) by weekly newsletter; (3) by monthly videotape; and (4) by closed-circuit TV. Sometimes project teams are formed with a leader selected by each team. Supervisors oversee and coach the teams.

Note to self: Why are PCBs a problem? Is there a legal limit? What are the effects of PCBs on people?

So how did the PCBs get there?

The lagoon has been used as part of our overall water-management plan and has never been used for the disposal of any industrial chemicals or wastes.

In the 1960s and 1970s, the lagoon water was used for cooling baths in the old forming operations.

We believe the contaminants were released when the cooling water was recycled back into the lagoon.

The forming operation has since been relocated and an oil/water separator has been installed; so there is no danger of further contamination.

We can say tests of the lagoon sediment revealed the presence of PCBs (polychlorinated biphenyls) . . . that company engineers believe the lagoon was contaminated during the 1960s and 1970s when its waters were mixed with a petroleum-based lubricant for cooling metal in the old forming facility . . . that this facility has been closed for fourteen years, so there is no danger for further contamination.

The lagoon was constructed in 1959 to be used as cooling water for molds in the old metal-forming operations. This was discontinued in 1981 when forming operations moved. The lagoon is currently used as fire water for the sprinkler system and also for the discharge of cooling waters from the current forming operation.

What's the plan to deal with the situation?

The company hired BBEO Remediation and Construction Company to close the lagoon.

This New Jersey–based company has experience in cleaning hazardous waste, including PCBs.

The state Department of Environmental Resources (DER) is overseeing the cleanup.

Work will begin May 15 to clean the lagoon.

Our engineers and BBEO personnel have developed a detailed closure plan.

The water will first be pumped from the lagoon.

It will be treated, tested, and then discharged into a connecting stream.

The sediment will then be excavated from the bottom of the lagoon.

It will be filter pressed to remove excess water, tested, stored in sealed containers, and removed by rail for disposal.

The area will then be lined and used as a storm-water retention basin.

Possible quote: "Work is scheduled to begin May 15 to clean the lagoon . . . the area will be closed, and strict access and safety guidelines will be followed during the project . . . workers will be wearing protective gear which will be cleaned and disposed of daily throughout the process . . ."

So we can say the water will be pumped, treated, tested, and then released. The polluted sediment will then be excavated, stored in leak-proof containers, and removed by rail for disposal. The area will then be used for storm-water retention.

Let's go over the plan once more.

BBEO Remediation and Construction has been contracted to close the lagoon . . . they have previous experience in dealing with PCBs . . . work will begin May 15 . . . the project is expected to take six to eight weeks . . . after bringing in their equipment (no company equipment will be used) they will close off the entire area . . . only select BBEO and company personnel will be permitted to enter the cleaning site . . . workers will wear protective suits, gloves, boots, and respirators, which will be cleaned and/or disposed of each time they leave the closed zone surrounding the lagoon . . . the water will be pumped, treated, and released into a connecting stream . . . the sediment will then be excavated, filter pressed to remove excess water, tested, stored in sealed containers, and removed by train for disposal . . . the area will then be lined and used for storm water retention.

Will this operation present any kind of safety hazard?

The closure plan includes strict safety guidelines. Throughout the project, access to the lagoon site will be allowed for authorized BBEO and company personnel only. All equipment, materials, and safety gear will be either cleaned or disposed of immediately after use.

Do employees know about all of this?

Employees are not yet aware of the discovery of PCBs in the lagoon.

Who knows about it outside the company?

We are working with the state Department of Environmental Resources, but county and city government officials don't know about the discovery yet.

What kind of relationship does the company have to city and county government?

Distant, at best. We need their cooperation to complete permits for our expansion plans. But we haven't done much in the way of building relationships. They're going to get a lot of questions from the public. How's that?

The lagoon is visible from the city expressway that leads into the city. People working on the site will be wearing "moon suits" or hazardous materials protective gear and will be seen especially during rush hours by people entering and exiting Douglas.

The plan has three parts or phases

(1) mobilization and site preparation—that's when BBEO brings and sets up equipment (start date May 15; finish date May 24).

(2) site remediation activities—lagoon dewatering starts May 25 and finishes June 16; sediment removal starts June 1 and finishes Aug. 9; belt press dewatering starts Aug. 8 and finishes Aug. 23; post-removal sampling starts Aug. 24 and finishes Aug. 30; preparation for structural backfill starts Aug. 31 and finishes Sept. 4.

(3) demobilization and closeout activities—removal of temporary facilities and controls starts Sept. 5 and finishes Sept. 11; demobilization starts Sept. 12 and finishes Sept. 13; and there will be a closeout meeting Sept. 20. Will taking care of lagoon slow down the plant expansion work?

Possible quote: "The project might slow plant expansion work, but that will be resumed right after the lagoon is closed." Also: "Our expansion plan is important and will give a boost to the local economy. But our first interest is cleaning up the lagoon." [could expand on this]

When all of this gets communicated who is going to field questions?

Casey Dilena, Manager of Human Resources, (717) 393-XXXX.

COMMUNITY RELATIONS CAN FACILITATE CORPORATE GROWTH

Community relations—how much is enough? Chief executives of companies, especially those on a fast track in the new economy, should know the answer to this question. Senior managers today are running their organizations lean, mean, and fast. Like astronauts, they are bearing on targets and defying the odds of colliding with the unexpected. Little do some leaders realize that effective community relations is low-cost insurance for keeping their companies from colliding with the unexpected and incurring potentially crippling costs.

By establishing effective community relations, executive managers facilitate corporate growth. How do they do this? One way is by giving managers in the communities in which they operate the credibility they need to deal with and recover quickly from a crisis situation. This is particularly important to managers in charge of plants that use substances that pose a potential threat to the health and safety of people residing near manufacturing/production plants. Plant managers with effective community relations programs are visible participants in local affairs and trusted spokespersons and representatives of their respective organizations. Unknown managers from unknown facilities with unknown risks have no credibility with community residents in a crisis situation. The consequences of a poorly managed crisis can paralyze an operation by restricting operating permits, plant modifications, and expansion plans.

Another way effective community relations facilitates corporate growth is by giving executive managers foresight into matters affected by public policy. Manufacturers around the world are learning that long-term contracts for power, for example, are not absolute entitlements. They are learning that public opinion can affect contract power rate changes, as well as the future supply of electricity. Taxes, transportation, and education are among other major public policy areas never to be taken for granted.

Managers who are well connected with the communities in which they operate are not likely to be blindsided by public initiatives. Instead, they are welcomed as participants in the public policy-making process. Statesmanlike collaboration with lawmakers and regulators usually results in acceptable policy with sustainability, in contrast to high-handed power plays that eventually cave in to the public interest in one way or another. By taking an active part in government processes, an executive manager can have an influence in shaping public policy and regulations as they affect a particular facility.

Another way effective community relations facilitates corporate growth is by affording executive managers flexibility. Well-managed facilities with effective community relations do not have to fear the threat of labor activities and various adverse external pressures.

Public support can provide extraordinary management flexibility and access to resources when residents of a community value a facility in terms of its economic contribution in wages, taxes, and local purchases, and in terms of its respect for human values and the quality of life.

Effective community relations facilitates corporate growth by giving executive managers the ability to deal with and recover quickly from a crisis situation; by giving executive managers foresight into matters affected by public policy, by welcoming their participation in the public policy-making process; and by affording them extraordinary management flexibility.

Arts Promotion

Nihonga

This is a case of promoting the premier showing of Nihonga art in the United States. The exhibit comprises a world-class collection of 50 contemporary works of Japanese masters. Showing of the exhibit was arranged by the mayor of Townsville, U.S.A., for the purpose of promoting greater understanding of the Japanese culture in a community attracting businesses based in Japan. To the Japanese, Nihonga exemplifies the solidly traditional merged with the new. The name *Nihonga* essentially means Japanese style of painting, as distinguished form Chinese style or Western style, and describes a blend of graphic style from the Chinese with the Western-influenced use of perspective. The imagery shown in the exhibition illustrates how the Japanese are able to reconcile old and new, to adapt a traditional discipline to embrace new ideas. For this case, you are to assume that your pubic relations firm has competed for and won a contract with Townsville, U.S.A., for services to promote the exhibit. Details of your work on this case are contained in a contract with the city of Townsville, U.S.A., on pages 100–102. Additional information follows the city contract, including an article about how to attract and retain volunteers.

TEAM ASSIGNMENT

Your team assignment is to develop a public relations plan that meets the specific requirements of the contract between your public relations firm and Townsville, U.S.A.—to promote attendance at the exhibit, promote community involvement in three exhibit programs, and recruit volunteers.

INDIVIDUAL TEAM MEMBER ASSIGNMENTS

Each team member is to complete a different one of the following items that might or might not be included in the design of your plan. (See Chapter 7: Samples of Effective Public Relations Writing.)

1. Write for the town a news release announcing that Townsville, U.S.A., will host an exhibit of Nihonga art. See case information for dates, cost of admission, and other details. Assume that visitors to the exhibit will receive a designer-type ticket with a large souvenir portion to be retained that features a Nihonga painting, that they will be greeted and guided through the exhibit by one of more than 350 docents trained by Townsville Art Museum director Ron Hawkins, shown a five-minute videotape, and given a color brochure about Nihonga art.

2. Write briefing notes for Mayor David Green to use in talking about the exhibit of Nihonga art on a local television talk show. Prepare the mayor's notes in the form of sound-byte responses to questions in the order they are most likely to be asked by a talk-show host. Answers should be short and conversational. Every response should work to entice people of all ages to see the exhibit and participate in exhibit activities. Responses should be organized with labels so that topics are easy to spot.

3. Write a letter of invitation from the mayor to major donors. Assume that the mayor decides to precede the public opening of the exhibit with an exclusive dinner (paid for by private sources) and a private showing of the exhibit for 16 donors who made major contributions in support of the exhibit. The event is an expression of gratitude from the mayor on behalf of the town so use your imagination to describe in the letter an elegant affair in terms of location, guest transportation, menu, entertainment, and, of course, the private presentation of Nihonga art.

4. Write a persuasive letter from Nancy Walker, president of Educational Service District #12, to superintendents of public school districts within the organization's service area encouraging them to make Nihonga Classroom Experience programs available to schools (kindergarten through

12th grade) throughout their respective districts. The president's letter must have compelling reasons for superintendents to use the programs as the ESD is a service organization and has no authority to direct the work of superintendents.

5. Develop a backgrounder exclusively on Nihonga art, drawing on Internet sources for information. The backgrounder should be organized in stand-alone paragraphs that journalists can easily select to copy and paste into articles about the exhibit.

6. Write a news release for Townsville to announce that it is accepting applications for volunteers to be trained to serve as docents for the exhibit. The release should center on quotes from the mayor that present this volunteer experience in irresistible terms. For ideas on what motivates people to volunteer their time and energy, see the article, "How to Attract and Retain Volunteers," on page 106. The city needs to recruit 350 docents to staff the exhibit. Volunteers are required to complete training provided by the Townsville Museum of Art. It will include five, one-hour lectures on Nihonga art, instruction on the correct approach to conducting tours, and a bibliography of readings. The cost of training will be covered by the law firm of Swallow, Finch and Robin, one of the exhibit's major sponsors. For their service, docents will receive commemorative gold pins in the form of the Japanese alphabet characters for "Nihonga."

7. Write a radio news actuality promoting the exhibit.

CONTRACT

This is a contract between Townsville, U.S.A., and (Your Public Relations Firm) by which your firm agrees to provide certain public relations services to Townsville in connection with an exhibit of Nihonga art.

WHEREAS, Townsville will be host to an exhibit of Nihonga art from July 1, through September 14,

WHEREAS the exhibit was assembled and offered for display by Japan City, sister to Townsville,

WHEREAS this collection of 50 contemporary Japanese paintings in traditional style, known as Nihonga, will be shown for the first time in Tokyo, Yokohama, Osaka, and Nagoya, then on to its premier showing in the United States at Townsville, launching its world tour that will include London, Paris, and Barcelona,

WHEREAS this first of its kind collection assembled by a sister city and provided by masters of the art is seen by citizens and officials of Townsville as an effective way to promote greater understanding and appreciation of the Japanese culture in a town that is growing faster in its relationships with businesses on the Pacific Rim than in its personal relationships among citizens of Townsville with its increasing Asian population,

WHEREAS to prevent the widening of a culture gap, citizens and city officials set as their objective the showing of a world-class exhibition of Nihonga art in Townsville as a stimulus for local residents, and people throughout the area, to learn more about the history, customs, and national character of Japan,

WHEREAS on this day, December 10, Mayor David Green makes an official announcement of the Nihonga event and calls for the establishment of a town team, including about 1,500 volunteer individuals and representatives of civic, service, and professional organizations to develop programs around the exhibit, prepare for its arrival, and help manage its public showing,

WHEREAS the public of which 50,000 visitors are expected, will be able to view the Nihonga art from 10 AM to 6 AM, daily at the Townsville Arts Center,

WHEREAS for the exhibit event to be the success that it should be, it has been and will be necessary to contract with a public relations firm to promote attendance and community involvement in the exhibit, and (<u>Your Public Relations Firm</u>) is qualified and willing to provide such services

NOW, THEREFORE, IT IS HEREBY AGREED AS FOLLOWS:

1. That (<u>Your Public Relations Firm</u>) will promote (exclusive of the use of paid advertising) exhibit attendance among people of all age groups throughout the Greater Townsville Area, securing publicity about the exhibit, preparing all of the materials necessary to work with the news media, such as a fact sheet, backgrounder, and news announcements, and cooperating with Townsville staff and elected officials on all questions or issues involving the exhibit event and public relations.

2. That (<u>Your Public Relations Firm</u>) will generate community involvement in the exhibit specifically by promoting three educational programs:

- Nihonga Artists on Location

- Nihonga Classroom Experience

- Nihonga Town Seminars

each of which is described in the Attachment to this contract.

3. That (<u>Your Public Relations Firm</u>) will help the town recruit approximately 1,500 volunteers as tour guides (docents), gift shop keepers, program coordinators, and others to assist with the exhibit.

For services under this agreement (<u>Your Public Relations Firm</u>) will present Townsville with invoices and proper vouchers, documenting time spent on such services at standard public relations rates for total compensation not to exceed $50,000, plus documented out-of-pocket costs not to exceed 10 percent of such professional fee. Major promotional items, such as direct mail pieces, video productions, and classroom materials, are to be presented separately and will be approved as funding sources are secured. (<u>Your Public Relations Firm</u>) is to begin its work by providing Townsville with a public relations plan for promoting attendance for the exhibit and community involvement in the three aforementioned educational programs and for helping the city recruit 1,500 volunteers to help with the exhibit. The plan should include a proposed budget. Major promotional items should be shown as line items marked "TBF" (To Be Funded) in place of a cost estimate.

DATED this 10th day of December.

TOWNSVILLE, U.S.A., a municipal corporation

By: _____

David Green

Title: Mayor

_____

T. Tom Plumb, Town Clerk

By April Rostkemper, Deputy Town Clerk

_____

(<u>Your Public Relations Firm</u>)

Approved as to form:

_____

Alfred A. Apple, Town Attorney

ATTACHMENT

CONTRACT
ATTACHMENT A

NIHONGA ARTISTS ON LOCATION

Townsville Museum of Art will host the visit of four Nihonga artists. The purpose of this program is to give people an opportunity to converse informally (through an interpreter) with students of Nihonga, to learn about the history of the art, the painting techniques used, and about the way in which the artists select and approach their work.

The student artists will be in residence for six weeks beginning the second week in June. The artists' programs will include workshops and demonstrations of painting techniques; informal discussions with American artists; visits with educators and summer workshop students; studio time for the artists to work on a current or new painting and for visitors to observe; and time for the artists to produce art work of their own to take back to Japan, possibly inspired by the greater Townsville environment. The schedule will be developed cooperatively between the artists and the museum staff member responsible for the Nihonga Artists on Location program.

NIHONGA CLASSROOM EXPERIENCE

The Nihonga Classroom Experience is a student lesson using Japanese art to generate interest in learning more about Japan—its culture, history, and national heritage. Lessons are being prepared for students in three groups: ages 4 to 6; 7 to 11; and 12 to 18. Instruction packets for each age group will contain a teacher's lesson guide, appropriate classroom activities, videotape, and Nihonga brochure, all of which will be enclosed in a program folder imprinted with a sponsor's name. Instruction packages could be available to all public school buildings. The classroom program will have a potential audience of 55,000 children. Additional packages could be available, upon request, for schools throughout the state.

One way to reach teachers is through Educational Service District (ESD) #12. The president, Nancy Walker, could send a letter to superintendents of schools in the service area introducing Nihonga and describing the classroom experience program and materials. President Walker could indicate that interested teachers would be invited to an in-service, credited, training session on the use of the Nihonga Classroom Experience lesson.

Prior to summer recess, ESD #12 could distribute colorful, promotional posters (about 10,000) announcing the exhibition and inviting children to participate in Nihonga summer workshops. Three workshops, offered for three age levels extending from kindergarten through 12th grade, could be offered during the exhibition by specially trained instructors.

When students return to school in the fall, their teachers could be reminded by the ESD to take advantage of the Nihonga Classroom Experience program. The videotape will be, essentially, a guided tour of the exhibition for children who were unable to see it during the summer. Curriculum units for the classroom lesson and summer workshops are being developed, professionally, as follows:

Purpose: To promote a better understanding of the Japanese people—their customs, culture, and national heritage.

Curriculum units: designed for children of ages ranging from 4 to 6 years; 7 to 11 years; and 12 to 18 years. Each unit will include three activities. Individual activities will take one to three hours each. These activities will include the following components, which emphasize instruction and content that promote greater understanding of the Japanese culture.

I. Instructional Components

    A. Goals and objectives.

    B. Good, clear directions so that nonspecialist teachers can readily translate the materials.

    C. A range of activities that appeals to different learning styles.

    D. Activities that stress collaborative learning.

    E. Activities that foster higher level thinking skills.

    F. A concluding activity that engages students in evaluation of their own work and/or their peers' work.

    G. List of materials—specific.

II. Content Components

    A. A general background and history of the activity as it relates to the Japanese culture, as expressed, for example, in Nihonga.

    B. Introduction to the appropriate Japanese words that relate to the activity.

    C. A geographical orientation to the activity—for example, Where in Japan does this activity take place/originate?

    D. An introduction to stories, music, dance, art, drama, and/or games of Japan that enhance the activity.

    E. An exploration of Japanese life surrounding the activity—for example, Where would students find this? At home? In school?, For what age group is it appropriate?

Each curriculum unit will be packaged in folders appropriate for each grade level and will be used during the Nihonga children's workshops, as well as in regular classrooms. ESD #12 will help coordinate development of the classroom program. A curriculum director has been retained to develop the lessons, to provide in-service training for area teachers, and to help with the summer workshops.

NIHONGA TOWN SEMINARS

The Nihonga Town Seminars will be designed to introduce mature students and adults to a broad range of subjects. They include Tea Ceremony, Japanese Cuisine, Japanese Flower Arranging, Raising of Koi, Bonsai Demonstration, Myths & Customs of Japan, Japanese/American Woman, Kimono Demonstration/Fashion Show, and Japanese Business Etiquette.

Each seminar will be presented by a qualified leader. There will be a different seminar each Monday evening at the Townsville Art Museum and possibly other locations during the exhibition. There will be six to eight seminars in the series.

Additional funds are being sought to enhance the stature of the seminar series by featuring a Nihonga artist for one of the sessions. Each of the seminars will be videotaped for use by colleges and universities and civic and professional organizations. The following sources have been contacted for help in identifying qualified seminar leaders:

Japan American Society	University of Washington
International Examiner	Regional art institutes
Asian Arts Council	Regional art museums
Council General of Japan (state office)	Academy of Art College, San Francisco
California Institute of the Arts	California State University, Los Angeles
School of Music and the Arts	
San Francisco Art Institute	Pacific Northwest College of Art
United States International University	University of Southern California
Western State College	University of California
World Affairs Council	University of Hawaii
Japan-American Society (state office)	Others

Notes about Nihonga Art

- a technique whose roots extend back more than a thousand years

- a term created in the nineteenth century to distinguish traditional Japanese painting methods from Western-influenced art

- often synonymous with art of the past

- incorporates time-honored materials, such as silk, rice-paper, ground semi-precious minerals, gold and silver leaf

- employs only materials fully derived from natural sources (brushes, paper, Chinese ink, mineral pigment, and animal glue)

- paintings retain close harmony with nature

- the technique has become one of the principal art forms of Japan

- one distinctive feature of this medium is the subtle control of detail that it allows—fine variations in line thickness and nuances in color attainable in Nihonga require painters to maintain close observation of their subjects

HOW TO ATTRACT AND RETAIN VOLUNTEERS

It might come as a surprise that corporations use volunteers, more commonly referred to as *interns*. Why are some organizations more successful than others in attracting and retaining volunteers or interns? I'm going to answer that question by relating a personal experience I had working for a Fortune 500 company.

One of the first volunteers I had the pleasure of working with was a student named Ellen. The company I was working for at the time had established a good rapport with colleges and universities throughout the United States. These institutions were the company's chief source of volunteers.

"Could you use a student intern for the summer?" the company headquarters asked.

"Yes!" I said instantly. "I have at least a dozen projects for a good project coordinator."

"Could a student handle the work?" asked headquarters.

"I happen to have a job description. I'll fax it to you and you can have the student decide for herself if she can handle it," I replied.

Now think about this. A person was volunteering help. And I was ready to accept it.[1] I had a list of tasks.[2] I had a job description,[3] and even a job title.[4]

Before the student reported for work, I alerted her coworkers that we were going to have an intern.[5] I didn't want anyone to feel threatened by a new person. In fact, I asked members of my staff to conduct parts of the student's orientation.[6]

When the student reported for work, she was introduced to coworkers.[7] She was given a work area.[8] And the work area was set up with all the tools she needed to do her job.[9]

We gave her a schedule for her first day.[10] It included a tour of the facility[11] and time to look over a list of people[12] she would be working with. The list identified who the people were, why they were important to her, and it had their phone numbers. There also was time on the schedule for her to read publications describing our operation.[13]

As a volunteer, she was interested in gaining job experience to list in her resume that would eventually help her get established in the job market. With the job title we gave her, she could say on her resume that she worked one summer as project coordinator for a Fortune 500 company.

There was no question in her mind about what we expected her to do. The job description identified who she reported to, what standards were expected, how her internship was to contribute to our overall goals, and it outlined 12 specific assignments. When I reviewed it with her, I asked about her professional ambitions[14] and explained how her assignments would contribute to her personal goals.[15]

I said to myself at the time, if she completes half of the 12 assignments, it would be quite an accomplishment for an intern and of significant value to the company. During the internship, we gave our volunteer periodic critiques[16] of her work and personal written notes of praise that she could attach to her resume.[17] To my delight, Ellen completed all 12 assignments in an outstanding manner.

If you noticed the superscript numerals placed throughout this article, you probably realized that you were given 17 suggestions—17 surefire ways to attract and retain interns and volunteers.

Media Relations
Charlie Zurlock

Working with the mass media in seeking publicity or responding to their interests is a major function of public relations. This case, a challenging exercise in media relations, requires more than establishing and maintaining a good working relationship with the media. It involves counseling a company whose lack of understanding of how to work with the media has resulted in an unending saga of negative publicity. The case also involves addressing relationships with government and with company employees. The challenge presented here is to educate the client on the basics of media relations, take immediate steps to end the negative publicity, provide the client with measures that will begin to restore and establish external relationships that will serve to reduce the chances of generating negative publicity in the future. Details of the case unfold in a script, which can be used as a classroom or professional workshop role play, that shows how the company got into an adversarial relationship with a newspaper reporter (see page 111). Additional case materials appear after the script. For a broad perspective on media relations see the article, "What Is a Media Relations Strategist?" on page 121.

TEAM ASSIGNMENT

Charlie Zurlock, owner of Custom Parts Company, has hired your team, a local public relations agency, to help with a situation created by his company's poor handling of media relations. The situation is taking its toll on the reputation of his family-owned business in his home community. Charlie is used to telling people what to do within his organization. However, he has yet to learn that his authority does not extend to the media or to any level of government, as you can see by his demands of your agency. He said, "I want you to put an end to the negative publicity we're getting and see to it that it never happens again. I want you to set state government straight on this health issue. And I want you to keep my employees from getting overly excited about so-called health risks in the workplace." Charlie believes that the media can be controlled, that state government can be told what should or should not be investigated, and that employee relations is a matter of giving everyone a Starburst glazed ham for the holidays.

Your team must develop a public relations plan for Charlie Zurlock that is responsive to his objectives. However, the plan must provide for educating Charlie in the basics of media, government, and employee relations. In the situation analysis of your plan, you must identify the company's shortcomings in dealing with the health issue, but the rules for writing the analysis are clear about not being judgmental or attributing blame to individuals or to the company. Consulting in public relations requires firm but tactful criticism and advice.

INDIVIDUAL TEAM MEMBER ASSIGNMENTS

Suppose that your agency decides that the company's management of relationships requires special guidance to raise standards and, as part of your plan, you offer guidelines. Each team member is to complete a different one of the following items that might or might not be included in the design of your plan. (See Chapter 7: Samples of Effective Public Relations Writing.)

1. Draft for Charlie a memo to employees establishing guidelines governing the company's working relationship with the news media. The memo should explain how the company is to work with the media and how employees should respond to inquiries from journalists. Because this is intended to be general company policy, there should be no reference to the company's current situation with the media. See Random Thoughts about Working with the News Media on page 116 as a resource for writing this memo. Select points that help shape your proposed guidelines for Charlie. (Use memo format—To: All Employees, From: Charlie Zurlock, Re: You and the News Media.)

2. Draft for Charlie a memo to his staff about how the company is to work with all levels of government—local, county, state, and federal. See Random Thoughts about Working with Government on page 116 and select points that help shape your proposed guidelines for Charlie. (Use memo format—To: Management Staff, From: Charlie Zurlock, Re: Working with Government.)

3. Develop a backgrounder on "effective employee communication." Use Internet sources to include some of the latest research on how today's employee wants to be treated. See Random Thoughts about Effective Communication among Individuals on page 118. The backrounder might be used by your PR firm in counseling Charlie.

4. Draft a memo from you, as head of the account team, to Custom Parts management providing guidance on how to discuss matters of risk with employees and the community. The memo should point out that there are some basics they should know to communicate matters of risk without getting people upset. See Random Thoughts about Communicating Matters of Risk on page 119. (Use memo format—To: Custom Parts Management, From: (Your Name), Re: Talking about Risk.)

5. Draft a media advisory addressed to editors and news directors (of print and broadcast media) calling their attention to an up-coming event commemorating the start-up of new environmental control equipment at Custom Parts Company and launching of the company's new program, "Clean Air Awareness." You make up the details for writing the advisory that must answer the journalist's W's—Who? What? When? Where? Why?—and describe an irresistable photo/video opportunity (PhotoOp).

6. Draft a news release announcing the hiring by Custom Parts Company of a director of public relations. Make up the details of the announcement to include the name of the individual, job experience, professional awards, education, and major job responsibilities. Include two substantive quotes from the new director that would be especially appreciated by local journalists. Use an appropriate news release form. Search the Internet for examples of personnel announcements.

7. Develop an information sheet providing an overview of the state's environmental protection agency. It is to be used to brief Charlie and his staff on the agency's director, the director's views on air quality (from testimony on the Web site), the agency's mission and goals specifically related to clean air, key staff members, and other background to promote a better understanding of the government's role in environmental protection. For

purposes of illustration use the Web site for the environmental department of any state government.

GETTING BAD PRESS AT CUSTOM PARTS COMPANY

Cast

Dorothy, Secretary
Student's Name, Reporter
Robin Jackson, Plant Engineer
Jessica Murray, Director, Department of Ecology
Charlie Zurlock, Owner
Dr. Emerson, State Physician
Nancy White, Human Resources Secretary
Dan Peopleton, Director, Human Resources
Narrator

NEWSROOM—DAY

NARRATOR: A reporter lifts the telephone receiver. Calls Custom Parts Company. Asks for the owner. Secretary answers.

DOROTHY (Secretary): Charlie Zurlock's office, this is Dorothy. How can I help you?

Student's Name (Reporter): Hello Dorothy. This is (your name) with the *Messenger.* I'd like to speak to Mr. Zurlock about your pollution problem.

DOROTHY (Secretary): (Instructively) Mr. Zurlock said if anyone calls about that citation, they should talk to our plant engineer. Would you like me to transfer you to her line?

NARRATOR: The reporter, somewhat concerned about the owner's refusal to speak to the media about environmental health and safety, agrees to talk to the plant engineer.

Student's Name (Reporter): Yes, What's his name?

DOROTHY (Secretary): (Boldly, correcting the reporter) **HER** name is Jackson. Robin Jackson. Just a minute please.

NARRATOR: Phone rings. Robin Jackson answers.

ROBIN (Plant Engineer): (Sounding annoyed) Hello. Robin Jackson here.

Student's Name (Reporter): Hello, Ms. Jackson. This is (your name) with the *Messenger.* Your title, is it plant engineer?

ROBIN (Plant Engineer): That's right. What do you want?

Student's Name (Reporter): I'd like your reaction to the Department of Ecology's announcement. The agency said it appears that 5 out of every 10,000 people living around your plant stand a good chance of getting cancer.

ROBIN (Plant Engineer): (Defensive; takes a shot at the government agency.) There are plenty of ways that a government bureaucracy can interpret its data. We've conducted our own health studies of our workers. There's been no increased incidence of cancer.

Student's Name (Reporter): (Aggressively interjecting) But the government,

NARRATOR: Plant engineer interrupts; tries to impose the results of a "company-paid" study that has yet to be completed; tries to minimize the health risk.

ROBIN (Plant Engineer): Listen. We just launched a new study. And we are predicting that by year-end, the findings will show that our emissions pose no more risk than smoke from a cigarette in an auditorium.

NARRATOR: Aghast! The reporter thinks: this engineer must have a crystal ball! She knows the results of a study before it's conducted. Wonder how much the company is paying to get the findings it wants.

Student's Name (Reporter): If you're so sure your emissions are harmless, why did the government target your operation for an impact study?

NARRATOR: Plant engineer attempts to sidestep the issue; takes another shot at the state agency; points a finger at other companies.

ROBIN (Plant Engineer): They're picking on us because we're nearby. We're just on the outskirts of town, you know. Practically under their office window. Hey look, we're not the only plant around here with emissions. The other plants like ours are tuned into this issue. You can bet on that! Sorry, I've got to take another call.

NARRATOR: The reporter, irritated with having been cut off, calls Jessica Murray, director of the state's Department of Ecology. Feeds back to the state Department of Ecology what the Custom Parts engineer said about the pollution fine and about the department.

Student's Name (Reporter): Hello, Jessica, this is (your name) with the *Messenger*. I tried to talk with Custom Parts about the pollution citation and fine that it got from you. The plant engineer, Robin Jackson, disagrees with you. She says their emissions pose no health risk. She implied that your agency is manipulating the data. She said that your agency is picking on Custom Parts because the plant is conveniently close to your offices.

NARRATOR: Upset with the accusation that her government agency is lazy and manipulative, the department head strikes back with a sweeping unsubstantiated, but quotable opinion.

JESSICA (Director, Department of Ecology): I think we're going to be able to show that emissions from that plant, and every one like it, pose a substantial health threat.

NARRATOR: The reporter ends the call to the state Department of Ecology and calls Custom Parts, this time getting through to the owner, Charlie Zurlock.

Student's Name (Reporter): Hello, Charlie Zurlock?

CHARLIE (Owner): Yes, this is Zurlock.

Student's Name (Reporter): I'm (your name) with the *Messenger*. I'm doing a story on your plant and yesterday's announcement by the state Department of Ecology.

I talked earlier with your engineer, Robin Jackson. But I have a few more questions.

CHARLIE (Owner): Get on with it. I've got a busy schedule, don't ya see, don't ya see?

Student's Name (Reporter): (Not about to be rushed) The state Department of Ecology thinks it's going to be able to show that emissions from your plant, and plants like it, pose a substantial health risk to employees and people living nearby. Exactly how much toxic material is your plant emitting?

NARRATOR: **Ignoring the public's legal right to know about toxic emissions, the owner hesitates . . . clears throat.**

CHARLIE (Owner): I can't recall the amount. Even if I could, I wouldn't want to tell you.

Student's Name (Reporter): (Disgusted with the owner's arrogance) Aren't you even a little concerned that your emissions might be endangering the health of your own employees and the community?

CHARLIE (Owner): (Tries to minimize the risk) I'm telling you . . . Our emissions are no more harmful to the human body than smoke from a wood-burning stove.

NARRATOR: **Reporter calls the state's Department of Health and reaches the state physician.**

Student's Name (Reporter): Hello, Dr. Emerson. I'm (your name) with the *Messenger*. I just spoke with the owner of Custom Parts Company. He claims that their emissions are no more harmful than smoke from wood-burning stoves. How harmful do you think the effects really are?

NARRATOR: **Not pleased to hear the company minimize a health risk, the physician offers an unsubstantiated but quotable opinion and refuses to let the company off the hook.**

Dr. EMERSON (State Physician): I think there is occupational exposure at the plant causing more cases of cancer. At this point, I can't tell you what it is—whether it's the emissions or other toxic chemicals. But I am working on a lot of different possibilities.

Student's Name (Reporter): You mentioned the increased incidence of cancer. How many cases have been reported?

NARRATOR: **The state physician offers an opinion based on hearsay, which is quotable.**

Dr. EMERSON (State Physician): Over the past several years, I've heard of at least nine workers at the plant who had cancer of the blood-forming organs. But this information came to me by word of mouth.

NARRATOR: **Reporter calls Custom Parts and this time, for some unknown reason, is referred to the Human Resources Department. A secretary answers.**

NANCY (Human Resources Secretary): Human Resources. Nancy White speaking.

NARRATOR: **The reporter tries to speak to the owner.**

Student's Name (Reporter): I would like to speak to Charlie Zurlock. I'm (your name) with the *Messenger*. I'm doing a story on your plant. We understand that at least seven employees at the plant have been diagnosed with cancer of the blood forming organs over the past several years. I'd like Mr. Zurlock to confirm this.

NANCY (Human Resources Secretary): (Acting as though she is an authorized spokesperson for the company) Well, I'd like to help. But we have no comment.

Student's Name (Reporter): I'd like to speak to Mr. Zurlock.

NANCY (Human Resources Secretary): No way, José.

NARRATOR: Reporter is upset with the brush-off. Calls the state Department of Ecology and describes the company's arrogance.

Student's Name (Reporter): Hello, Jessica? This is (your name) at the *Messenger*. We spoke earlier about the Custom Parts plant. I'm not getting much cooperation from them. I understand that your agency has ordered the company to do emission studies; you want them to determine the possible threat of cancer to employees and those living near the plant. How severe is the threat of cancer?

NARRATOR: The head of the agency offers the strongest statement yet of unsubstantiated but quotable opinion.

JESSICA (Director, Department of Ecology): The risk of getting cancer to employees and people outside the plant could be substantial.

NARRATOR: Reporter tries once again to reach Charlie Zurlock.

DAN (Director, Human Resources): Hello, Dan Peopleton, Human Resources.

Student's Name (Reporter): I'm (your name) with the *Messenger*. We're doing a story on your plant. I am trying to reach the owner, Mr. Zurlock. According to the state Department of Ecology, your plant's emissions are jeopardizing the health of workers and community residents. I need to know more about that.

NARRATOR: The director of Human Resources also thinks he has psychic powers and predicts the results of a study yet to be done, then takes a shot at state government.

DAN (Director, Human Resources): Sure, I'll be happy to comment. We're confident that at year-end our research will show that any cancer cases were not caused by working at the plant. Hey look, Clark Kent, if you want some advice, don't pay so much attention to the Department of Ecology. They haven't done a thorough job of studying our emissions.

BACKGROUND

Custom Parts Company

Custom Parts Company (CPC) is located in Capital City, U.S.A. It produces custom parts for industrial machines using steel, titanium, and various carbon composite materials. It employs 231 people. The employees, about 198 people, are members of a union, represented by the All Trades Council. CPC is privately owned by the Zurlock family and run by Charlie Zurlock. Its products are marketed throughout the United States. The company is not involved in the local community, except for Charlie's wife, Helen, who is a major donor to and board member of the Women's Association.

The company has been in operation for 28 years and has a record of eight citations by the state Department of Ecology (DOE) for air pollution. The DOE doesn't make a special effort to publicize its fines unless the subject of a fine fails to cooperate and adhere to environmental regulations. On March 1, 20XX, the DOE cited Custom Parts Company for exceeding toxic emission limits once a week since the beginning of the year. DOE fined the company $10,000 and mandated that an independent study be conducted (at CPC's expense) of worker health and of the health of residents, living within two miles of the plant. It is true that the company had excursions of toxic emissions once each week from the beginning of the year to the end of February. No excursion lasted more than 10 minutes, but each one expelled more than two tons of foul-smelling particulate matter into the air. The emissions were big in volume and highly visible. It's true that the company has not been very responsive to the government.

New control equipment has been ordered, but for some reason not in time to meet regulatory deadlines. It has not as yet arrived and no one seems to have even an estimated delivery date. Meanwhile, company engineers have tried to fine-tune existing controls, but the effort has not produced consistent results. The company maintains that the worker environment is absolutely free of any health risk. However, the company is in the process of hiring an independent laboratory, True-Test Labs, Inc., to conduct a health study of employees and local residents. It is true that the company does not have a perfectly clean record for environmental control. However, Charlie has updated the company's pollution control equipment, once in 1960 at a cost of $2 million and again in 1980 at a cost of $3 million. Employees are loyal to the operation, not because of the Starburst glazed ham their families get from Charlie and his wife each year, but because their skills are specialized and limited to Charlie's operation. In other words they couldn't get work anywhere else.

The local newspaper was informed of the citation and fine in a news release issued by the DOE. The reporter contacted the company for a statement. The reporter talked with several different people (refer to classroom/professional workshop role play) who seem to have an adversarial attitude toward state government and newspaper reporters. Reports of the company's alleged cancer-causing emissions have alarmed employees and have resulted in two weeks of negative publicity for the company. Employees feel, "Just because Charlie says it's safe doesn't mean nothin'."

Random Thoughts about Working with the News Media

Employees are largely responsible for the reputation of an organization. . . . A company's reputation makes qualified people want to come to work and stay with an organization. . . . Reputation has an influence on customers' buying decisions. . . . A reputation contributes to investor decisions in buying stock. . . . Financial institutions that loan money for business development are influenced by a borrower's reputation. . . . Government officials are more likely to treat an organization fairly and journalists are more likely to write accurately about an organization if the name is respected. . . . A good reputation helps an organization to be a welcomed part of the communities in which they operate. . . . Employees help form an organization's reputation because, to outsiders, employees are the organization. . . . How employees feel about the organization and what they say about it are the basis of attitudes others hold toward the organization. . . . In going about their daily work or personal activities, employees represent a powerful influence on their employer's reputation. Employees may have occasion at one time or another to speak with a representative of the news media. It's important to bear in mind that to the media, employees are the organization. . . . Whatever an employee says could easily be broadcast or printed as a statement from the employee's employer. Some organizations have guidelines for employees if they are contacted by any of the media (newspapers, magazine, radio, TV). These guidelines might include telling employees to immediately refer all contacts by the media to a designated spokesperson. This enables an organization to gather any necessary information and respond promptly to media inquiries. . . . Responses to the media usually require some research, review of information by appropriate individuals, including an organization's attorney, and clearance by executive management to release the information to the media. . . . Media requests must be acted on promptly because reporters are usually working against tight deadlines; they often need specific information quickly. . . . A neglected press call could mean losing an important opportunity for comment or clarification of an issue. . . . Some guidelines discourage employees from engaging in idle conversation with reporters because the journalists decide what is quotable and what is not. . . . Some guidelines stress that complete and accurate information is best given by an organization's spokesperson. . . . Some guidelines say that if it has been determined by the organization that it is appropriate for an employee to engage in an interview with the media that it is essential for the interview to be monitored by another organization representative who can listen to the conversation and help ensure that there is an accurate interpretation and understanding of information discussed.

Random Thoughts about Working with Government

Organizations want to have effective working relationships with local, county, state, and federal government officials—elected representatives as well as government agency personnel. Well-run organizations debate issues on the basis of their merits and will not engage in any combative behavior over any matter with government. . . . Well-run organizations make an effort to become acquainted with and helpful to government representatives who have an interest in various aspects of business—from health and safety to environmental control. They take government representatives through their operations and meet with them in their offices to discuss current business issues and problems, particularly those involving government measures or the need for them. . . . Well-run organizations attend or send a representative to public hearings on public policy relating to the organization's interests. They offer to testify at hearings on matters of particular concern. They encourage employees to serve on business committees, local boards, commissions, and civic groups. Where appropriate, they invite officials to make presentations (e.g., a public safety director or fire chief might be asked to be on hand to mark a new record of consecutive no-accident days; environmental protection agency officials might be invited to start up a new piece of recycling equipment). . . . Well-run organizations encourage communication with government that fosters mutual understanding and respect. They welcome government officials for firsthand inspections of operations and to meet employees on the job. They host government representatives for meetings with management to discuss issues and, at the same time, apprise them of the organization's contributions to the local and regional economies: number of people employed; average annual payroll; products manufactured; annual sales revenue and how it is allocated for supplies, rent, depreciation, payroll; state and local taxes paid; property tax and personal income taxes paid by employees; uses made of profits for plant improvements, new equipment, research, employee benefits, aid to schools, hospitals, and other local organizations and causes; special local programs and services provided, such as day care, diversity training, continuing education; participation in community improvement projects; employee benefits provided; plant environmental problems and cleanup efforts; amount of energy consumed in daily operations and energy-saving measures implemented; safety and health standards in the operation; new protective equipment facilities or technology; security standards used for plant protection; utility requirements for water, sewage, and waste disposal; employees who serve on local boards and commissions, and so on. . . . Well-run organizations expect managers to be current on issues of public policy affecting the organization. . . . The organization is expected to be an active participant in the public policy process—in other words, when regulations or laws are being considered the organization wants to take an active part in discussing and debating points of interest to help shape policy that is fair, practical, and cost-effective. This means the organization will be alert to the potential effects of proposed legislation and determine a course of action in light of those effects; determine if others are getting involved or if the organization must take the initiative; identify supporters and opponents of a proposed measure; make personal contact with elected representatives to express a position and present the organization as a source of information; consider offering to testify at hearings about how an action will affect the welfare of the organization, employees, and community; develop support from other political bodies; inform employees of legislation that would affect their well-being and consider enlisting their aid in contacting elected representatives; monitor day-to-day developments so that the company's action will be absolutely relevant. . . . Well-run organizations are interested in early identification of issues of importance. When appropriate, the organization will reach out to organizations with common interest in an issue to form a coalition so as to speak with a stronger voice in getting a message across to government officials. . . . The organization will join and support organizations whose charter is to represent and lobby for public policy that supports the responsible growth and development of business. . . . The organization will host visits with government representatives to set the stage for mutual understanding between the public and its representatives on a continuing basis. . . . Facility tours initially tell government officials that an organization is a member of his or her constituency; it also helps government representatives to know and understand an operation. . . . Follow-up is important. Efforts must be made to ensure that government officials continue to be aware of an organization's operation. Such efforts should include a note of thanks reemphasizing key points made during a visit, answers to remaining questions, expression of interest in an elected official's or regulatory representative's activities, and requests to be put on mailing lists. Organization members who accompanied representatives on a visit should express interest in keeping in contact with them. . . . Government visitors should receive copies of photographs taken with employees, a plant or office manager, labor leaders, and others during the visit, along with copies of newspaper or plant newsletter articles detailing the visit. . . . A well-run organization continues to inform government representatives of key activities, continuing challenges, and concerns about upcoming legislation.

Random Thoughts about Effective Communication among Individuals

What does it mean to have effective communication among individuals? It means showing respect for each other regardless of position. . . . It means recognizing individuals as intelligent, well-meaning and responsive. . . . It means sharing information about all areas of an organization and its interests so everyone is informed. . . . It means talking to each other in an informational rather than judgmental way. . . . It means being in the loop—getting information on a regular basis. . . . Effective communication is two-way and two-way communication in an organization must be encouraged. . . . Effective communication among individuals requires a team orientation. Job-oriented dialogue among team members is essential for achieving productivity goals and high quality standards. Effective communication among individuals also means frequent face-to-face meetings. . . . It means talking and thinking about communication. . . . It means planning together and executing plans with precision. . . . It means everyone striving to be clear, direct, and open with each other. . . . It means revealing the bad and celebrating the good. . . . It means accepting responsibility for mistakes and providing plans to correct them. . . . It means telling it like it is. . . . It means rejecting the notion that there is power in hoarding information. . . . It means nurturing the notion that having common knowledge about an organization makes work meaningful. . . . Effective communication among individuals means challenging each other to be knowledgeable enough to be good ambassadors of an organization who can provide complete and accurate information to others. . . . It means being completely truthful. . . . It means sharing information about an organization's outlook, future plans, policies, and practices affecting daily work, about challenging local and regional issues, employee benefits, how an individual's work fits into the big picture, personnel changes, where and how an organization's products and services are used, where the organization stands on issues affecting its industry, about cash flow and the bottom line, what competitors are doing, and activities in other parts of the organization. It means cultivating genuine working relationships that provide a sense of security. . . . Effective communication among individuals means listening to understand and letting others know that it is OK to show compassion.

Random Thoughts about Communicating Matters of Risk

A red flag should pop up in your mind when you, as a public relations practitioner, have to communicate to others matters of risk to human health, safety, and the environment. Risk communication is a special area of expertise based on a body of knowledge developed by individuals and organizations that have invested major resources in studying the dynamics of how risks are perceived and how citizen outrage can be avoided when sensitive subjects are raised to a plane of public discussion. I had the privilege and pleasure of working on several risk communication projects with the nation's preeminent risk communication consultant, Peter M. Sandman, a Rutgers University faculty member since 1977. A wealth of information can be found on Dr. Sandman's Web site: www .psandman.com. Dr. Sandman founded the Environmental Communication Research Program (ECRP) at Rutgers in 1986 and was its director until 1992. During that time ECRP, now called the Center for Environmental Communication, published more than 80 articles and books on various aspects of risk communication, including separate manuals for government, industry, and the mass media.

I have learned that there are four especially important factors to keep in mind when communicating matters of risk. One is that people are more receptive to receiving information about risk to their health or safety if the communication comes from a familiar source. The source must be trustworthy and have the good sense and compassion to recognize people's feelings and address them before getting to the facts of the matter.

The second factor is control. People feel uncomfortable and threatened by risks over which they seem to have no control. People today know they are entitled to be made aware of any serious threat to their health, their safety, and their environment. Such threats are viewed not only as wrong, but morally wrong. Emotions intensify if these threats are controlled and/or imposed by someone else. One way to provide control in a risk situation

is to invite oversight by an established authority, such as a government agency or service such as a public fire and rescue unit.

The third factor is answering questions. When it comes to personal risks, people want all of the answers, not just some or those considered most important. For example, if a person is in a public meeting and is discussing a matter of risk, it is imperative that the individual stay as long as necessary to answer every question, respectfully, down to what might seem unimportant and trivial. It is equally important to find out what is of greatest concern to

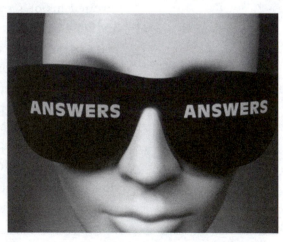

people, because a risk can be perceived in many different ways and it is essential to focus accurately on the concern that is uppermost in mind.

The fourth factor of importance in discussing matters of risk can be referred to as evidence. Does the person discussing risk have credibility? Is what the individual is saying backed by evidence? It would not be effective for a company executive, for example, to assure community neighbors of their safety if the executive's company has a long and continuing record of industrial injuries and accidents. In discussing risk the source of the information must have a credible basis from which to speak.

WHAT IS A MEDIA RELATIONS STRATEGIST?

Working with the media is a complex and demanding job. People in the public relations profession who have responsibilities in media relations take this aspect of the job in their stride. It would be rare to find a reference in their job descriptions to performing six functions of a media relations strategist. And yet that's what they do and they deserve recognition for doing it effectively.

When a person says he or she has responsibility for the media, most people think that involves issuing news releases and answering press calls. However, if someone were to create the job of media relations strategist, I believe it would have, among others, six important functions, each requiring knowledge of media operations and a full range of skills—from journalistic writing to thinking and speaking spontaneously and making strategic use of media opportunities. Following are the six key functions of a media relations strategist.

1. Originates news by knowing media needs and how to develop information to fill them.

2. Addresses the news by responding to news reports and inquiries, by knowing how to take a position as a news source, by knowing what to say and how to say it or have others say it.

3. Diffuses situations before they become news by knowing how to recognize in advance issues with news potential and how to use conflict resolution and accommodation measures to resolve them before they become of public interest.

4. Disseminates news by knowing how to prepare information professionally and to arrange for its instant distribution on a local, regional, national, or global level.

5. Corrects news by knowing news production and appropriate procedures to set the record straight on erroneous news reports so that misinformation doesn't keep recurring in print or electronic form.

6. Develops strategies to orchestrate the release of messages through a variety of channels by various means to influence the behavior of one or more target publics or audiences.

Many public relations practitioners starting a new job have an opportunity to shape the job according to their individual skills and the needs of their respective organizations. Often that entails drafting or editing a job description. Should you have the good fortune to be given this opportunity, consider including the six key functions of a media relations strategist. A public relations practitioner with media relations responsibilities deserves to be appropriately compensated for performing the role of a media relations strategist.

Public Relations in Public Schools
I'm Getting to That . . .

This is a case of a peaceful school environment that unexpectedly explodes with emotions, taking administrators, faculty, staff, parents, and even many students by surprise. School districts have a responsibility to develop crisis plans. However, the range of traumatic events that districts experience has increased significantly over the years from temporary disruptions to highly publicized events. Educators are greatly challenged to obtain the training needed to deal effectively with today's diverse range of crisis situations. While many schools have plans to deal with the unexpected, their plans must employ more than a top administrator and a small response team. Today's problems require broader involvement of all members of the school community. They require the involvement of outside support services, from fire and rescue personnel to professional counselors. They require plans with provisions to meet the physical and psychological needs of individuals in every stage of a crisis situation—from trauma through recovery.

In this case your team will be a school district's public relations staff. Your challenge will be to come to the scene after the initial shock of an incident, assess the situation, and help strengthen relationships so people are able to solve problems constructively.

Details of the case unfold in a script dramatizing a confrontation between worried parents and a high school principal (see page 125). The narrative is suitable as a role play for the classroom or for a professional workshop.

TEAM ASSIGNMENT

For this case, assume that your team is the public relations staff for the South County Public School District and that the incident described in the classroom or workshop role play took South County High School and the district by complete surprise. The district superintendent has instructed your public relations team to get involved immediately in assisting the South County High principal by providing and helping to implement a public relations plan with the goal for South County High to be functioning normally with mutual respect and trust among all members of the high school community. As you will see in the role play on page 125, emotions have errupted and attempts to get a difficult situation under control are off to a bad start. To turn things around you will have to focus not only on the situation but on two important dimensions of leadership—courage and trust. The case provides an opportunity to show how you would support a leader, the high school principal, in ways that strengthen the person's courage to stand up and do what's right. You will also need to show how you would enable an individual to earn the trust people require of a leader who is to guide them through a difficult situation. The principal of South County High needs public relations direction and support to communicate the district's four-point action plan. Your team must plan how to support the principal in communicating the district's four-point plan of action to all of the high school's key publics.

INDIVIDUAL TEAM MEMBER ASSIGNMENTS

Each team member is to complete a different one of the following items that might or might not be included in the design of your plan. It is up to you to decide what the content should be for each element.

1. Opening remarks for the high school principal to make before a student assembly; the remarks will set the tone and tenor for addressing the school's crisis situation (90-second duration in speaker's form).

2. Letter from the superintendent of South County Public Schools to parents as a follow-up to last weekend's parent meeting with South County High School principal.

3. Opening remarks for South County High School principal for a meeting with the editorial board of the town's local newspaper (90-second duration in speaker's form).

4. A memo from Principal Burdick to faculty and staff informing them of the school's four-point action plan, which is summarized by the superintendent in the role play that follows these assignments.

5. A question and answer sheet for school faculty and staff to use in responding to phone calls by anyone interested in the current situation. The sheet should cover the basics and refer individuals to the school's Web site for a complete and accurate description of the incidents that occurred and for details of the school's plan of action for addressing the situation.

6. A phone script to be read by a school secretary inviting officers of South County High's Parent Teacher Association to a meeting with the principal.

7. A tip sheet to be sent by the school to the local media on what parents should tell their children to help keep them safe at school. Search the Internet for "violence in schools" and related subjects.

EMERGENCY MEETING AT SOUTH COUNTY HIGH

CAST

Sally Edwards, Parent
Tom Edwards, Parent
Nadel Harper, Parent
Paul Burdick, High School Principal
Irritated Parent No. 1
Irritated Parent No. 2
Irritated Parent No. 3
Irritated Parent No. 4
Irritated Parent No. 5
Irritated Parent No. 6
Clark Cantwell, Reporter
Rose, Teacher
Ellen, Teacher
Alex, Science Teacher
Maxine Gradeletter, District Superintendent
Narrator

NARRATOR: A stream of several hundred cars flows into the parking lot at South County High. Doors slam shut, one right after another as parents leave their vehicles and head for the walk to the auditorium. A journalist asks an officer to reposition her patrol car and turn on the strobe lights for a more dramatic camera shot. Tom Edwards and his wife Sally are among the parade of parents.

SALLY (Parent): (Nervous, with a worried expression) Tom, I'm worried. We've never been summoned like this to attend a meeting. Oh, my! An "emergency" meeting they said on the phone! Tom!!

TOM (Parent): (Trying to be reassuring.) Now, Sally, let's not jump to conclusions. It's probably just a precaution.

SALLY (Parent): Precaution!!

TOM (Parent): Calm down, dear. It's probably about some party that got out of hand.

SALLY (Parent): Get real Tom. It's not about six-pack shenanigans down on the Chattahoochee. These days it's about hostage-taking, sniper attacks, murders, terrorist activities, and bombings. Oh my, Tom!!

NARRATOR: The Edwards reach the auditorium entrance with others. No one is at the door to meet the anxious visitors, which adds to an already empty feeling in the pits of nervous stomachs. Tom Edwards takes a seat, turns his head to the left and is eye to eye with Nadel Harper, another parent.

TOM (Parent): Hello. I'm Tom Edwards and this is my wife Sally.

NADEL (Parent): (Looks with a raised eyebrow) Hey.

NARRATOR: Finger tapping thumps over the sound system. Thump. Thump. It's more an expression of nerves than a test of the microphone. Thump. Thump. Thump. The high school principal speaks.

PAUL (Principal): (Staring, not at the audience of 600 parents, but down at notes on the podium) Several years ago we established a program for diversity in our school . . .

SALLY (Parent): (Talking to her husband, John) He could have at least said hello. He makes us come to this meeting at nine o'clock on a Saturday morning and doesn't even acknowledge that we're here.

PAUL (Principal): (Continuing his remarks) Included in our diversity program were students, faculty members, administrators . . .

NARRATOR: An irritated parent stands to address the high school principal.

IRRITATED PARENT NO. 1: (Interrupting the speaker) Paul, would you mind just telling us why we are here?

IRRITATED PARENT NO. 2: (Adding to the interruption) Yes! What is the emergency? What's this all about?

PAUL (Principal): (Raising his eyes, but not looking far into the audience) Yes, I'm getting to that. Last Thursday a boy, who is not a student, came to the school to see a girl. It was during lunch. He tried to distribute Ku Klux Klan patches. He was apprehended quickly and escorted off the campus.

IRRITATED PARENT NO. 3: (Interrupting the principal) So what's the big emergency, Paul?

PAUL (Principal): Yes, I'm getting to that. That incident on Thursday started a lot of students talking about race, freedom of speech, about the boy being apprehended and sent away from the school.

NARRATOR: Thump. Thump. The principal figits with the microphone.

PAUL (Principal): Emotions got somewhat intense. On Friday morning there were random acts of vandalism in the school.

IRRITATED PARENT NO. 1: Like what? Give some examples?

PAUL (Principal): Yes. In wood shop, about sixty birdhouses were glued solid to the workbench. In the home economics room, a door was glued shut. The most serious incident happened in the band room. Students argued over race, free speech . . .

IRRITATED PARENT NO. 2: Just how bad did it get? Don't hold the details. You're talking to hundreds of us who came here to find out what's going on.

IRRITATED PARENT NO. 3: (Shouting out.) I'll tell you what happened! I heard that a tuba got thrown out a window. A trombone was wrapped around someone's neck. Nearly strangled him. A student got struck in the head with an oboe and went to the hospital.

IRRITATED PARENT NO. 6: (Interrupting) I heard teachers and two parents just stood and watched. That's when Jamie got hit in the head with an oboe.

IRRITATED PARENT NO. 3: (Interrupting) My daughter ran down to the office to call home. They wouldn't let her use the phone . . . said it was school policy.

PAUL (Principal): (Breathing heavily, visibly shaken) Yes. Yes. I'm getting to that . . .

IRRITATED PARENT NO. 4: (Acting somewhat restrained and reluctant to talk) What about the gun reports? Are you going to tell us about the gun reports?

IRRITATED PARENT NO. 5: (She screams . . . gasps repeatedly for air . . . calls to her husband) Arnie! Oh, Arnie! They've got guns!!!

PAUL (Principal): Yes. I'm getting to that. I mean, no, I wasn't going to bring that up. We checked those reports thoroughly and found no basis for them. Now, I'd like to introduce Jeri Johnson, my secretary, who will collect questions. I would like those of you who have questions to write them on a slip of paper. We will pick out the most important ones to answer because we can't answer every question.

IRRITATED PARENT NO. 1: (Barking at the principal.) NO! We're not going to do that! And YES, you ARE going to answer questions. We are staying until every question is answered!

IRRITATED PARENT NO. 3: I'm not sending my child to school until I know exactly what's behind all this and that it's safe for my child to be in school!

IRRITATED PARENT NO. 6: (Interjecting) So what's the plan, Paul? How is the school going to deal with this? What are you going to do to make this place safe for our children?

PAUL (Principal): Yes. I'm getting to that. We are going to announce the banning of any clothing that disrupts education. We are going to have security personnel, city police visible and in uniform, and metal detectors at the main doors.

IRRITATED PARENT NO. 4: (Interrupting) How many entrances are there?

PAUL (Principal): There are six.

IRRITATED PARENT NO. 4: Then we want SIX metal detectors!

IRRITATED PARENT NO. 5: (With an expression of disgust) There doesn't seem to be any plan.

IRRITATED PARENT NO. 2: (Stands up) Well, here's the plan, Paul. We want every measure necessary to secure the safety of students. We want an 800 help line for any student who is troubled about anything. We want to review the dress code. I'm sure many of us are willing to volunteer to . . .

PAUL (Principal): I appreciate that. We also want to involve the students in helping to solve this problem.

IRRITATED PARENT NO. 6: (Interrupting) That's the LAST thing we need. This is for ADULTS to straighten out.

IRRITATED PARENT NO. 3: I don't agree with that.

CLARK (Reporter): Excuse me, Mr. Burdick. I'm Clark Cantwell from the Spotlight News. I would like to know . . .

PAUL (Principal): (Interrupts.) I'm sorry Mr. Cantwell. The press wasn't invited. This is, well, it's a private meeting with parents.

CLARK (Reporter): You can't be serious! A private meeting? At a public school? With parents! A student riot! You might not want to answer my questions, but you can be sure that every comment made today will be in tomorrow's paper.

NARRATOR: The meeting finally adjourns after nearly three hours of emotionally charged dialogue. Parents are leaving the auditorium feeling frustrated and upset. Small groups gather outside talking. The Edwards walk toward the parking lot.

SALLY (Parent): So, we're called to an emergency meeting, given no useful information on the phone OR at the meeting.

TOM (Parent): This is shocking! There was no indication of any kind of festering problems. It's the largest high school in the district. Students come from upscale suburban developments.

SALLY (Parent): Everyone seemed to be getting along. What's the minority population, Tom?

TOM (Parent): About 15 percent, I think.

SALLY (Parent): Paul Burdick doesn't do very well under pressure. I thought he was going to have a heart attack.

TOM (Parent): He tried to avoid telling us about the incidents. He want on and on about diversity. He ducked the gun reports. He tried to duck the press.

SALLY (Parent): Worst of all he didn't address our biggest concern—safety.

TOM (Parent): I thought his action plan was . . . Well, it wasn't even a plan. He didn't have a plan!

SALLY (Parent): And what about the way he tried to control discussion! He says write down your questions and we'll pick the ones we want to answer.

TOM (Parent): Where was the district? I can't believe no one came from the district. Where was the superintendent? (Tom closes the car door) Heads are going to roll. Sally. Heads are going to roll.

SALLY (Parent): We're not sending Jessica back until this mess is straightened out.

TOM (Parent): That's for sure!

NARRATOR: Three teachers are standing in a hallway near the auditorium talking about the meeting and wondering if any parents are going to let their children go to school on Monday.

ROSE (Teacher): This is a mess. I don't know what's going to happen on Monday.

ELLEN (Teacher): I'd say we're all a little short on facts.

ALEX (Science Teacher): Does anyone know exactly what happened? How accurate are these stories? Is that true about the fight in the band room?

ELLEN (Teacher): No. I'm in the room next door. Things have been kicked up a notch. They're not accurate.

ROSE (Teacher): Why didn't we anticipate what they were going to ask? Why the big meeting? Seems like we could have taken the initiative to head off the rumors. We still could. Parents were begging for some plan of action.

ALEX (Science Teacher): I'd like to know more about what's behind all this pent up emotion. What's forcing the steam out of the volcano? What are the core issues? What's the whole story?

ELLEN (Teacher): Poor Mr. Burdick. He's no coward. But he let fear get the best of him instead of letting it bolster his courage. He needs to step up to the tough questions, be more open with people. He was so nervous he didn't see how desperately parents wanted him to talk about keeping their kids safe.

ROSE (Teacher): No question. He missed an opportunity. The school has to be more responsive. There are too many unanswered questions for parents, for us, for the students. Parents trust Burdick. He's always shown respect and compassion for everyone. He just needs to be clear, to give everyone a chance to work on the problem.

ALEX (Science Teacher): Well, he had better be quick about it. This mountain is puffing steam. The magma is moving.

ELLEN (Teacher): It's not like the district to get so caught off guard. Knowing the superintendent, there will be an action plan on the table before anyone sleeps tonight.

ROSE (Teacher): I think you're right. We'll see details on building security, notification procedures, intervention. There will be an investigation of the current issues, open forums for kids and parents, and individual counseling. I know this superintendent. He's thorough. We'll have a plan that let's everyone know that the problem is being managed.

ALEX (Science Teacher): I hope you're right, Rose. The mountain is . . .

ELLEN (Teacher): That's enough about the volcano, Alex.

ROSE (Teacher): What do you expect from a science teacher?

ALEX (Science Teacher): I'm serious. This is a crisis.

NARRATOR: Three hours have passed since parents left the high school auditorium. An emergency meeting is coming to a close in one of the classrooms. Participants include the principal, the district superintendent, a student body president, representatives of faculty and staff, president of the Parent Teacher Association, a member of the local law enforcement office, and the district's PR director. The district superintendent, Maxine Gradeletter, is summarizing a short-term emergency action plan developed by the group.

MAXINE (Superintendent): We need to consider this situation a wake-up call to our cultural responsiveness. I would like to see us turn this incident into a learning opportunity for the whole school. But for now, I believe we agree on these points for an action plan:

- Point One: SECURITY

  On Monday there will be six uniformed, but unarmed, resource officers walking designated routes on campus. They will be visible to students upon arrival and throughout the day. There will be a memo in the mailbox of every faculty and staff member from Principal Burdick indicating that we have increased video surveillance at all entry points; it will describe our identification, response, and notification procedures for dealing with intruders. There will be increased liaison with local law enforcement authorities.

- Point Two: LEADERSHIP TEAM

  We have expanded the leadership team here to work directly with Principal Burdick. A task force from the central office will review our district policies on cultural diversity. We will make certain they are current. We will ensure that the district has the training necessary to implement the policies, adequate resources to communicate them and the consequences for failing to follow them. We will also be certain that the mechanisms are in place to enforce our zero tolerance rule on harassment and violence.

- Point Three: A SCHOOL INITIATIVE IN
                CULTURAL AWARENESS

  In brainstorming about cultural awareness and responsiveness to diversity issues, student body president Mitch Rivers made a suggestion that we get students to think of ways to recognize diversity as a strength. He suggested contacting a flag vendor about donating a flag for every nation represented in the high school. Mitch would like to see the flags on display as a visual, prideful reminder of our diversity. In this school there would be nearly 40 flags to display.

• Point Four: A COMMUNITY ENRICHMENT SYMPOSIUM

This is an emergency action plan to respond to the immediate situation. However, we agree that there should also be a broad-based community enrichment symposium. The primary goal of the symposium would to promote awareness of the various ethnicities represented within the student body and engender a sense of pride in our community's diversity.

I believe that we all concur on this four-point action plan. It's up to the PR staff to have this plan communicated to everyone Monday morning.

PAUL (Principal): We need to make clear that the acts of violence described at the parent meeting were highly exaggerated. Sixty birdhouses were glued to the workbench in the wood shop. One refrigerator door was cemented shut in the home economics room. And there was some pushing and shoving in the band room. A student was bumped in the head with an oboe. No one went to the hospital. Nothing else happened and things were settled quickly. I have to admit that I overreacted in calling the parent meeting. I'm not trained in dealing with anything like this.

MAXINE: Thank you, Paul. You have been a good principal here for the past five years and I know you have the respect of students and their parents. You're just going to need some extra support from all of us to get through this and lead everyone in showcasing our cultural differences rather than fighting over them.

Sports Marketing
IndyCar Racing

This case is an introduction to sports marketing with a focus on auto racing, the most popular sport in the world. It provides insights to corporate sponsorships of IndyCar racing teams and to how businesses participate in and profit from these high-profile activities. There are essentially three groups to consider in the marketing of professional sports—athletes, owners, and fans. However, as you focus on a particular activity, such as IndyCar racing, the picture gets more complicated. You must consider the racing team owner, the driver, the crew, the title sponsor and secondary sponsors (usually corporations), fans at large and corporate fans (including employees, customers, suppliers, and investors), the general media, the business, financial, sports, trade print media, and broadcast media. All of these interests surround the sport in a complex configuration of relationships and are drawn to it by an incredible aura of competitive excitement. The distinctions between these groups are basic and straightforward. Spectator sports generate about $60 billion in revenue annually, a clear indication of the tremendous involvement they draw from both businesses and individual consumers. Corporations purchase billons of dollars worth of sports-related products annually, commonly in the form of advertising and sponsorships. Managing a title sponsorship can become a public relations responsibility with requirements similar to managing a multimillion-dollar business. This case is your opportunity to explore many facets of sports marketing by seeing what your team can do with the title sponsorship of an IndyCar Racing League (IRL) team. Be sure to read the case background and the article on page 137, "Stefan Johansson Motorsports and an Introduction to Motorsports Marketing," provided courtesy of race-car driver and team owner Stefan Johansson.

TEAM ASSIGNMENT

Your team assignment is to (1) select an existing publicly traded company that fits this case (focus on the company's business-to-business relationships, not retail sales) or make one up; (2) select an Indy race-car team and driver from the Indy-Car Racing League Web site, www.indyracing.com; and then (3) develop a public relations plan that shows how the title sponsorship could be used to benefit the company, a plan that you would propose to the chief executive officer. The plan should focus only on public relations activities with a budget of up to $1 million for one racing season. Use the current or upcoming racing season for your plan and assume that it is about to begin. Read the case background information and the article, "Stefan Johansson Motorsports and an Introduction to Motorsports Marketing" on page 137.

INDIVIDUAL TEAM MEMBER ASSIGNMENTS

Each team member is to complete a different one of the following items that might or might not be included in the design of your plan. (See Chapter 7: Samples of Effective Public Relations Writing.)

1. Write a news release announcing your company's sponsorship of the Indy race-car team. The announcement should include a quote from your CEO and a quote from your IndyCar driver.

2. Write 90 seconds of remarks for your CEO to use to introduce your company's Indy race-car driver before a gathering of all of the company's headquarters personnel. The remarks should relate IndyCar racing to your company in the areas of teamwork, precision, and quality.

3. Write an article for your company's employee newsletter announcing the company's decision to sponsor an Indy race-car team, introducing the race-car driver, and providing some background information about Indy-Car racing and sports marketing. The article may include a picture of the race-car driver and/or one of the race car. Possible message point: teamwork, precision, and quality.

4. Draft a media advisory (or media alert) that entices the media to interview your race-car driver and see the team's show car. Use your imagination to stage the event at a place other than a race track and at a time that assures maximum public exposure, such as a shopping mall at noon or a bank lobby at 10 AM on Saturday. Include activities that put the driver and car to good use in attracting attention and providing great photo opportunities, such as showing people taking turns sitting in the race car.

5. Draft a letter to be signed by the company's corporate secretary (officer-level position) in response to a letter from Don Gilmetter, a company shareholder. Mr. Gilmetter states in his letter that rather than sponsor a race car the company should share its success by paying dividends to the stockholders. He states that he has a hard time understanding how the sponsorship of a race-car team could benefit the company. He says he's trying to be open-minded but knows that racing involves "big bucks."

6. Use a photo of your race-car driver from the Internet and develop a photo news release announcing that the driver and show car will appear at an annual community charity auction. You may make up all the details for a complete announcement.

7. Draft a biographical sketch of your team's race-car driver.

BACKGROUND

The chief executive officer of the company you serve as public relations director decides to sponsor an Indy race-car team for the upcoming IndyCar Series. The CEO asks you to think about how the sponsorship could benefit the company.

You think to yourself that the CEO essentially has asked you to manage what amounts to a $6-million-a-year business. That's roughly the average cost of being a title sponsor of an Indy race-car team (about $5 million for team operating expenses and $1 million for hospitality). You know that the CEO expects a preliminary plan and budget in one week.

It would be safe to assume that, ultimately, the CEO wants the company to be managing the title sponsorship of an Indy race-car in specific ways that benefit the company. Obviously, the benefits had better be significant for the board of directors to support this sports marketing initiative. You think that this initiative should come as a recommendation from the marketing or sales department. You learn, however, that such initiatives sometimes derive from the personal interests of executive managers.

You think one way the sponsorship could benefit the company is if it were used to strengthen the company's business-to-business relationships with its customers. The CEO has a natural talent for building relationships. He's admired for his business acumen. He's personable, has a great sense of humor, and enjoys socializing. However, his routine is so busy that he seldom takes time to really get to know the heads of customer companies. If he were to commit time to hosting customers at the races, that would certainly build stronger relationships in terms of customer loyalty and increased orders.

The company is publicly owned. The stock is held primarily by large institutional investors—large funds. You have heard the company's chief financial officer say, on more than one occasion, that it would be beneficial to broaden the shareholder base and to have a more diverse mix of shareholders. Trouble is, this is a business-to-business company and it doesn't have much public name recognition. So, maybe another way the sponsorship could benefit the company is if it were used to broaden the shareholder base. While most of the company's stock is held by funds, there still are thousands of potential individual shareholders for this multibillion-dollar company. With greater public exposure to the name, the company would have a better chance of attracting the interest of potential investors. Of course, you would have to make strategic use of the media to accomplish this objective to archieve greater public recognition of the company name.

What about inside the company? You think to yourself, could the sponsorship help us internally? There has always been some distance in the relationship between first-line supervisors and managers. It's a situation that has always existed and no one has ever tried to bring the working relationships closer together. What if, on a selective basis, supervisors and managers were asked to help host races that are held near their respective plant operating areas? It would be an opportunity for them to work together in a different environment. There certainly could be some creative ways to address this situation with the race-car program. And employees could be brought into the sponsorship if the company were to provide a block of tickets to each of the races. So, another way the sponsorship could benefit the company is if it were used to improve the working relationship between supervisors and managers.

As you think through ways that the sponsorship could benefit the company, you begin to shift your focus to the different hospitality activities that could be used in developing a plan. The program provides many activities, but how they are packaged and presented to guests is what makes the racetrack experience memorable. So in your plan you will want to show some creativity in the possible strategic use of these and other activities.

Your sponsorship entitles your company to any of the following activities:

- Title sponsors may obtain general admission tickets for up to 100 people at each race of the season, usually a one-day event. Title sponsors extend special hospitality privileges to guests. They include admission to a hospitality tent with food and beverages, to the team's transporter that is a truck trailer equipped to carry two race cars in an overhead compartment and a workshop below, to the team's private motorcoach, and to the pit area and stand where the team owner communicates with the driver during the race.

- In the hospitality tent, the team's driver might give guests a briefing on the track and how it must be driven. The driver might pose with guests for photos and provide autographs. Of course, there are photo opportunities everywhere and the chance to meet world-famous race-car drivers and team owners. Some teams provide guests with caps and t-shirts or other memorabilia. Team also provide briefings on the use of technology in Indy-Car racing.

- Teams usually have at least two show cars (race cars without engines) for sponsors to use for customer-, employee-, and community-relations purposes. An example would be having a show car for display (sometimes with the driver) at an employee picnic, a charitable community event, or a customer's headquarters. People can sit in the car, have their pictures taken, and sometimes be photographed standing with the driver.

In reading the activities, you see that an extraordinary feature of a title sponsorship is the Indy 500 race. There's a general description of the weekend. Guests arrive at Indianapolis (at their own expense) Friday and check into a hotel room booked and paid for by the sponsor. The event usually is planned for couples. That evening guests might be entertained in the team's garage where tables with black-and-white checkered tablecloths and a red carpet runner transform a race-car garage (which is always kept as clean and organized as a hospital's operating room) into a party room with live entertainment and a catered dinner and dancing.

Guests can enjoy brunch Saturday morning in the team's hotel hospitality room. They socialize with the team owner, driver, and company hosts. The driver provides a briefing on how he or she will drive the race on Sunday. Guests have the afternoon free to visit the IndyCar Museum and other places of interest. Saturday evening the guests can board tour-class buses that take them to a country club or other resort for a theme party (Western/International/European).

Sunday, following brunch at the hotel, guests can board buses that mainline the route nonstop with a police motorcycle escort to the track. Guests are led to a hospitality suite with outdoor seating for 100 people and an indoor area with food, drinks, and a TV monitor showing ESPN coverage of the race. Guests can obtain passes from the team at any time that provide access to the pit and other restricted places on the track, such as the team's transporter and motorcoach areas. It can be arranged for selected guests to take a ride around the track before the race with a race-car driver in one of the official race cars. Guests are returned to the hotel after the race and the weekend is concluded. Some companies keep guests connected with the team by faxing or e-mailing a race report immediately after each race and/or by mailing a bulletin or newsletter with feature stories about the team and its progress throughout the season.

Finally, title sponsors may obtain 100 tickets for general stadium seating at each race, including the Indy 500. Those tickets oftentimes are used for employee incentive programs.

Your preliminary research provides a general idea of hospitality expenses as a guide for developing a plan budget.

Budget Item	Cost
Hospitality (per race)	$15,000
Hospitality (for the Indy 500)	$150,000
Publications (e.g., information kits)	$15,000
On-car TV camera (5 races)	$100,000
Media monitoring (to determine amount and value of TV coverage)	$5,500
Merchandise (catalogue costs: production, printing, mailing)	$20,000
Indy 500 stadium tickets (100)	$19,000
Photography	$5,000
Newsletter (production, printing, and postage for six issues)	$47,000
Show car appearances (5)	$10,000
Contingency	$60,000

Having read this background, broaden your understanding of sports marketing with the following article, "Stefan Johansson Motorsports and an Introduction to Motorsports Marketing," and begin your plan.

STEFAN JOHANSSON MOTORSPORTS AND AN INTRODUCTION TO MOTORSPORTS MARKETING

Motorsports is the fastest growing sport in the world. It is watched, in person or on TV, by more people than any other sport including soccer. Motorsports exudes glamour and drama and is unquestionably, the ultimate sports and entertainment spectacle. It is the pinnacle of high-tech, state-of-the-art machines and the challenge of man to control them.

That challenge has fascinated us for many decades. Throughout that time, as today, the drivers are revered for their bravery, athletic ability, and charisma and truly are the personalities that make the sport so special. The result of this fascination with speed and spectacle is that motor racing draws a highly desirable

Stefan Johansson has been a key part of many of the world's top racing series in a storied driving career. Johansson began his major-league driving career in 1983 with the Spirit/Honda Formula 1 squad and earned his first World Championship points in 1984 while with Toleman. He earned podium finishes for Tyrrell and Ferrari and gave the Onyx team its first podium in 1988. He moved to Champ Cars in 1992 with Tony Bettenhausen and made seventy-three starts, earning four podium finishes in five seasons. He launched his Dayton Indy Lights team in 1997 but stayed in the cockpit, racing sportscars, winning the 12 Hours of Sebring and the 24 Hours of Le Mans in 1997. He was also the European champion of the American Le Mans Series. He has now cast his lot with the Champ Car World Series as he joins the Bridgestone Presents The Champ Car World Series Powered by Ford with a new two-car team.

demographic profile. The most recent trends show an increase in the number of women and families attending the races and watching at home. Due to its reach and effectiveness, motorsports has become, in its own right, one of the world's premier and most desirable marketing properties. Worldwide, the popularity of racing has skyrocketed over the last five years. This dramatic growth has resulted in the development of new racing series as well as race facilities, which in turn, has brought more racing to more people and created new fans.

Without a doubt, the popularity of the sport has been assisted by the dramatic increase in televised coverage of racing events. All the major networks broadcast racing and, in addition, channels such as SKY, Eurosport, ESPN, Fox Sports Network, ESPN2, Sports Channel, Speed Vision, and TNN are firmly dedicated to carrying races as well as the multitude of race-related shows. Motorsports enjoys participation by a wide variety of supporters. Long gone are the days when racing was solely supported by automotive companies and related products. Race weekends are attended by the Who's Who of international and U.S. business as well as celebrities from other sports and entertainment forums.

Today, companies form all disciplines support this sport for a variety of business reasons. Consider the wide spectrum of products and services provided by the companies that participate in racing. Why are these companies involved in this sport? They are involved simply because they are meeting and exceeding their marketing and business goals through a motorsports platform. Motorsports allows a company to break through the marketing clutter with creative promotions that reach a very targeted audience. Whether they are launching a new product, increasing name recognition, vying for the fiercely product-loyal race fan base, or for business-to-business reasons, companies are receiving a return on their investment, which keeps them coming back year after year. This article outlines what Johansson Motorsports (JMS) is all about. It further explains the benefits of a properly executed motorsports marketing program and delineates our team's role with its marketing partners. Reviewing this article should prove entertaining, but, most importantly, it will leave you with a better understanding of how and why motorsports so effectively builds business and drives sales.

Consider how motorsports attracts the interest of such diverse companies as Ameritech, Anheuser-Busch, Bell South, Beecham Braun, Casa Fiesta, Casino Queen, Coca-cola, DKNY, Duracell, First Alert, Gatorade, GE Capitol, Gillette, Hewlett Packard, Holiday Inn, Kleenex, Lanier, Marathon, Mercedes Benz, Microsoft, Mobil 1, Motorola, Nextel Omega, Planters, PPG, and Sears.

Genesis of Stefan Johansson Motorsports

For over two decades, Stefan Johansson has been one of the top drivers in the world of international motorsports. He has been successful in Formula –1, Indy-Car, and Le Mans–style sports cars, recently winning both the 1997 12 Hours of Sebring (Ferrari) and the 24 Hours of Le Mans (Porsche). He again drove for Porsche in the 1998 24 Hours of Le Mans and in other international endurance events. Throughout his career, Stefan has driven for some of the most prestigious teams and manufacturers in the world including: Ferrari, McLaren, Porsche, Mercedes, Toyota, Nissan, and Mazda.

Over the years Johansson has accumulated a superlative degree of knowledge and experience regarding race team operations as well as technical issues. Stefan remains very active with his driving career and is constantly evaluating opportunities to use his experience and knowledge about the sport. One such avenue is in fulfilling his ambition to own and run his own race team. In this manner, he brings to JMS over 20 years of racing experience. Stefan has a clear picture of what he desires in his team. To this end, he is instrumental in all facets of the team from choosing drivers to designing the team's headquarters in Indianapolis. Detail oriented, Stefan stays in touch with everything and allows little to pass by. When not overseeing the team or tending to his own racing career, Stefan is something of a Renaissance man with interest in art, design, business, and music. He is an accomplished painter with several exhibitions under his belt.

In design his talent runs the gamut from creating all the watches for his H III watch company to the furniture for the race shop and logos for his products. His business acumen focuses not only on his U.S.-based businesses, such as his European style indoor go-karting track in Indianapolis, which is currently under nationwide partnership offering, but also on international concerns. Well liked in the racing and business communities, Stefan is key in generating world-wide business contacts, which continue to expand the JMS networking portfolio.

Goals and Objectives

The goal of Johansson Motorsports is to be the premier team in every category in which it participates. This includes not only the results on the race track but also those off the track. To accomplish this JMS has assembled a group of the most competent and talented personnel available in the business. Today, every effort continues to be made to select the best people in their particular field. In this quest, JMS searches for top talent from around the world, as it sees these people as an essential investment in the team's future. Additionally, only first-rate equipment and tools are provided to the team so that it can perform its tasks at peak levels. Presentation of the team and its members is meticulous with every effort being made to adhere to the team's philosophy and goal to be the most professionally presented company in the business.

The same philosophy applies to the team's home base. JMS is headquartered in a 15,000-square-foot state-of-the-art race factory located on Gasoline Alley in Indianapolis, Indiana. The facility design clearly expresses the team's philosophy and goals. As the showcase of JMS it was important that the facility be designed with the same attention to detail used when the focus is on the team itself. Outside of the practical nature of the facility, its second purpose is to create a confidence in all who visit that Johansson Motorsports represents absolutely the best the racing industry has to offer.

These efforts combine to forward the main objective of JMS, which is to win every race and championship in which it participates. The focus of each team member is to put forth every possible effort to achieve this goal. In turn this attitude will give JMS's drivers the confidence that every time they get into the car, they will have the best-prepared equipment at their disposal. The motor racing platforms for JMS to implement its goals and objectives shall include, but not be limited to, the 24 Hours of Le Mans race, the American Le Mars Series, and the European Le Mans Series. Currently JMS focuses on Le Mans–style racing with the ALMS series. This series offers premier venues, highly desirable demographics, and, of course, intense competition.

Motor Racing Series ALMS

Every year millions of spectators, broadcast viewers, and listeners from around the globe focus on the Sarthe region of France to witness a 24-hour motor racing event that dates back to 1923. The 24 Hours of Le Mans tests both man and machine in what is arguably the world's most prestigious automobile race. In an effort to expand on the rich history and tradition of the 24 Hours of Le Mans, the Automobile Club de l'Ouest (ACO), organizers and rights holders for the trademarks and rules for the twenty-four-hour race, agreed to license their internationally famous brand name and rules to successful businessman and entrepreneur Donald E. Panoz. In addition to the licensing rights, the ACO agreed to grant prequalifying exemptions for the 24 Hours of Le Mans each year to three class winners in each of the three major territories (Americas, Asia, and Europe).

This represents nine of a total of twelve prequalifying exemptions for the 48-car starting field. Such an incentive is sure to attract major teams and manufacturers from around the world. With these rights, Panoz founded the American Le Mans Series in 1999 with an eight-race schedule. In 2000, the schedule was expanded to twelve races: eight in the United States, one in Canada, two in Europe, and the season finale in Adelaide, Australia.

Each race will have a minimum purse of $200,000 with 10 percent of each purse going to the privateer fund to be distributed at the end of the season. Prize money from the race purses is distributed exclusively among privateer teams. Our domestic and international television and Internet distribution is unprecedented in American sports car racing history.

American Le Mans Series

A survey of American Le Mans spectators held by Peter Honig Associates yielded the following facts:

- Almost 30 percent of fans plan nearly a year in advance to attend race events.
- Sports car racing, followed by Formula 1 and IndyCar racing, is the most popular type of racing. At a lower level is a second group led by stock car

racing/NASCAR racing, followed by a third group that includes drag racing, sprint car racing, other stock car racing, midget racing, and truck racing.

- Nearly 80 percent of those interviewed liked all three classes of cars in the same race. This is true for those whose favorite racing is sports car racing as well as those favoring IndyCar and Formula 1 racing.

- The cars are the stars! Most fans rank seeing the cars they are interested in, together with passing and speed attributes, as the number one point in racing. Manufacturer participation is next most important, followed by driver interest.

- Avid fans—those attending the most races—and stock car fans are most likely to be thirty-five or older and married.

- Sports car fans are more likely to be college educated and have higher incomes than stock car fans.

- Many of the world's most prestigious sports car brands intend to compete in the Le Mans series: BMW, Panoz, Chrysler, Viper, Corvette, Cadillac, Prosche, Ferrari, Bentley, Volkswagen, and Audi.

- The Le Mans Series license is worldwide.

Following is a sample showing the numbers of media impressions generated by the American Le Mans Series:

Sebring Speedvision 28.9 million
Fox Sports Net 54 million
Charlotte NBC 28.9 million
Speedvision 100.8 million
Silverstone Speedvision 28.9 million
Nurburgring Speedvision 28.9 million
Sers Point Speedvision 28.9 million
Mosport NBC 28.9 million
Texas NBC 28.9 million
Portland NBC 28.9 million
Atlanta Speedvision 28.9 million
Laguna Seca Speedvision 28.9 million
Las Vegas Speedvision 28.9 million
Australia NBC 102.2 million

The Motorsports Marketing Platform

A motorsports marketing partnership provides a company with an opportunity to become a part of the fastest growing and the most popular sport in the world. Motorsports provides brand awareness and customer loyalty unlike no other sponsorship venue. Jim Schiemer, CART racing program manager for Shell, puts it best, "[motorsports] has become one of the leading spectator sports in the country with growing media attention given to the drivers, the teams, and the sponsors, building enhanced brand awareness and increased customer loyalty for those companies involved." The importance of Schiemer's remarks becomes more apparent when one considers that in a competitive consumer market, a brand associated with motorsports will win the business over another, all other things being equal, when the customer has an interest in motorsports. It is widely accepted that on average, 65 percent of race fans consciously purchase the products and services of the companies that sponsor motorports. This is a compelling statistic when one considers that a full 30 percent of any cross section of the general public expresses a strong interest in motorsports. Motorsports is a powerful multimedia marketing platform that a company can use to communicate its desired image. A motorsports partnership provides a company access to tens of millions of potential customers in the United States and hundreds of millions worldwide that fit within that company's demographic profile. Corporate hospitality and entertainment programs are other ways a company can benefit from a motorsports program. Again, Schiemer states that, "Shell hospitality is a way to put your best foot forward for dealers and jobbers, or potential new customers. They can meet the drivers and team members, and experience the excitement of getting a firsthand look behind the scenes in the pits and garages."

Marketing Partner Growth Objectives

Johansson Motorsports has a vision focused on the future. JMS knows that to develop a solid long-term relationship with a company, it takes time for that entity not only to understand the many benefits that a motorsports marketing platform can provide, but just as important, how that platform can efficiently and effectively be used to attain its goals. Without this understanding, a marketing partner may not be able to justify expending the resources required to continue its affiliation with our team. Johansson motorsports is looking for marketing partners who will grow with the team. JMS provides an option to marketing partners to start in American Le Mans Series racing as a way to "get their feet wet" without spending a tremendous amount of marketing resources.

During such an introduction to motorsports, a company can learn how to maximize this multimedia marketing platform to accomplish its goals. Whether the goal is to sell more product, develop business relationships, or build a strong corporate image, it can be accomplished through motorsports. But the bottom line is knowing that JMS wants to grow with its marketing partners so that each will understand the needs and abilities of the other, thus developing a win-win relationship.

The Motorsports Marketing Partnership

It is important to note that before JMS begins any program with its marketing partners, it completes an exhaustive analysis of that partner's needs. As with racing, a strong marketing partnership is won back at the workshop and office with proper planning and preparation. The planning and preparation does not end when the season begins because we view the relationship with our marketing partners as an ongoing process. We continuously evaluate the program to ensure that our marketing partners are achieving their goals, maximizing their involvement, and continually benefiting from the opportunities that arise through their participation with JMS. In this manner, special attention is focused on the following:

- clearly defining objectives

- creating a cost-effective program

- establishing guidelines for an effective program

- delineating an internal communication policy

- monitoring program effectiveness on a per-venue basis

- evaluating potential opportunities

- assisting in the development of a total promotional package

- determining media strategies

- continuously planning and evaluating programs

Beyond these tasks and upon implementation of a marketing plan, the focus with our marketing partners is twofold: first, to maximize a company's marketing resources; and second, to create measurable results—new or increased business. It is JMS's goal to offer our marketing partners much more than simply placing their logo on a winning car.

Maximizing marketing resources is JMS's way of assisting a company to create a motorsports program using the least amount of that company's market dollars. JMS's approach creates an opportunity for a company to become involved with the team without having to increase its marketing and advertising budgets. JMS knows how to identify potential synergistic partners and how to maximize their benefit as a cooperative marketing partner. This is accomplished through forming strategic alliances with a company's vendors, suppliers, franchises, the media, and other companies. This leveraging of relationships increases the effectiveness of a company's marketing resources and results in generating "free" marketing dollars as well as improving relationships with the company's cooperative marketing partners. Measurable results of a motorsports marketing program come from the forming of new business relationships and/or the increase in sales of products or services. JMS provides to a marketing partner access to its global portfolio of business partners and relationships. This proves effective in generating new business both domestically and abroad.

Benefits of the Motorsports Marketing Partnership

Motorsports is the number one sport in attracting corporate sponsorship dollars, with 25 percent of all sponsorship money being directed to racing. Why? It is number one because it allows a company to break through the marketing clutter with creative promotions that reach a very targeted audience. Motorsports brings to a company a broad market. Involvement alone will generate millions of impressions for a marketing partner. To maximize its involvement, Johansson Motorsports will assist a company in the development of any race-related merchandising program, which could include but is not limited to

- promoting a sponsor supplement with a major racing magazine designed to build lists and establish a company as a major brand name in motorsports.

- developing a sweepstakes series that is designed as a self-funding promotional program to build lists and generate floor traffic.

- providing show cars designed to increase floor traffic and to be used as a general promotional tool.

- assisting in the development of a marketing partner's team fan club as a promotional tool designed to build lists and loyalty.

- assisting in the development of the direct mail program of a marketing partner's team. The goal of this program is to build a loyalty/affinity program based on developing a lifestyle list.

- assisting in development of authentic sponsor team merchandise. The goal of this program is to build loyalty and impressions.

- delivering race weekend event marketing programs for a company to use as VIP hospitality to build trade relations and top-of-mind awareness on the part of the buyer and distribution channel executives.

Business-to-Business Sales

Many of the business-to-business objectives apply equally well to the business-to-consumer process. The potential marketing benefits that accrue from the association with a race team can be focused on maximizing specific business-to-business relationships and audiences. These audiences are

- potential customers
- existing customers

- trade press, media, and market opinion makers

- the company's employees and families

- the company's vendors

There are many marketing and hospitality programs that can be developed to

- build a competitive and leading-edge image

- create product and/or market distinction

- crack hard to reach accounts in a neutral environment

- trigger buy decisions

- reward customer loyalty

- enhance relationships and promote bonding with key accounts

- build a distinct identity with the trade media

- drive morale and team building

- build distinct commercial sales programs

- use the Johansson Motorsports facilities as an unusual and dramatic customer demonstration, reference, and/or meeting site

Information Courtesy of Stefan Johansson Motorsports

Government Relations
Give and Take Back

Citizens elected to positions in state government—from state representative to governor—have a responsibility for the state's economic health. States compete among each other to attract investments, such as the building of a plant or headquarters relocation that will strengthen a state's economy by providing revenues in terms of wages, taxes, and local purchases. State competition includes providing incentives, such as tax credits, infrastructure improvements and additions, land packages, expedited permit processing, worker training programs, and so on. Companies base their site selections, in part, on these state government incentives.

In this case, some members of a state's legislature are proposing to rescind an incentive once given to companies that selected the state for their operations. The CEO of the company you serve is not about to stand idly by and give up the incentive that was promised to the company.

As you will see in the case background on page 148, ChannelGate Electronics needs to be a strong leader. To learn how professional writers can help create a commanding presence for leaders you will want to read the article, "Does Every Chief Executive Officer Have a Ghostwriter?" on page 149. It would be useful also to search the World Wide Web for information on how a bill becomes a law in state government.

TEAM ASSIGNMENT

Your team comprises the public relations department of ChannelGate Electronics, Inc. located in Overton, Anystate. Norman Gate, ChannelGate CEO, has instructed your department to see that the state legislature does not approve H.B. 3540, a proposed measure that would rescind tax credits that were granted to electronics companies as an incentive for locating their operations in the state. Gate wants to see a public relations plan that develops for his company enough political clout to eliminate H.B. 3540 from further consideration by legislators. He wants his company to be operating with the benefit of tax credits indefinitely. Your plan must be developed right away and must include provisions for orchestrating support—individuals and organization heads who will testify in favor of maintaining the tax credits during the public hearing on H.B. 3540, which is scheduled one work week from today at 3 PM in the state capital.

INDIVIDUAL TEAM MEMBER ASSIGNMENTS

Each team member is to complete a different one of the following items that might or might not be included in the design of your plan. (See Chapter 7, Samples of Effective Public Relations Writing.)

1. One-page letter from your CEO to the head of the Association of Anystate Businesses urging the organization to take a position against H.B. 3540.

2. A one-page letter from your CEO individually addressed to every member of the Anystate House of Representatives urging them to oppose H.B. 3540.

3. A legislative alert to ChannelGate employees urging them to write to their elected representatives in the House and asking them not to consider H.B. 3540.

4. A one-page information sheet for use in developing a coalition to defeat the proposed measure. It should give information about H.B. 3540, identify its sponsors, and provide reasons for opposing H.B. 3540 and instructions for contacting members of the House. This should be a persuasive document in the form of a fact sheet.

5. Text for a pocket point card with facts about H.B. 3540, reasons why it should not be considered by the legislature, instructions for contacting members of the house, and your organization's contact information.

6. A one-page letter from your CEO personally addressed to individuals and organizations that supported incentives, such as a tax credit, to recruit your

company to locate in the state. The letter should express appreciation for their support in recruiting your firm, describe the current situation with the proposed H.B. 3540, and ask them to contact your CEO to confirm that they will testify in support of retaining tax credits at a public hearing scheduled for (make up the date) at the state capital.

7. Write 90 seconds of opening testimony against H.B. 3540 to be given by Norman Gate before members of the House Revenue Committee chaired by Oscar Harrison.

BACKGROUND

Six elected representatives of the state legislature are sponsoring a measure that would amend legislation passed in 1995 that gave ChannelGate in Overton, Anystate, and six major electronics firms in Circuitville, tax credits for an understood indefinite period as an incentive for locating their operations in the state. The incentive amounts to a 50 percent credit on each firm's state business and occupation (B&O) tax. The six state representatives are working aggressively to eliminate the tax credit granted to the electronics firms in 1995 because of the state's dire financial position.

The managements of ChannelGate and the other six affected electronics firms were surprised and upset about the initiative to eliminate what once was promised as an incentive for the firms to locate in Anystate. The annual contribution of the seven electronics firms to the state's economy in terms of wages, taxes, and local purchases—totaling $552 million—far exceeds the tax credit—totaling $24 million. The firms question how reneging on the incentive would look to other firms considering Anystate as a place to locate a business. The CEO of ChannelGate, Norman Gate, insists that his PR department block any measure to take away the firm's tax credit. Your team is ChannelGate's PR department and has responsibility for government relations. Your department head is a registered lobbyist in Anystate.

You begin to assess the situation. First you consider home base. Your area of the state is represented by three elected officials—two members of the House of Representatives (Alfred Peabody and Charlie Bismark) and one member of the Senate (Holly Green). When your firm was considering Overton for its operation, Mayor Helen Fish and the entire city council welcomed ChannelGate with opened arms. Included in the grand welcome was the Overton Chamber of Commerce headed by George Harman, the Overton Economic Development Council headed by Sandra Dollars, as well as the town's many service clubs, particularly the Rotary Club of Overton led by 86-year-old Charlie Dobetter. As you assess the situation you are thinking about developing as much political clout as possible by bringing key contacts and possible coalitions together on the issue to rally to your cause.

Looking beyond home base you consider that ChannelGate is a member of the Association of Anystate Businesses, a statewide organization of businesses headed by Randy King. And your CEO, Norman Gate, is a member of the influential Anystate Business Roundtable in Appleton led by Executive Director Butch Bartolli. Your state representative, Alfred Peabody, is a member of the Revenue Committee of the House of Representatives. The governor of Anystate is Elsie Greenbach.

The elected officials sponsoring the measure to eliminate the B&O tax credit are Bruce Fisher and Allen Giverback of Plum Valley; Molly Wantsmore and Jim Glover of Artichoke Hill; and Byron Bick and Karen Greedy of Crabapple. Your CEO is so upset about the situation he wants you to send individualized letters to every member of the House.

The measure to eliminate tax credits, H.B. 3540, is expected to be sent to the floor for a vote of the House of Representatives sometime within the next three weeks. A public hearing on the proposed measure is scheduled one work week from today at 3 PM in the state capital.

As a seasoned lobbyist, the head of your public relations department knows that it is always best to take the high road—to work as a statesman and to argue positions on the basis of their merits. Your director knows to attack the issue and never its supporters because opponents today might be needed as allies tomorrow. It is not unusual for your director to argue an issue intensely with an opponent in a public hearing and relax afterwards with the same opponent over wine and dinner. Your director proudly regards maintaining respectful relationships as a mark of good statesmanship.

DOES EVERY CHIEF EXECUTIVE OFFICER HAVE A GHOSTWRITER?

We probably will never have a definitive answer to the question: Does every chief executive officer have a ghostwriter? CEOs who have good writers are not inclined to talk about it. However, many CEOs do have talented, highly skilled ghostwriters. And for reasons that will become obvious, such writers are an invaluable resource.

A highly skilled ghostwriter can give a CEO a commanding presence in any situation. In any situation? A commanding presence? How do ghostwriters do that? How do they know what to write? How do CEOs find ghostwriters? I can help you discover answers to these questions because I was a ghostwriter for corporate executives of Fortune 500 companies for more than 30 years.

In what kinds of situations do ghostwriters give CEOs a commanding presence? Highly skilled ghostwriters give CEOs a commanding presence before members of the board, before industry analysts, before shareholders, with customers, before employees, with journalists, with government officials, with potential investors, and before many other important audiences.

How do ghostwriters give CEOs a commanding presence in such diverse situations? In what they write highly-skilled ghostwriters are able to give CEOs a commanding presence in virtually any situation because they

- have experience in working with CEOs and have learned to think like CEOs;

- are able to assimilate the mindset of CEOs and can write in ways that reflect their character, values, beliefs, and goals;

- are adept researchers and are able to gather even the most complex and technical information, organize it, and translate it into plain English;

- keep abreast of management trends and jargon and incorporate current management thinking into their writing to help keep CEOs on the cutting edge;

- provide CEOs with ideas and concepts that help shape policy, crystallize visions, solidify goals, and articulate positions;

- stay connected with and analyze the attitudes and beliefs of important CEO audiences and in their writing enable CEOs to effectively influence the attitudes and beliefs of these audiences.

How do ghostwriters know what to write? Ghostwriters usually get their direction directly from the CEOs. Talented ghostwriters require surprisingly little direction from CEOs, provided that the CEOs give their writers ample opportunity to get to know and understand who they are, what they stand for, and where they are heading. Once a working relationship is established with a ghostwriter, a CEO is able to make assignments in terse form and expect, with little or no further discussion, first-class results in an appropriate form. The final product might be a keynote speech, formal letter, informal remarks, testimony, presentation narrative or script, position paper, by-lined article, or just a list of talking points.

With a good ghostwriter, all that a CEO needs to say is, "I would like . . .

- to make these three points before this audience in a 20-minute presentation;

- a by-lined article on this subject for this magazine;

- a position paper on this issue to submit to this congressional committee;

- talking points in preparation for my interview with this reporter;

- a draft of my letter to shareholders for the annual report;

- a technical paper and scripted presentation with visuals to give before this trade conference;

- a response to this shareholder's letter;

- a proposal on this for the board;

- informal remarks for the upcoming employee awards dinner;

- a persuasive argument in opposition to this issue for my meeting with the head of this government agency.

How do CEOs find talented ghostwriters? Shopping for a ghostwriter is not something done easily by an executive recruiter or by a human resources director. Ghostwriters can come from various disciplines, such as public relations, marketing, law, human resources, and finance. Their background must include certain skills and characteristics. They should be skilled editors, writers and researchers, good listeners, and interviewers. They should have strong intuitive qualities, a sense of what leadership is all about. They must respect and appreciate the value of corporate reviews and clearance procedures. And, above all else, they should have good chemistry and unshakable trust with CEOs.

Many CEOs do have ghostwriters. Many CEOs have more than one. For busy executives, good ghostwriters are an invaluable resource, an indispensable capability. Highly skilled, experienced ghostwriters can give CEOs a commanding presence in any situation.

Crisis Communication
Community Alarmed

Crisis is a time of great danger, a time of serious trouble. It's a decisive time, a crucial time. Most important, a crisis is a turning point because the way it is dealt with will determine its consequences. Answers to how an organization should handle a crisis can be found in a plethora of books. However, it is the court of public opinion with its own set of expectations as to how a crisis should be handled that is the ultimate judge of crisis management. It doesn't matter if the crisis is real or perceived, the situation must be managed as a crisis. In this case a reputable company is about to be thrust into the public spotlight for its use of hazardous chemicals. Case details are presented following the team and individual assignments in a series of news reports. The heads of organizations must be visible leaders, especially in times of crisis, and you will understand this imperative better after reading the article, "CEOs Must Be Visible Leaders," on page 158.

TEAM ASSIGNMENT

Your team has been hired as a public relations agency by Wafermaker, Inc., one of many silicon wafer manufacturers, to develop a public relations plan to address mounting concerns among community residents about health and safety risks associated with the company's use, storage, and transportation of hazardous chemicals. Tensions are so high among residents that the company expects its association with hazardous chemicals to surface in the news media at any time in a way that could put the company on the defensive and possibly tarnish an otherwise sterling reputation as a corporate citizen.

INDIVIDUAL TEAM MEMBER ASSIGNMENTS

Each team member is to complete a different one of the following items that might or might not be included in the design of your plan.

1. Your agency is asked by Wafermaker to draft a letter from the Parks Elementary School principal, Henry File, to parents inviting them to an informational meeting to be held at the school (you select a date). School officials and officials of Wafermaker, Inc., will be at the meeting to provide information and answer questions. You are to draft the letter for the principal's signature.

2. In deliberations with your agency team, Wafermaker officials consider calling a press conference or briefing. In considering such an event, Wafermaker officials discuss what they might say in opening remarks at a conference or briefing to set the tone and tenor for their response to what is sure to be an intense community demand for information. You are to write ninety seconds of opening remarks for George Sanders, Wafermaker vice president for manufacturing, for a press conference or briefing. (You decide if it is to be a press briefing or press conference and what Sanders should say to put the company in the best light before the media and the community.) In your remarks you will want to welcome reporters and thank them for coming and tell them why you called the meeting (briefly recap the fire incident, the mention of chemicals in news reports, and the resulting concern in the community, especially among parents of children attending nearby Parks Elementary School). The remarks are to lead up to a briefing by company representatives about its use, storage, and transportation of chemicals. Set the tone of the conference by making known the company's desire to provide complete and accurate information, about the company's standing in the community, and how it wants to uphold its

reputation by being completely open and forthright in its communication with the public. Be careful not to try to persuade the media of anything; let the information presented in the meeting stand on its own merits. Your remarks should close with the line, "And now I would like to present the staff members who will provide you with a briefing."

3. In deliberations with your public relations agency team, Wafermaker officials discuss possible communication with customers. Assume that it is decided to contact customers. Draft a letter from George Sanders, Wafermaker vice president for manufacturing, to customers. Assume that Sanders told you to acknowledge the incident and assure customers that it would not have any bearing on the scheduled shipments of their orders or on the quality of the silicon wafers. The same letter is to be sent to every customer but will be addressed to individuals. In the letter you will want to acknowledge the fire so that customers learn about it firsthand from Wafermaker, but you will not want to provide details that will unnecessarily cause concern among customers.

4. In deliberations with your public relations agency team, Wafermaker officials agree that you should develop a fact sheet listing the chemicals it uses with two or three practical, common, worthwhile applications for each chemical. For this assignment you will have to research the uses for the following: acetic acid, hydrochloric acid, hydrofluoric acid, nitric acid, sulfuric acid, ammonium hydroxide, potassium hydroxide, sodium hydroxide, sodium sulfide, methanol, trichlorethane, trichlorosilane, argon, nitrogen, hydrogen, hydrogen chloride, oxygen, diborane, phosphine, hydrogen peroxide, chromium trioxide, potassium dichromate, isopropyl alcohol, and silane.

5. In deliberations with your public relations agency team, Wafermaker officials request that you develop a list of all questions (including rude ones) that might be asked at a news conference or briefing. The list is to form the basis of a Q & A sheet.

6. Wafermaker officials ask your agency to develop a one-page backgrounder describing silicon wafer production in terms that can be used easily by journalists. (Search the Internet for information.)

7. Draft a list of messages that would be important for Wafermaker to make to each of its stakeholder audiences.

In developing communication to parents, the media, and customers, it is best not to make assumptions about what people know or how they feel. Also it is best not to try to persuade anyone of anything. To influence behavior it is most effective to provide information and firsthand experience that will enable people to persuade themselves. It is best to provide complete, objective, and factual information. For example, you might begin your communication, "On Friday, January 11, Wafermaker had a fire that was believed to be caused by a faulty heater. No one was injured; damage was estimated" and so forth. Resist the temptation to promise more than you can deliver (e.g., "students are perfectly safe"); to make assumptions, especially negative ones (e.g., "no reason that the plant might have to be moved"); to presume what people know or don't know (e.g., "many of you think . . ."); to guess how people feel (e.g., "many of you are afraid"); to speak on behalf of something over which you have no control (e.g., it is not acceptable for the school principal to write: "You can rest assured that Wafermaker operates safely.").

BACKGROUND

A series of unexpected events creates a crisis situation for Wafermaker in Oakleaf, U.S.A. As you read the news reports that follow imagine how quickly emotions must begin to intensify among community residents. Consider how easily a company's hard-earned reputation can be seriously damaged. Try to empathize with Wafermaker management as they contemplate a situation with which they have no experience. Try to share management's feeling that at any minute issues can come into the public eye, and Wafermaker with its sterling reputation as a model corporate citizen can be put on the defensive by the same people who earlier welcomed it to the area with open arms.

The region had aggressively recruited electronics plants, considering them to be safe, clean, and nonpolluting, a preferred alternative to traditional basic industries. There were no known reasons why such plants could not be integrated into the community in business parks and on property sharing borders with stores, schools, and residences. However, an incident in India focused world attention on industrial hazards and an incident in Oakleaf brought the matter of concern even closer to home.

DAY 1

Gas Kills 300 in India Gas from a pesticide plant escaped into a city in central India this morning and killed at least 300 people and injured thousands more.

DAY 5

Top Executive Arrested, Then Freed The chairman of an American company whose plant was associated with a gas leak that killed more than 1,600 people was taken into custody by India police today. He was released later.

DAY 7

Death Toll in India Hits 1,900 from Gas Leak The official death toll from a poison gas leak at a pesticide plant rose to about 1,900 yesterday.

U.S. Company's Reputation Severely Damaged Reputation of the US company with a majority ownership in the pesticide plant in India where leaking of a deadly chemical cost more than 2,000 lives has suffered substantially in the eyes of the American public.

DAY 9

Fire Damages Wafermaker Plant A fire today damaged the Wafermaker plant in Oakleaf. Firefighters entering the plant were sprayed by what at first was feared to be chemicals but later was confirmed to be water from the plant's sprinkler system. Damage was estimated to be about $1 million.

DAY 10

Mention of chemicals in the news reports was the first time that the community became aware of the use of chemicals in electronics plants, such as Wafermaker's. Parents of the 500 children enrolled at Parks Elementary School located near the Wafermaker plant were particularly interested in the reference to chemicals. When parents talked about the plant at home, their children told how they looked through the school windows at people in baggy suits moving big barrels behind the plant. They told about how trucks bring barrels and take barrels away.

DAY 12

Phone calls began pouring into the principal's office at the Parks school. Parents wanted to know more about the school and its safety procedures should there ever be a chemical accident at the Wafermaker plant. Phone calls of community residents to the silicon wafer manufacturer also increased and became more emotionally intense as callers pressed for information about chemical use.

DAY 14

Wafermaker management requests professional public relations advice.

ADDITIONAL BACKGROUND

Wafermaker employs 700 people at its Oakleaf plant.

Wafermaker makes silicon wafers for the computer industry.

The fire caused about $1 million in damage, according to company officials.

Cleanup work is under way.

The company does not expect any of its employees to be off the job because of the fire.

About 30 people will be used in the cleanup operation. Another 50 to 75 workers will move their operation to a nearby warehouse while duct work is replaced at the plant and soot and dust are cleaned up.

The fire was started by a malfunctioning electrical switch.

Most of the damage was from smoke. About 20,000 square feet of the plant's 200,000 square feet were affected by the fire. Damage to walls and equipment was minimal.

The cleanup process will affect the silicon wafer polishing area, final inspection area, and the packaging operation.

Some machinery has already been moved to temporary quarters.

The plant manufactures silicon wafers used in making computer chips.

Numerous chemicals are used at the facility, but none of the chemicals was burned or released during the fire.

The fire was nearly out by the time firefighters arrived, but it produced extensive smoke.

Wafermaker operates in an ultraclean environment. Manufacturing the wafers and maintaining the clean environment involves the use of chemicals. Because of possible chemical contamination of workers, the facility has safety showers. A worker who is accidentally contaminated can enter a shower that releases a large volume of water to promptly wash off any chemicals. Wafermaker said the majority of chemicals used there are potentially hazardous, but if handled properly are safe.

Employees handling chemicals are required to wear protective suits to prevent any possible harm to themselves.

Wafermaker said a worst-case scenario would involve liquefied hydrochloric acid. If it escaped all safety systems, a gaseous cloud would form and depending on the weather could hang over the area. People would know to move away because of the odor. Prolonged exposure could be harmful to people, according to the company.

Wafermaker said it takes every possible precaution and safeguard to protect its employees, the environment, and neighbors.

The company spent more than $6 million on environmental control systems for the plant.

Fearful of the chemical hazard, some parents wanted to keep their children from going to the Parks Elementary School near the plant.

Leaders of the Parent Teacher Organization began contacting local, county, and state government agencies to learn more about the plant's use of chemicals.

Most chemicals are stored in tanks in an area that has concrete walls and floors painted with an acid-proof resin. Pipes carry the chemicals to work areas through a concrete tunnel also painted with the acid-proof resin. Wastes are piped through the tunnel to a treatment facility in a similarly secure area, according to Wafermaker.

Acids and bases are neutralized and piped into the city sewer system. Nothing is disposed of on plant property except purified water used in the manufacturing process.

A chemical spill is highly unlikely, according to the company.

The company emphasized that the plant was designed to operate in close proximity with a community and, therefore, its safety systems are the best available. Plant managers and workers live in the community and have children who attend area schools.

Wafermaker was aware that its use, storage, and transportation of chemicals were under intense scrutiny by the community, that rumors were rampant, and that the company could expect media attention any day or any minute.

CEOS MUST BE VISIBLE LEADERS

The watchword for every organization in today's environment is preparedness. We are looking to our leaders for information, direction, safety, and moral support. Our leaders include the chief executive officers of American business.

Chief executives have a responsibility to visibly lead their organizations back to a state of business as usual. By stepping up to this responsibility, CEOs have an unprecedented opportunity to earn an extraordinary measure of employee respect, admiration, and commitment.

Why must CEOs be visible leaders? For employees to take up work as usual under the looming threat of terrorism requires strong assurances from the highest authority that all precautions are being taken to safeguard employee health and safety in the workplace. Health and safety in this uncertain environment cannot be relegated by CEOs to personnel and security departments. Securing the workplace under the shadow of terrorism requires executive oversight on a daily basis to enable CEOs to make crucial decisions in time to protect employees from potential harm. In addition, employees need reassurances that their organizations have leaders at the helm who are in control of the communication and the resources necessary to take the organization through a crisis situation. In an uncertain, challenging environment overcommunication is impossible. Employees reach out for evidence that the situation is being addressed with care and competence. People feel comforted and more in control when they are connected to others through communication. The frequency of communication is just as important as its substance. Waiting to communicate until there is something to say is anything but comforting.

What should CEOs do to be visible leaders to employees? Chief executives must provide more face time with members of their organizations. They can do it personally to some extent, electronically to a greater extent, and they can do it throughout the organization by encouraging management face time with employees at all levels of supervision.

Practices, such as Hewlett-Packard's Management By Walking About (MBWA), are particularly important. This practice is exemplified in the public sector by the highly commendable leadership of former mayor of New York Rudy Giuliani. Communicating the presence of leadership and responsible, caring management, as Mr. Giuliani did so diligently after the terrorist attacks on September 11, 2001, is something that people under duress need to hear over and over in every way possible.

Chief executives should encourage managers to communicate in meaningful gestures—greeting employees in the morning, visiting employees in their lunch setting, offering a friendly comment at the coffee machine, and sending an unexpected e-mail message, such as, "Let's all have a good day and enjoy working together." These various forms of communication enable employees to stay connected with those who have the authority and resources to help ensure their health and safety.

Why can't CEOs delegate the leadership responsibility to others and just carry on the way they have in the past? Any one of America's CEOs could be thrust unexpectedly into managing a crisis situation. Real or perceived, their organization will be in danger. The chief executive will have 45 minutes to 12 hours, at most, to set the direction for the way in which the situation will be managed. If the crisis is managed poorly, there could be employee injury or loss of life, as well as long-term damage to an organization's image, reputation, profitability, and stock value. If the crisis is managed properly, there is potential for employee well-being and public admiration. The CEO's organization can garner great respect for disclosure, candor, prudent action, total regard, commitment, and contrition as appropriate.

Contrary to public belief, many organizations do not have crisis communication plans ready to implement at a moment's notice. Many chief executives take the risk of hoping a crisis will not occur. Chief executives unprepared for managing a crisis fall into a reactive, defensive mode that gets communicated instantly by the news media sometimes throughout the world.

What is expected of a CEO in a crisis? The role of a CEO in a crisis situation is not defined by the CEO, the board, or industry peers. The role is defined and evaluated by the general public. In a crisis situation, the public expects an organization's top leader to

- step forward immediately, publicly and take charge;

- provide information completely and truthfully as soon as it becomes available;

- own up to responsibilities;

- lay out immediate action steps;

- show concern for everyone's needs;

- cooperate with the news media, give lots of "face time," communicating regularly and frequently.

Business leaders have an extraordinary opportunity to bond with employees in taking organizations back to business as usual. By stepping up to these leadership responsibilities, chief executive officers can earn an extraordinary measure of employee respect, admiration, and commitment.

Corporate Communication
Downsize

This is a case of closing a major production facility. It is representative of a phenomenon commonly referred to as *downsizing* that ran rampant in the 1980s and 1990s and continues to appear, especially in the manufacturing sector.

What is downsizing? It's the act of reducing the size and complexity of an organization. How is it done? It's usually done by any one or combination of the following: decreasing the number of employees, closing facilities, exiting selected markets, dropping product lines, shedding activities unrelated to a firm's core business. In business, this activity is given various names, such as restructuring, reengineering, reorganizing, redesigning, and reinventing.

Why do organization's downsize? Reasons frequently offered: escalating domestic and or global competition, increasing costs, declining markets, weak economy, increased use of technology. Reasons never offered: overstaffing, overestimating, overspending.

What are the benefits of downsizing? We have yet to see a definitive answer to this and other questions, such as, If jobs are eliminated to improve a company's competitive position will employee morale and/or productivity also improve? If a company reduces its workforce and sheds activities outside its core business will its stock price increase? If a company simplifies its operations will there be an actual cost savings? Will reducing a workforce temporarily and rebuilding it when market conditions improve automatically restore an organization to its original strength? Are the benefits of downsizing shared by everyone in an organization? Benefits have to be assessed on a case-by-case basis. In general, benefits are arguable. Nevertheless, the practice continues. What is known is that the process imposes multiple pressures that produce stress that is real and can be harmful and expensive. These effects can be mitigated to a significant extent through thoughtfully planned and professionally implemented communication and by heeding the lessons learned by others who have experienced the process.

TEAM ASSIGNMENT

Your team assignment is to develop a public relations plan for closing Houston Operations, one of eight production plants owned and managed by Supercore International, Inc., a leader in the design and production of structural products for commercial buildings. Background information for this case begins on page 163 and is in the form of transcripts of the chief executive officer's assignment to the public relations director and of discourse among executives of a core group in private communication planning meetings.

INDIVIDUAL TEAM MEMBER ASSIGNMENTS

Each team member is to complete a different one of the following items that might or might not be included in the design of your plan. It is up to you to decide what the content should be for each element. Information for these elements is included in the case background beginning on page 163 in the transcripts and in the correspondence among core group members, which follows the transcripts. (See Chapter 7: Samples of Effective Public Relation Writing.)

1. Develop a news release announcing closure of Supercore's Houston Operations.

2. Draft a memo from the Houston Operations plant manager, Bill Cabot, to employees announcing the company's decision to close the plant in indefinitely.

3. Draft the business rationale for closing Houston Operations.

4. Draft a Q & A sheet addressing employment matters for use by human resource personnel.

5. Draft a fax announcing the plant closure to be sent to Supercore's distribution centers.

6. Draft a Q & A addressing the plant closure for use by supervisory and management staff throughout Supercore International.

7. Draft a letter from the CEO to all employees announcing the Houston closure and reasons for making the decision.

BACKGROUND

DOWNSIZING

Transcript of Monday Meeting, July 8, 20xx

George Waters, CEO
David Maple, Public Relations Director

GEORGE: I want to talk to you about a move we are about to make. This is highly confidential. You are only the sixth person to know about this decision.

DAVID: I understand.

GEORGE: We are going to close the Houston plant. This will affect about 200 employees. I want to do this in keeping with the reputation we have for upholding quality and acting responsibly. I want to have this announcement made and to be operating with minimal negative impacts from the closure on the overall business.

DAVID: I'm sure we're doing this for good business reasons. But I'd like to know more specifically about the rationale for closing this particular plant.

GEORGE: Tom Oaks will give you those details. I want the announcement to be made in three weeks.

DAVID: Who will I be working with?

GEORGE: There will be a core group of five, including you.

DAVID: Will that include the plant manager?

GEORGE: Yes. I've known Bill Cabot for more than 15 years. I trust him completely. He'll do what's right for the company. You can work with Bill, Tom, Gayle, and Harvy. I want to have a communication plan from this core group by noon Friday.

Meeting Adjourns

Transcript of Tuesday Meeting of Core Group, July 9, 20xx

Tom Oaks, VP Operations
Gayle Hopkins, VP Marketing/Sales
Harvy Collins, VP Human Resources
Bill Cabot, Plant Manager Houston Operations (not included in this meeting)
David Maple, PR Director

TOM: David, communication planning is your area; how should we prepare for this announcement?

DAVID: We don't have a track record in closing plants. Not this company. In fact, this will be our first experience. But other companies have closed more than one facility and have some good advice to offer. I called the resource center of the Public Relations Society of America (PRSA) in New York. Had them send articles about Fortune 500 companies and what they learned about announcing plant closings. I have ten lessons learned based on this research. These points go beyond communication, but they're all important considerations.

TOM: A lot of people are going to take an interest in this announcement, not just employees.

DAVID: That's a good place to begin, Tom. Let's identify those audiences. Within the organization we have Houston Operations employees, including sales, customer service, and estimating personnel. Externally, we have Houston's customers and key suppliers. In the community we have community leaders, government representatives on the local, county, state, and federal level. And we have the media—local, business, financial, and trade press. We're privately owned so we don't need to worry about investors. This points to the first lesson learned by others: We need to be first to communicate fully to everyone concerned.

HARVY: It's going to take some time to reach all of those groups.

DAVID: It has to be done all at once. I'll show you how we're going to reach everyone in a single morning. That's the function of a good plan.

GAYLE: So how do we decide what to tell these different groups?

DAVID: That's a key question, Gayle. We have to have a crystal clear business rationale for the decision to close Houston. That rationale will be the basis of every communication. Our credibility with all of these audiences depends on the soundness of our rationale for closing the plant. Tom, if you will provide me with the basic information, I'll draft the rationale. If we can't explain the business reasons for a closure to ourselves, we can't expect anyone else to understand why the facility must be shut down. The rationale will be at the heart of every communication we develop. In our next work session, tomorrow, we need to decide on key message points for each audience.

GAYLE: What about Bill? Isn't he supposed to be working with us?

DAVID: That happens to be third on my list of lessons learned. It's essential to have full support of the plant manager. George said we can trust Bill Cabot completely and that he will do what's best for the company, even though he will be retired in the process. We would have to alter our strategy if we had a different manager. A manager could take issue with the decision or resist talking about the decision. Most people would rather avoid confrontation and controversy. Think about a plant manager who has been operating for years in the comfort zone of a routine operation. Suddenly he gets thrust into having to confront people in and outside the plant about shutting down. He could have a very difficult time talking about that. It's much easier, even with someone as loyal as Bill, to follow a solid plan.

HARVY: One of your points must focus on the 200 employees who will lose their jobs.

DAVID: Yes. Every Fortune 500 company I read about emphasized the importance of putting a high priority on human needs. You will need a Q & A on HR stuff. We're talking about job information . . .

HARVY: . . . relocation opportunities, if any, early retirements, jobs training. You're right. We're going to want to provide financial, family, career counseling, psychological counseling for managers. We will need to provide letters of recommendation, help with resume writing and whatever placement services are needed. You know this announcement can also cause people to jump ship. We need to make sure that we identify and contact people we want to keep elsewhere in the organization.

DAVID: Another lesson learned is to protect against demoralization elsewhere in the organization. Employees easily identify with one another. How the Houston employees are treated will be of great interest to every employee in the company. They will draw conclusions about how they might be treated. That reinforces the importance of having a sound business rationale for the decision to shut down. Another thing we have to protect is the safety and security of everyone at Houston. It's another lesson point. What's the physical layout at that plant?

TOM: If it's what you're thinking, the operation is wide open. Someone . . .

HARVY: Like an emotionally distraught employee?

TOM: Yes. Someone like that could walk right in the front door and have dozens of production people in his or her sights. We'll take a look at security. We also have to think about the unlikely possibility of vandalism, looting, sabotage, and any other form of reprisal. David, according to my notes, that's six points.

DAVID: I have four more. One is keeping the planning confidential with a core group, which we have. Another is having a comprehensive plan. We're working on that. Once we have a plan we have to commit to following it. The plan will have to have contingency provisions for dealing with problems like leaks and rumors. A third one is in your area, Harvy—meeting all local, state, and federal laws for closing a facility. The fourth is leaving the community in a way that the community would welcome our return in the future. This closure will impact the local economy in terms of revenue from wages, taxes, and local purchases. The community needs to understand our decision and not feel that it could or should have done something to secure the plant's future. We might even consider gifting the community some property, park equipment, or public improvement.

Let me wrap up this part of our meeting with a summary of lessons learned:

1. Have a crystal clear rationale.

2. Work confidentially with a core staff.

3. Follow a comprehensive plan.

4. Place a high priority on human needs.

5. Have full support of the person in charge of the facility to be closed.

6. Meet all local, state, and federal requirements.

7. Protect against demoralization elsewhere.

8. Ensure safety and tight security.

9. Leave the community in a way that the community would welcome our return.

10. Be first to communicate fully to everyone concerned.

TOM: We have to regroup tomorrow . . . here, nine o'clock.

**Tuesday night in the office of
PR Director David Maple**

Maple is reviewing his research on plant closings from PRSA headquarters in New York. The experience in plant closings by more than a dozen Fortune 500 companies reveals 10 important *communication* points. Maple decides to present them at Wednesday's planning meeting in a PowerPoint presentation. He finishes the last slide and checks his e-mail before leaving the office. There's a message from VP Operations Tom Oaks and a file attachment. The message reads: The information you wanted for drafting the rationale is in the attached file. Maple opens the file, which is in a memo format:

SUPERCORE INTERNATIONAL, INC.
Interoffice Correspondence

CONFIDENTIAL

JULY 9, 20XX

TO: DAVID MAPLE
FROM: TOM OAKS
COPIES: George Waters, Harvy Collins, Gayle Hopkins, Bill Cabot
RE: BUSINESS RATIONALE

Following is the information you will need for developing a statement of our business rationale for closing Houston Operations. Supercore International, Inc., has provided the standard of quality in structural products for commercial buildings in countries around the world for more than half a century. We are a leading international supplier of custom designed products and systems. We have 51 facilities. They employ 5,221 people in North and South America, Europe, and Asia.

We have been the market leader in North America and have been steadily increasing market shares in Europe and Asia. However, business conditions in our major market, specifically the United States, are causing us to adjust our production capacity. The U.S. commercial building market is experiencing a major recession. Volume of construction business has dropped dramatically over the past five years. Many parts of the country are overbuilt in commercial construction. Contractors are constrained financially. Financing for construction projects is hard to get. Supercore and its competitors have seen their market drop 37 percent in five years. Industry analysts expect that it will be another 18 months before this market begins to turn around and that there will be a further decline next year. Competition for the reduced volume of business has put enormous downward pressure on pricing. That, plus the cost of maintaining excess production capacity caused us to assess what could be done to reduce operating costs and still maintain the same high level of sales and service to our customers.

We decided our production capacity had to be brought in line with market conditions. By the end of this year Supercore will consolidate its manufacturing operations in the United States, reducing the number of production plants from eight to seven. Houston Operations was the likely candidate for an indefinite closure. The Southwest has had the weakest construction environment in the country for the past five years, and this has led to a substantial decline in the plant's sales volume in the past 10 years. The depressed regional economy, resulting from a major decline in oil prices and a rash of major bankruptcies, together with an oversupply of commercial buildings, has severely reduced market demand for our products. Houston has been operating significantly under capacity for several years. Work there can be handled easily by our other facilities.

Actually, the Southwestern market is relatively small and isn't expected to improve much in the foreseeable future, which is another reason we focused our decision on Houston. But the main reason we selected Houston over other plants was that its closing would be least disruptive in terms of the company's ability to serve its national dealer network.

We will serve the Southwest as effectively and aggressively as ever using the same sales organization. The Houston area sales districts and their distribution centers will become part of our Southeastern Area operations. We are confident that reducing our production plants from eight to seven will leave us ample capacity to supply customer needs for the coming years. Even with the closing of Houston Operations, Supercore will continue to be one of the largest international producers of structural products for commercial buildings. We are generally considered to be the industry's quality leader with service that outperforms our competition.

Our outlook is positive, despite current market conditions. Commercial building represents a big market in the United States and around the world. Our brand has enjoyed a major market position and we have always been a full participant in economic recoveries. We see excellent market potential in Europe and in developing parts of the world. We have built our organization not on business but on relationships with employees, suppliers, customers, dealers, the media, social and environmental activists, and with the communities and countries in which we operate.

****

David, that should give you something to work with in developing our business rationale statement.

T.O.

Transcript of Wednesday Morning Meeting of Core Group, July 10, 20xx

Tom Oaks, VP Operations
Gayle Hopkins, VP Marketing/Sales
Harvy Collins, VP Human Resources
Bill Cabot, Plant Manager, Houston Operations (not included in this meeting)
David Maple, PR Director

DAVID: Tom, I read your memo. Thanks for the information for the rationale. Last night I gleaned more helpful information from my research on lessons learned by other companies. This information focuses directly on communication. In the interest of time, I'll quickly cover 10 points that I have summarized in a PowerPoint presentation.

   1. Announce the closing according to a plan.
The logistics of getting key messages to a diverse number of audiences all at one particular time requires meticulous planning and scheduling. We must have a plan and follow it through to the last detail.

   2. Use prepared Q & As.
When it comes to work like this, I know from experience that only birds can wing it. We will need a Q & A on each major subject area and we will have to supply them to everyone who has a responsibility for communicating the information.

   3. Spike rumors.
We need to offer every company communicator guidance on how to spike rumors and deal with news leaks.

   4. Stay in touch with the media.
A plant closure is a major news item. We can expect calls from the local, business, financial, and trade press. We can minimize calls and conversations by developing a news announcement that anticipates and responds to what journalists will want to know about the closure. This will help ensure the accuracy of what is reported. No matter what we do there will always be more

questions, so it's essential that we stay in touch with the media until all information needs are satisfied.

5. Assess audience reactions.

The point here is that effective communication is a two-way process. We communicate. We listen. We respond to feedback. And the process continues until we're satisfied that the communication is complete and accurate.

6. Respond to problems.

When an announcement is planned properly, people involved in the announcement activities develop a sense of ownership and commit to identifying and dealing with problems to help ensure a successful outcome. We want everyone involved in this announcement to have confidence in the plan and all the information they need so they will feel compelled to help head off potential problems.

7. Communicate frequently with employees.

When an organization gets into a stressful situation, especially one that pertains to health, safety, or job security, people need face time with their leaders. They need to be in touch to have a sense that someone is in charge and providing direction. So it's important for managers and supervisors to be in touch on a personal face-to-face basis even when there is nothing new to communicate.

8. Show concern and commitment.

The way in which we make the announcement in Houston needs to show everyone affected by it that the company is taking an action that is absolutely necessary and that we are doing it with compassion, understanding, and a commitment to make good on every promise.

9. Generate positive follow-up publicity.

We have opportunities to follow the announcement with positive news by publicizing successful personnel placements and any goodwill gestures to the community like a donation of property or park equipment.

10. Leave the community in a way that would invite our return.

We need to make sure community leaders and government representatives are not blindsided by the announcement, that they are well informed and prepared to respond to questions from their constituents. We need to make known that we will continue to serve the Southwest market with products and services from our other facilities. We need to reposition, not sever, our relationship with the community.

GAYLE: Well, we're going to look to you for how we apply this. What do you need from us so we can get down to the specifics of developing the announcement plan?

DAVID: Gayle, I need you to provide key message points we want to make to distribution center managers, to field sales personnel, and to customers. We'll have to talk to Bill about the message points for Houston plant employees and key suppliers. Tom, I will need from you and Harvy message points for employees company-wide. I think I have what I need to draft the news announcement and the message points for community leaders and government representatives. If you all agree, I think we should take some time now to rough out a timeline that will become our communication schedule. Then let's meet again tomorrow morning [Thursday, July 11]. I will have a draft announcement plan and timeline for us to review. We should have a final draft by the end of the day. Tom, do you want to schedule a meeting with George for Friday [July 12]?

TOM: I'll do that. Let's get to this schedule.

DAVID: We need to bring Bill into the planning group. Why don't we have him join us on Monday, July 15?

HARVY: We have a lot of stuff to review, probably revise, and get approved. It might be good to schedule a three-day work session.

DAVID: What about doing that next week, Wednesday through Friday [July 17–19]?

TOM: That should include review and approval of an operations shutdown plan and timetable.

DAVID: It's also the time we should decide if this core group needs to be expanded and who that should include.

HARVY: I will have the retention plan ready. We can do a final review of government requirements for a closure. We can review the employment information Q & A. I will also have a description of employment assistance services we will be providing. And we can review security arrangements.

DAVID: We can finalize the communication plan and timeline. It will contain contingency provisions for handling news leaks and rumors. The business rationale and news announcement need to be reviewed and approved, as well as the communication to all of the various stakeholders.

For the announcement, I propose that we notify the general managers of each of our operations by phone on July 26 and send them information kits via courier to arrive the same day. We'll get Bill's opinion on how soon to notify key staff in Houston. We should courier information kits to sales reps and distribution center managers.

I think we should schedule the announcement for Tuesday, July 30. On announcement day we need to cover the following something like this:

- Bill Cabot personally notifies supervisors.

- Houston supervisors notify employees and distribute letter from Cabot.

- Facility managers company-wide distribute CEO letter to employees with business rationale attached.

- Bill meets with Houston customer service representatives and estimators.

- Headquarters faxes sales reps company-wide with instructions to notify Southwest customers by phone.

- News release to headquarters personnel (electronically) and to Houston media and via news distribution service to state wires, national business, financial media, and trade media.

- Bill and selected staff members call community leaders and local government representatives.

- Houston faxes government representatives at state and federal offices.

- Houston mails news release and letter to Houston customers and suppliers.

In the days following the announcement, Houston will be operating counseling services and employment assistance and we should be looking for opportunities to generate some positive publicity.

MEETING ADJOURNS

David Maple's notes for writing the news announcement:

Dateline should be from headquarters, Thyme, Ill., July 30, 20XX

indefinite closure

structural building products plant

to bring production capacity in line with market conditions

consolidating our manufacturing resources in the United States by reducing the number of production plants from eight to seven

This adjustment will enable us to reduce operating costs and still provide the same high level of sales and service to our customers

with the U.S. commercial construction market in the midst of a major recession, the market for the company's products has dropped by approximately 39 percent, nationwide, over the past six years

will be another eighteen months, with a further decline in the coming year, before this market begins to turn around

Supercore International will retain the same Southwest sales organization and distribution centers in Houston, Denver, and Wichita. These centers will be supplied by production facilities in Tennessee, Illinois, Alabama

Closure expected to be completed by year-end

will affect approximately 200 employees

some employees will have an opportunity to relocate to other Supercore International facilities

The company will provide employees with a severance pay package and job placement services

Houston has always had highly skilled, productive employees; closure is regretful; we will work hard to help them find other employement

The plant started operating in 1980

business grew rapidly

ran at near capacity during the building boom of the early 1980s.

Houston was well situated to serve the Southwest, and in particular, the Texas markets, which had major levels of construction back in that period

This period was followed by a virtual collapse of building activity in the region

Supercore gave Houston Operations some of the company's international work and jobs from other parts of the country; it still operated below capacity levels

Depressed conditions hit other regions and Houston's operating level was reduced further

Market conditions caused us to assess our situation in the United States

Supercore made a thorough analysis and concluded that of the eight production facilities, closure of Houston Operations would have the least effect on the company's ability to serve our customers nationally

Conditions are what they are and we have to adjust our production capacity

Houston plant was built in 1979

Supercore International, Inc., is a leading international producer of structural building products and systems for the nonresidential market

Headquartered in Thyme, Illinois

Supercore International has 50 facilities employing approximately 5,000 people in North America, Europe, and Asia.

David Maple's notes for writing a general Q & A:

We'll be asked why. We're closing one of eight U.S. plants to bring production in line with market conditions.

Some may think we're overreacting; they'll try to point to indicators that we're coming out of the recession. But commercial construction business in the United States is in the midst of a major recession. Construction work has dropped significantly over the past six years. Supercore and other manufacturers have seen their market drop by approximately 39 percent in the past six years. It will be another eighteen months before this market begins to turn around.

Not everyone understands why construction is in worse shape than the general economy. There's been substantial overbuilding in many parts of the country. Building activity is down substantially. Developers are constrained financially. They are unable to attract capital for projects.

We'll get plenty of questions on, Why Houston? Fact is, the Southwest has been the weakest section of the country for construction for the past six years. Why? Breakdown of the energy belt economy with the big drop in oil prices, consequences of the savings and loan crisis, and lots of bankruptcies. It's likely to be a weak market for the foreseeable future. But the major reason behind selecting Houston was that it would have a minimal effect on our overall operation.

We have been in Houston so long that it will probably seem to some that we are pulling out of this market. So we need to be direct in letting people know that we're going to serve this market as well as ever before. We will continue to operate our distribution center in Houston. That center and those in Denver and Wichita will be supplied by production facilities in Tennessee, Illinois, and Alabama. These plants can handle additional volume.

About 200 employees will be affected by the closure. Some will be given opportunities to relocate to other facilities.

Severance. We'll get some questions about the package. It has two elements. Employees will be offered incentive pay to work until their individual assignments have been completed. All employees will get a severance amount whether or not they work until their jobs end.

We might be asked about a possible employee buyout. That's not possible. We're not interested in selling these assets. We may have use for them elsewhere in the future.

The end date? Closing date? We haven't set an exact date. We have to allow enough time for transferring work to other plants. Should be able to have everything done before the end of December.

As for other plants . . . People will be wondering if other plants will be closed. The answer is no. According to our market outlook, we think this adjustment of reducing our U.S. capacity from eight to seven plants will give us the right capacity to supply customers for the near future.

We know this is going to have an impact on the local economy. We'll get questions about that. The Houston plant has contributed about $20 million a year in wages, taxes, and local purchases.

There will probably be people who expect us to somehow make up this deficit, this loss of income to the community. What can we say. We've been a solid contributor to the local economy for many years. We've provided good paying jobs. But business conditions no longer support this plant. We're in a position that many others are in. We can't justify our cost of operating here and there's no way to continue contributing to the economy.

We'll probably get asked about the possibility of reopening the plant in the future. The closure is indefinite. The Southwest building market is severely depressed. We expect it to be that way for quite some time.

Someone will probably persist and ask if it will ever be opened again. But who could possibly know what conditions will be into the long term? We can't make any projections, let alone commitments.

We have had such a good relationship with local and state government representatives that some of them are going to be wondering if there is anything they can do to change our decision. But there isn't anything they can do. The decision is based on business conditions in the Southwest and around the country.

I suppose someone could wonder if putting this plant here was a mistake in the first place. That certainly isn't true. It really took off into the mid-1980s and was well situated to serve the Southwest. Texas had lots going on then. Major construction projects were under way. But that period didn't last. Things pretty much collapsed. Who could have predicted the S & L debacle?

Employees at Houston had nothing to do with the decision. They always have been a fine team. Good, smart, hardworking individuals. They were always making suggestions on how to improve things, quality, and production. Other employers should take a hard look at the talent that will be available from this plant.

Employees at our other plants might wonder if any of them might get bumped by a relocated Houston employee. First of all, there will be a limited number of relocations. We place a high value on our human resources and will be very thoughtful in any placements.

That brings up the matter of employees who are not relocated. We will provide employment services, like preparing resumes and training for making a job search and how to interview. We'll be talking to local employers to describe the kinds of work people have been doing for us and how their skills might relate to other business operations. We'll give employees time off for job interviews. We will make a concerted effort to help everyone as much as we can.

The announcement may seem abrupt and someone might ask if we couldn't have given more notice. But we made the announcement as soon as we finished our analysis of the market situation. With the closure targeted for year-end employees will have an opportunity to work and be looking for other jobs for many weeks.

Let's see, we made the decision to close the plant in June, after our study was completed and assessed. The final decision came in mid-July. So there weren't any unusual delays in going thought the process and making it know publicly.

The Houston plant . . . We'll secure it, probably move the equipment and eventually sell the property. The Houston plant was built in 1979. It started up in 1980. It produces structural building products and pre-engineering building systems for the nonresidential market. It's not a union plant.

As for the outlook . . . We'll see an even greater decline in the market in the coming year and it will be at least 18 months before things begin to turn around. We will be stepping up our sales and marketing efforts. When things pick up we'll be in position to participate in the recovery as we have in the past.

****

SUPERCORE INTERNATIONAL, INC.

Interoffice Correspondence

CONFIDENTIAL

JULY 10, 20XX

TO: DAVID MAPLE
FROM: HARVY COLLINS
COPIES: George Waters, Tom Oaks, Gayle Hopkins, Bill Cabot
RE: INFORMATION FOR Q & A ON PEOPLE-RELATED ISSUES

Following is information you can use in writing a Q & A on people-related issues:

There will be severance pay for salaried and hourly employees. At the time of termination, each employee will receive a base severance payment. It will amount to the person's weekly pay times the individual's years of service up to 25 years. Partial years will be prorated.

There will also be an incentive severance payment for individuals who work up to a time we specify or when the particular job ends. Employees who qualify will be given $1,000 if they have less than two years of service and $2,500 if they have two or more years of service. The incentive will be paid when their jobs terminate.

The severance base pay and incentive pay will be payable to employees who are offered relocations to other plants, even if the individual does not accept the relocation offer.

Those who resign before their jobs end must give us two weeks' notice in order to get their base severance pay. There's some flexibility on this requirement depending on circumstances.

Acts of misconduct related to the company, customers, or other employees will disqualify a person from receiving severance payments.

We will get questions about benefits. Benefits end with job terminations. Hourly and salary employees may continue their medical insurance at their own expense according to COBRA provisions. We'll have more information on COBRA later.

As for retirement benefits . . . Individuals who qualify for retirement or early retirement under either hourly or salary retirement plans can do so and receive retirement benefits. We'll have more details on this later.

We will be pressed hard on how many Houston employees will be transferred to jobs in other facilities. Actually, we don't know at this point. We have to see what's needed at other plants and we'll have to see who is willing to relocate of those who could be offered the opportunity. As soon as the announcement is made other plants will be assessing their personnel needs. We will have a more accurate idea when we have reports from the other seven plants. It won't be a large number.

Likely transferees will be employees in managerial, supervisory, or technical jobs.

We'll probably be asked where the relocations could be. Most likely places would be Cilantro, Tennessee, Sage, Illinois, and Rosemary, Alabama.

As for when transfers might be made, I would say they would begin in September and go through the end of the year.

Unfortunately, most employees will not have an opportunity to transfer. There's no cutoff date for employment. It will be different for each individual. It depends on how their work relates to the transition and if they accept the incentive to work as long as we need them. We will try to be more specific about this in the coming weeks.

If salaried employees in managerial or technical jobs want to be transferred, they will be given an opportunity to complete a form that will be sent to appropriate personnel for consideration.

Transfers are handled differently for hourly employees. A transfer might be possible for employees with specialized skills. However, the individual would be responsible for moving expenses.

****

SUPERCORE INTERNATIONAL, INC.

Interoffice Correspondence

CONFIDENTIAL

JULY 10, 20XX

TO: DAVID MAPLE
FROM: BILL CABOT
COPIES: George Waters, Tom Oaks, Gayle Hopkins, Harvy Collins
RE: INFORMATION FOR MY MEMO TO HOUSTON EMPLOYEES

David, I'd appreciate a little help with writing my memo to the Houston employees. I've known many of these folks for more than a dozen years. If you would rough out something I will personalize it.

Some of the points I'd like to include are

- Very difficult; we have operated like a family

- Proud of the teamwork we've shown

- Struggled through some lean times together, but always recovered

- I personally believe the decision to close was justified from a business assessment

- Need to support each other as we prepare for looking in some new directions

- Can't help but wonder, why us? But there's nothing we could have done to alter the outcome. That's clear when we face the facts:

Supercore has too much underutilized production capacity and will have for some time to come

The market our plant serves is by far the softest in the country

Prices have eroded, profits are down, no way to cover the cost of operating this facility

Unfortunately for us, our customers can be easily served by other plants

The Southwest distribution center will serve to anchor Supercore's business in this market

I'll be talking with everyone in smaller groups as we move forward . . . we'll go over personnel concerns

I know we all have mixed emotions over this . . . we will have to make a special effort to rely on our professionalism to maintain the teamwork needed to work through the shutdown process

We have always given our customers a level of quality that always meets and often exceeds company standards . . . they deserve our continuing commitment and a smooth handoff to our other plants

you know the rapport we have enjoyed . . . nothing has changed in that regard . . . we will continue working together in an open, straightforward, totally honest relationship

in all honesty, I have to admit this is the most difficult memo I have ever had to write

See what you can do with that. Thanks, David.

B.C.

SUPERCORE INTERNATIONAL, INC.

Interoffice Correspondence

CONFIDENTIAL

JULY 10, 20XX

TO: DAVID MAPLE
FROM: GAYLE HOPKINS
COPIES: George Waters, Tom Oaks, Harvy Collins, Bill Cabot
RE: INFORMATION FOR MY FAX TO DISTRIBUTION CENTERS

I appreciate your help with this communication, David. I am providing the main points that I think should be written in my memo to be faxed to Supercore's distribution center managers.

> You were notified this morning about the company's decision to close Houston Operations
>
> I talked by speaker phone to the staff at the Houston distribution center. As you know, that facility will remain in operation. Southwest Area Sales will also remain as usual.
>
> We're all going to have our own thoughts about the shutdown and we're certainly entitled to that . . . we have a responsibility to fully understand and be able to discuss the business reasons for the decision . . . urge you to read and study the business rationale in your information kits . . .
>
> As members of the sales organization, our biggest responsibility is to maintain our current business and make every effort to keep from losing any business as other plants begin to supply Houston customers . . . to protect our position will require a stronger than ever commitment to the company and its strategic direction . . . I know we are up to the challenge . . .
>
> No matter how we plan, there will be some rough situations . . . some not easy or even possible to see . . . will place great demands on our ability to work together . . .
>
> Can't emphasize enough the importance of reading and studying all of the materials in your information kits . . . you must know this material well enough to show complete confidence in Supercore's decision about Houston . . .
>
> We need time to go over the transition plan in detail . . . plan to attend a meeting of all distribution center managers at headquarters on Friday, August 2, at 11 AM in the main conference room . . . your attendance is mandatory . . . we have a big job ahead of us and I know we can handle it when we tackle it as a team . . .

That's about what needs to be said, David. I'll look forward to your draft. Thanks.

G.H.

SUPERCORE INTERNATIONAL, INC.

Interoffice Correspondence

CONFIDENTIAL

JULY 10, 20XX

TO: DAVID MAPLE
FROM: TOM OAKS
COPIES: George Waters, Gayle Hopkins, Harvy Collins, Bill Cobot
RE: INFORMATION FOR MEMO FROM CEO TO ALL EMPLOYEES

David, we'll need a memo written from George Waters to all employees. I would see it containing these points:

1. For a company that holds its employees in highest regard, putting business realities ahead of our personal relationships is extremely difficult

2. I have a responsibility to our organization to keep us in a strong competitive position

3. Market conditions, as we all know, are heavily taxing our ability to generate the sales necessary to earn some return on investment . . . in the United States we have experienced swings from no orders to round-the-clock production . . .

4. The bottom line is that we have to face the reality of bringing our capacity in line with market conditions that are expected to remain depressed for the foreseeable future . . .

5. Because the situation is serious, I asked for a thorough market study and comprehensive study of our production capacity and operating options . . . it became evident that the way to restructure with minimal effects on our overall business is to shut down the Houston plant . . .

6. It is with deep regret that we have to pursue a decision that will affect nearly 200 hard-working employees, some of whom have been with us for more than a dozen years . . . we will provide severance and employment services, including working with Houston employers to make local placements wherever possible

7. So that everyone is able to know the details behind our decision to close Houston I have included with this letter to all employees a copy of our business rationale for this action

8. You will see clearly from the rational that Houston has always been a top performer and closure is entirely due to market conditions

David, let me have a draft by tomorrow. George asked for a draft ASAP. Thanks.

T.O.

Image Building
Superstar Entrepreneur

This is a case of image building and centers on a superstar entrepreneur. Much research has been done in attempts to characterize entrepreneurs. Many are driven by the desire to make a lot more money than they could with some other application of their skills and energy. What every entrepreneur must decide is whether the rewards of their respective enterprise will justify the cost, sacrifice, and risk involved in achieving some degree of success. George Bernard Shaw said, "The reasonable man adapts himself to the world; the unreasonable man attempts to adapt the world to himself. Therefore all progress depends upon the unreasonable man." The character of the superstar in this case lies somewhere between reasonable and unreasonable. You will develop this case using the public relations file notes that follow the team and individual team member assignments. As you do, think about what makes this superstar tick and how the personality traits of this entrepreneur can be put to good use in building a business. The article on page 186, "Work with Journalists and Make CEO Profiles Soar," should stimulate further thought in the development of your public relations plan.

...NMENT

For this case assume that your team has been hired by superstar entrepreneur Jan Overbrook. Your superstar has a tenacious spirit that has enabled her to turn some ideas into profitable ventures. Your team has collected information about Overbrook and has a file of interview notes that reveals secrets behind your client's successes and failures. Overbrook has hired your team to develop a public relations plan spanning 12 months that will promote her image as a superstar entrepreneur in ways that will propel the expansion of her latest business venture, Wellness Advocates, Inc. (WAI). Overbrook wants to expand WAI services, initially, throughout New York in towns with major medical centers—specifically Albany, the Bronx, Valhalla, Brooklyn, Buffalo, Stoneybrook and Old Westbury. She tells your agency that the PR budget is $50,000 plus out-of-pocket expenses. As part of the PR plan she wants your agency to engage the blogosphere to help establish her credentials as the nation's wellness advocate. She said her friend Jason, whose experience inspired WAI, and several of her WAI counselors have agreed to add a depth of experience and knowledge to her site by serving as resources to enable her to stimulate dialogue. She believes telling Jason's story would be a good way to reach out to other bloggers and to attract an audience of potential clients for WAI. She envisions her site to be the coffeehouse where people come to share their medical experiences—the good, bad and ugly. She said, "I want the PR plan to provide guidance on how to be successful in kicking off my blog." In one of your meetings with Overbook, she said, "By the way, did I tell you I have a book about to be published titled *Wellness Advocates, Inc.?*"

INDIVIDUAL TEAM MEMBER ASSIGNMENTS

Each team member is to complete a different one of the following items that might or might not be part of the design of your plan. (See Chapter 7: Samples of Effective Public Relations Writing.)

1. Draft a personality profile of the superstar.

2. Write a phone pitch script to an assistant program director to get TV coverage of the superstar.

3. Write a memo to the superstar client proposing an *unusual* attention-getting book-signing event/tour.

4. Write a pitch letter to get the superstar coverage in a national magazine.

5. Draft a backgrounder on Wellness Advocates, Inc., and the superstar.

6. Write a prompting sheet for the superstar to use for a TV talk show. Describe Wellness Advocates and its purpose. Use short conversational phrases. Ilustrate how WAI helps a person take responsibility for his or her

health using acid reflux disease as an example—describe what it is and list questions that a patient should ask the doctor about the condition and its treatment, as well as how to avoid the problem. Arrange the information in the order it might be asked for by the talk-show host.

7. Draft an op-ed article about the need for people to take more responsibility for their own health.

Client file on Jan Overbrook

Facts and interview notes 12/05/20XX

<u>Observations</u>: Overbrook seems to be a "pro" at getting things done. She obviously likes to run the show and make things happen. Her energy is boundless. We [the agency] had better be as precise about organization and detail as she is. When she goes for the goal it's done cost-effectively and on schedule. If there's one thing we learned at the last meeting, it was be prepared; she makes decisions! She's analytical and objective. She's also quick. And what we present had better be logical. Forget theory and any abstract ideas. Overbrook wants practical applications; she cares about what's here and now. She's outgoing and sociable; she's also matter-of-fact and direct.

<u>Random quotes from the interview with Overbrook</u>: I know I'm analytical and that can seem impersonal and uncaring to some people. So I have to remind myself to think about how others think and feel. I've been successful and I tend to get caught up in the success of things. I've surrounded myself with talented people and I have to remember to credit them and make sure they know they're appreciated. If this relationship lasts [with the agency], you'll see that I make rapid-fire decisions. I know I should spend time listening more, so if I get too far out in front I want you to tell me. Don't let me jump to conclusions when you have stuff that I should know. When the work is good, we'll be fine. When it's not, brace yourself because I don't pull punches when it comes to criticizing.

<u>Client's story of what inspired the new business</u>: My latest venture is Wellness Advocates, Inc. I started it a year ago, on January 1. The idea for it was inspired a year before that. A dear friend of mine, Jason Adams, drove himself to City Hospital as he was having a heart attack. He had been videotaping a friend's wedding and left the camera running so as not to disappoint his friend. He was transferred to General Hospital where they put a double stent in one of his arteries. Another artery was 80 percent blocked, but they decided to treat that with drugs. Bad decision.

Seven months later, on August 8, Jason had shortness of breath and chest pains. He was rushed to General. The double stent had failed but vessels near it had regenerated. A chemical-release-type stent was placed in the other clogged artery. No one volunteered to tell him the condition of other arteries and he finally had to press hard for answers before leaving the hospital.

On August 15, Jason awoke with tremendous pains in his chest. Off to General once again. Jason waved to friendly faces as he was wheeled on a gurney to critical care. The welcome got serious when they started the heart catheterization treatment. He said it was like some medieval torture chamber. Narrow bed. Doctors and nurses outfitted like Martians to fend off the radioactivity. A sharp jab in the groin with a long metal stick. Big cameras pointing down as he strained to hold the pose for 30 minutes. A shot of morphine eased the pain, but Jason begged for more and more. Meanwhile, down in accounting, the figure in the ledger was reaching into a sixth column.

He awoke to the voices of heart surgeons who said his heart was "fine." Jason said, "Great, so why all the pain?" They told him it must be his lungs or stomach. He said it was obvious their area of expertise and interest was the heart; stomachs and lungs were someone else's area.

Jason was released and sent to cardiac rehab at County Hospital. For half an hour he walked on a treadmill, rode a stationary bike, lifted weights, then passed out. His blood pressure fell to 64 over 50. He was rushed to the ER. Another battery of blood tests. By now his arm was numb from all the blood taking.

"Jason, your heart is fine," the doctor said. "The problem might be your liver." Liver? lungs? stomach? Heart? Totally exasperated, Jason's wife said, "Enough is enough!" She called the family doctor, told him the situation, and without seeing Jason at General, he told her to take Jason back to City Hospital and have them insert a scope to look at his stomach.

Jason had nothing to wear because he had thrown up on his clothes on the way to the ER. So he had to wear his General Hospital gown to City. A security guard at General saw Jason in his gown and hassled him because he thought Jason was trying to leave the hospital without permission. Finally he was admitted to City. They insisted on another full examination routine, telling him his heart was fine but that they could not perform the scope procedure right away because he needed to fast for 24 hours.

By this time Jason just wanted to go home. Enough doctors, hospitals, IVs, and blood tests. His weight dropped from 269 at the time of his first attack to under 200 and was continuing to decline.

Finally, the family doctor told Jason that his most recent attack was from acute acid reflux. Jason had never heard of it. Some of the symptoms are the same as those of a heart attack—chest pains, heavy breathing, nausea, even passing out. He was told more pills. More exercise. Better diet control. Better diet was a joke to Jason. He hadn't eaten anything of substance for the past three weeks.

The doctor scheduled the scope procedure at still another hospital, parkview, for September 23. But Jason decided he needed a new family doctor. He wanted a coordinated approach to his problems. He wanted someone to take a holistic look at his physical condition, to review the list of drugs (and potential interactions) that had been prescribed by a battery of different physicians. He wanted to see details of the many examinations. He wanted to know if he was in a life-threatening situation. He wanted better advice about diet and exercise and dreaded the thought of passing out again on some piece of equipment. He wanted to know more about acute acid reflux.

It was the experience of this very dear friend that inspired me to establish Wellness Advocates, Inc.

<u>Client's comments on the mission and operation of Wellness Advocates. Inc.:</u> The mission of WAI is to show clients how to take responsibility for their health and wellness. At WAI we have a staff of facilitators. They are not medical advisors. Their job is to show clients how to overcome any feelings of trepidation for white smocks and stethoscopes and become medically conversant about their health and wellness. That means suggesting sources of information and teaching them how to ask questions and insisting on satisfactory answers. It means showing them how to stay current on the latest developments in medical discoveries, new procedures, medicine, and research. It means showing clients how important it is to take a personal interest in everything they put into their bodies—from food to pharmacy products. It means showing clients how to take a holistic approach to their health and wellness and finding qualified medical professionals who subscribe to such an enlightened view.

At WAI we show clients how to create and maintain a personal medical file, what health indicators to track and record, what records to include, and how to obtain them.

We also provide support so that when a client feels like he or she is being led down a blind alley we can help them avoid an experience like Jason's by showing them how get complete and honest information to enlighten and ensure themselves that they are on the right course.

WAI has a staff of six facilitators who collectively are educated in a full range of medical subjects from diet to drugs. We have offices in New York City, Syracuse, and Rochester. We have over 700 clients. The fee for our service is $48 per month. We have a Web site. We have the private financial backing necessary to begin expanding the business nationally. We have an information kit that explains everything for potential clients. We have a stellar reputation. We are not widely known yet, but those who meet us and become acquainted with our mission in nearly every case become clients. Our service becomes so valuable that when we get together with a client the meeting always begins with a big hug.

<u>Observations and random client comments on managing a business</u>: When we first started I tried to do everything, because I feel better when I have complete control. Then we started to expand and I hired people who could carry out my ideas and my ways of working with clients. I've had other ventures, like a chain of gift shops in New York hospitals, a wellness newsletter published nationally, and a florist in Old Westbury that specialized in patient bouquets that were delivered by volunteer caregivers who spent five to 10 minutes talking with each hospital recipient. But WAI has, by far, been the most successful and most rewarding venture. What I love is meeting people, getting acquainted and getting hired by clients.

Trying to control everything is a real challenge, especially when I don't like the nitty-gritty accounting work and meeting all of the regulatory and other administrative requirements. Dividing my attention between serving clients and managing the business gets real stressful. But I'm determined to do this no matter what it takes.

I have an exercise routine and I try to spend time outdoors. But I hate the thought of taking time for a vacation. I love to work. I was married once and had two children. They were my primary interest. My husband died and the children are grown. I couldn't have ventured into my own business while they were growing up. I remarried. My husband, Banks, manages a venture capital firm. Convenient arrangement! Not really. The businesses are kept separate. He's a workaholic too. But we both plan to expand operations, hire staff, and quit killing ourselves. I feel good about the business. I have done well and I've been rewarded for a tireless effort. <u>Client's views on secrets of her success</u>: I'm results-oriented in a tenacious way. When I set a goal nothing discourages me from reaching it. When I make a commitment it is rock solid; you can count on it. You'd be surprised at how tough I can get. And I make good decisions. You have to be a risk taker. I have a good sense about things and know just how far to go. One way to uncover business opportunities is to look for dissatisfaction among consumers. Finding effective ways to eliminate dissatisfaction can lead to a viable business venture, just as Wellness Advocates responds to Jason's frustration with the medical community. I think you also have to know how your talents, interests, background, and values combine with your particular personality to enable you to do what you are most suited to do. Did I tell you I have a book about to be published called simply, <u>Wellness Advocates, Inc.?</u>

WORK WITH JOURNALISTS AND MAKE CEO PROFILES SOAR

Many chief executive officers would like high profiles in the media. The reasons for wanting or needing public visibility are diverse and far ranging. The need, for example, might be to show leadership in an industry. Or the desire might be to become better known in the local business community.

A CEO's success in getting media attention depends largely on the chief executive's attitude toward journalists. At one extreme, some CEOs regard journalists as a necessary nuisance. At the other extreme, CEOs see journalists as gateways to important audiences.

Having worked with the news media for more than 30 years, I can tell you that having an effective relationship with the media requires consistent cooperation with journalists. Responding to reporters through others with, "Tell him I'll call him back," or "Tell her I will have to make some calls to get the information," and not responding is not an expression of cooperation.

Journalists, like securities analysts and others in the information-gathering business, have a job to do. Helping them accomplish their work by consistently being an accessible, responsive, useful source of information goes a long way in developing mutually beneficial relationships.

One way to ensure consistent cooperation with the media is for CEOs to treat journalists as they would treat customers. By treating journalists the way major customers are treated CEOs can watch their public profiles soar.

So, what must a CEO do to treat journalists the way major customers are treated? When a journalist calls, a CEO must respond promptly, not when it's convenient. Yes, that means walking out of an important meeting to take a press call, just as the CEO would respond promptly to a major customer who needed information. A missed call is a missed opportunity for publicity and for developing a working relationship with a reporter.

When a journalist schedules a meeting, a CEO must be there on time. Would a chief executive leave a major customer waiting in the lobby for 10 or even five minutes? A CEO must show the same respect for a reporter or news crew as would be shown for a major customer.

When in an interview, a CEO must participate with undivided attention. Would a chief executive interrupt a meeting with a major customer by responding to intercom messages, phone calls, or executive assistants passing written notes? The task at hand is to convey information thoughtfully and accurately and that demands uninterrupted concentration.

When a journalist asks for information, a CEO must provide details, including background that might help the journalist complete the assignment. Would a CEO expect a major customer to make purchasing decisions with incomplete information and unanswered questions? Reporters are expected to develop articles regardless of their depth of knowledge of a particular event or business development. Effective reporters have the acumen to ask the right questions to get the background and information they need to write a story. A CEO who takes the time to assist a reporter with an assignment takes a giant step forward in becoming a valuable news source.

When a photojournalist—a news photographer—wants to take pictures, a CEO must relax and allow ample time to enjoy the session as one would enjoy being photographed with a major customer. Claiming to be under tremendous pressure with no time to spare will result in a news photo of a stressed executive whose clock has run out.

When journalists call, a CEO must make a concerted effort to recognize frequent callers by name and affiliation just as a major customer would be acknowledged. It's an important part of the relationship-building process.

Like major customers, journalists need timely contact, useful information, undivided attention, and respectful recognition from CEOs.

This advice applies to the heads of public, private, and not-for-profit organizations. Many such organizations have public relations personnel responsible for media relations who handle much of the day-to-day work. However, to achieve a high public profile, a chief executive must work in partnership with public relations personnel and actively share the media relations responsibilities.

By treating journalists the way major customers are treated, CEOs can watch their public profiles soar.

Employee Communication
Quality Out of Control

All businesses, service as well as manufacturing, have one objective in common—to deliver quality in whatever they have to market. Quality is the cornerstone in building a business and so over the years many different quality programs, such as Total Quality Management (TQM), have been put to work to ensure quality in products and services. TQM means, essentially, that there are quality requirements in every phase of providing a product, such as taking orders, purchasing materials, manufacturing, shipping, billing, and so on. This case points out what many companies have learned—without effective communication you will not achieve a high standard of quality even if you have checks and balances in every phase of the business. Details of the case, including a chart summary of research findings, appear after the team and individual assignments. Read the article, "Does Your Company Have the 'Write' Stuff," on page 194 to see how something as basic as effective writing can contribute to an organization's ability to make money.

TEAM ASSIGNMENT

Your team is the public relations department of a company that manufactures various forms of paper packaging. The manager of one of the company's plants that manufactures paper shopping bags for grocery stores asks you to meet with him to discuss a serious problem. At the meeting he says, "I have been talking quality around here for months and it's like talking to a brick wall! Quality seems to be lacking in everything we do and I don't know what more I can do. We're beginning to lose customers. We get reports about handles falling off bags and bottoms falling open. One lady is suing us for letting a jar of Bobos Bread & Butter Chips fall through a bag and break her toe. We have had everything tested and we know the problem is not with paper or glue. It's a problem with how we work together to run the equipment that makes the product. It's a very serious situation, and just when I'm getting ready to retire. I don't want to reinvent this place at this point in my career. I'm just asking you, as our PR experts, to see if your expertise in communication can help get my quality message across to everybody."

Your team begins its work by interviewing members of the plant management staff. A sampling of research findings is summarized in the chart on page 193. The chart shows one- or two-word responses to interview questions that reveal the chief reasons for the plant's quality control problem: There is no consensus among managers on management's primary focus, its top priority, the plant's immediate needs, what the quality standards are, or who sets them. Your team makes the following recommendations to the management staff:

Reconcile your differences. Agree that

- management's focus is on quality.

- management's top priority, next to safety and health, is quality.

- management's greatest immediate need is to improve quality.

- to have plant-wide ownership in a quality improvement program everyone must participate in defining quality standards and meeting them once they are established.

The management staff agrees to your team's recommendations and asks for a public relations plan for internal communication that enables the plant to achieve the goal to be using effective internal communication for increasing plant-wide quality control.

Your plan must be designed to communicate to all employees management's commitment to quality and must include a strategy for involving all employees in helping to develop quality standards for all departments. The plant manager also wants the plan to include a recurring special event for employees to celebrate progress in achieving higher quality standards.

INDIVIDUAL TEAM MEMBER ASSIGNMENTS

Each team member is to complete a different one of the following items that might or might not be included in the design of your plan.

1. Draft a memo from the plant manager to sign and send to staff members enlisting their cooperation in being interviewed by members of the public relations department. (Use memo formant—To: Management Staff, From: Tom Jones, Re: Interviews.) The memo should state the plant manager's concern with quality, say why the public relations department is involved, and ask for the staff's cooperation in being interviewed and in being forthright in providing information.

2. Write in memo form a summary of the findings of your research in interviewing staff members. In other words describe in broad terms what you could reasonably conclude from the responses shown in the chart on page 193. (Use memo format— To: Tom Jones, From: Your Name, Re: Research Findings.) You should be working as a team player and therefore should not single out individuals, cast blame, or in any way be condescending or act as an authority on the subject of quality. Report the findings objectively, in general terms. Key off the questions. For example, "There does not seem to be a consistent understanding among staff members as to who establishes quality standards."

3. Write a backgrounder on the subject of managing for quality. Do not use information from the case or try to relate the backgrounder to the case. The backgrounder is to be a general discussion about the subject of managing for quality. Search business management sources on the Internet for information.

4. Write scripted remarks (90 seconds in speaker's form) for a member of your PR team to use in a meeting with plant staff members at which you briefly recap your assignment, the research you conducted, and conclusions based on the findings. You are sharing your findings with colleagues as a team player. So be careful not to set yourself apart from the plant staff with comments that might be perceived as judgmental, dictatorial, or instructive. Be careful not to appear like a knight on a white horse charging in from headquarters with all of the answers. The remarks should lead up to introducing a staff member who will present your department's plan as a proposal. You must win acceptance of your plan for it to be pursued in earnest by the management staff.

5. Write the first draft of a basic mission statement for this plant that would serve as a central message to focus, unify, and motivate employees. Search

the Internet for sample mission statements as a reference. Your draft statement would be used to begin serious discussions about the plant's mission and would require input of all employees for achieving a final version.

6. Write a news release announcing the hiring of a quality-control manager for the Better Bags plant. The release is to be issued by the plant so use an appropriate dateline. It should contain two quotes from the plant manager that would be especially appreciated by customers of Better Bags. As a resource, search for an announcement example at Businesswire.com or PRNewswire.com. Also, for guidance, search the Web for "quality control manager." Use information from the Internet search and make up details, including the name of the individual, job history, education, professional memberships, personal interests, and so on.

7. Write 15- and 30-second public service announcements urging people to reduce waste by using paper grocery bags over and over again— using them creatively by turning them inside out for wrapping or drawing paper, then depositing them for recycling.

FACTS

Company name: Better Bags, Inc., Paperville, U.S.A.

Employees: 276

Product: Paper grocery bags with paper handles

Customers: Grocery stores—chains and independents

Established: In business since 1972

Manager: Tom Jones, 64; 30 years of service; degree in mechanical engineering from the University of Technology

Bag Operation

The bag operation is automated. Movement of material is along an assembly line of machines that cut, fold, glue, and attach paper handles. The equipment adjusts to changes in temperature. Paper jams are infrequent, but require set up and adjustment time. While the equipment is automated it must be closely monitored, which requires diligence on the part of equipment operators, accurate reading of gauges, recording of data by workers, and coordination between shift supervisors. Sometimes the equipment runs 24/7. To reach an optimum operating level that results in efficiencies that produce a margin of profit, managers, supervisors, and workers must operate as a team, focusing on quality standards that are demanding of the equipment and the entire workforce. Similar bag operations in other company locations have shown that to achieve optimum production levels, quality

SAMPLING OF RESEARCH FINDINGS

	Priority[1]	*Focus*[2]	*Standards*[3]	*By Whom*[4]	*Met*[5]	*Need*[6]
Plant Manager	Yes	People	Customers specify	All	Good	Money
Printing Supervisor	I think so	Quality	?	Supervision	Yes	Quality control
Production Manager	Yes	Production	?	History	Reasonably good	Communication
Second shift supervisor	Not sure	Safety	Try to make best product	Supervision	We try	Fix floor congestion
Mechanical Engineer	Used to be	Production	Fluctuating	Supervisor, production manager, superintendent	Pretty well	Communication
Superintendent	Don't know	People	?	Supervision	No	One-on-one communication
Second Shift Supervisor	Yes	Service	?	Top management	Depends	Resolve personnel conflicts
Personnel Manager	Yes	Profit	None	Superintendent customer service	Hit/Miss	More decisive management
Bottoming Supervisor	Think so	?	Talk quality	Tony	Few rejects	Better communication
Production Scheduler	Used to be	Appease customers at all costs	Inconsistent	Top management, supervisor	Mostly OK	Leadership communication
Warehouse Supervisor	Depends	Safety	Fine, different for each operation	Everybody	Not bad for the United States	Replace the production manager

1. Is quality one of the plant's main priorities?
2. What seems to be management's main focus?
3. Describe the plant's quality standards.
4. Who sets the quality standards?
5. How well are the standards met?
6. What is the greatest need for improvement in this plant?

standards must be clearly defined and effectively communicated. It has also been learned by industry that many factors are to blame for poor quality, including company politics, shortsighted thinking, and poor management. However, at Better Bags, Inc., product quality at six of the company's plants was improved substantially and measurably just through improved communication.

Communication

The plant operates three shifts:(1) 7 AM to 3 PM; (2) 3 PM to 11 PM; and (3) 11 PM to 7 AM. On each shift employees are given a 20-minute lunch break. Supervisors conduct safety meetings every day at the beginning of each shift. Supervisors also conduct communication meetings once each month. The plant manager talks to employees quarterly by shift. The most effective ways to communicate with employees are (1) through supervisors; (2) by weekly newsletter; (3) by monthly videotape; and (4) by closed circuit TV. Employees function in work groups and, for special efforts, in terms. Team members can select a team leader. The team effort is coached by the shift supervisor.

DOES YOUR COMPANY HAVE THE "WRITE" STUFF?

Now why would an executive manager want to give an organization a writing test? To increase profitability. That's a good reason. Just when you're beginning to think that "reengineering" was the last great hope to increase profitability, someone comes along with the simple suggestion that improved writing skills can improve an organization's bottom line.

So, how can something as basic as good writing impact financial performance? I'll illustrate the point six ways. Once you begin to think about it, you will discover more ways that are specific to your business.

(1) **Customer Service** Why are your customer service costs as high as they are? Don't ask your customer-service department; its goal is not to reduce or eliminate itself. Make your own assessment. Is the volume of customer calls high because product instruction sheets are unclear; because product manuals fail to adequately explain product features; because special offers, discounts, or ordering procedures are confusing? The goal should not be to improve customer service, but rather to reduce the need for it with more clearly written materials.

(2) **Web Presence** Why hasn't your Web site reduced expenses as you originally expected? You set up a station somewhere in cyberspace thinking that it was going to save you money. Instead you find that customers are like shooting stars. They can appear at your cyberspace station as quickly as they can disappear from it. Why? If they can't find what they're looking for

quickly, they can go instantly to competing sites to find what they want. The goal should be to have your Web site messages written so well that customers can easily find and navigate to exactly what they want.

(3) **Competitive Information** Why aren't your employees sharing information that could benefit the company? Information that employees acquire in doing their jobs can be extremely valuable to your business. In fact, most of the competitive information you might like to have is probably right under your own roof. The goal should be to show employees writing practices and forms that encourage interpersonal communication and greater sharing of information throughout the organization.

(4) **Stock Value** Why aren't investors recognizing the full value of your company? Your company's most valuable assets are its core competencies. If you ask industry analysts, investors, and potential investors to name your company's core competencies, could they do it? The goal should be to ensure that written materials communicate strategically with financial audiences.

(5) **Competitive Bids** Why haven't you been winning a greater number of business bids? When no one asks a single question after your company's sales presentations, is it because the presentations are so thorough as to answer every conceivable question? Or is it because they didn't stimulate any interest? The goal should be to have presentations and proposals written that are highly persuasive and compelling enough to win new business.

(6) **Quality Control** Why are your error rates higher than they should be? If you asked each of your employees to describe what is meant by "quality" in your particular operation, would you hear one concise definition, consistently, throughout the organization? Or would each person have a different idea of what is meant by quality in your organization? The goal should be to have standards clearly written and understood by the entire organization.

I have raised questions about profitability in six areas of your business. You won't find answers to my questions in financial statistics, such as return on investment, net earnings, and total debt to invested capital. You don't need to hire an MBA from Harvard to find the answers. You just need to give your company a "writing test." Make a simple assessment in each area covered above, asking yourself or your customers, securities analysts, investors, and other important audiences, "How well is it written?"

Assess your company's writing skills and how effectively they are applied, then take steps to raise the bar to its highest level of proficiency. You are likely to find more than one significant opportunity to improve profitability through good writing.

chapter 7

Samples of Effective Public Relations Writing

*t*his section of the book presents professional samples of public relations writing that were provided courtesy of many different sources. The samples were chosen specifically to illustrate the different types of writing required by the writing assignments in the case section of the book. The samples are not shown as templates, because some are formatted for use on the Internet. Rather, they are instructive in showing the approach, diction, and tone of voice that are appropriate in communicating with a variety of audiences, such as employees, parents, government officials, staff members, clients, and others. For specific guidance in developing news releases, media alerts, speeches, backgrounders, and other tools of the trade it is best to consult any of a number of outstanding textbooks on public relations writing.

PUBLIC RELATIONS WRITING SAMPLES

FEDERAL EMERGENCY MANAGEMENT AGENCY (FEMA)

Backgrounder: Terrorism

EMERGENCY INFORMATION

1. Before the September 11, 2001 attacks in New York and the Pentagon, most terrorist incidents in the United States have been bombing attacks, involving detonated and undetonated explosive devices, tear gas and pipe and fire bombs.

2. The effects of terrorism can vary significantly from loss of life and injuries to property damage and disruptions in services such as electricity, water supply, public transportation and communications.

3. One way governments attempt to reduce our vulnerability to terrorist incidents is by increasing security at airports and other public facilities. The U.S. government also works with other countries to limit the sources of support for terrorism.

U.S. TERRORIST INCIDENTS

WHAT IS TERRORISM?

Terrorism is the use of force or violence against persons or property in violation of the criminal laws of the United States for purposes of intimidation, coercion or ransom. Terrorists often use threats to create fear among the public, to try to convince citizens that their government is powerless to prevent terrorism, and to get immediate publicity for their causes.

The Federal Bureau of Investigation (FBI) categorizes terrorism in the United States as one of two types—domestic terrorism or international terrorism.

Domestic terrorism involves groups or individuals whose terrorist activities are directed at elements of our government or population without foreign direction.

International terrorism involves groups or individuals whose terrorist activities are foreign-based and/or directed by countries or groups outside the United States or whose activities transcend national boundaries.

BIOLOGICAL AND CHEMICAL WEAPONS

Biological agents are infectious microbes or toxins used to produce illness or death in people, animals or plants. Biological agents can be dispersed as aerosols or airborne particles. Terrorists may use biological agents to contaminate food or water because they are extremely difficult to detect. Chemical agents kill or incapacitate people, destroy livestock or ravage crops. Some chemical agents are odorless and tasteless and are difficult to detect. They can have an immediate effect (a few seconds to a few minutes) or a delayed effect (several hours to several days).

Biological and chemical weapons have been used primarily to terrorize an unprotected civilian population and not as a weapon of war. This is because of fear of retaliation and the likelihood that the agent would contaminate the battlefield for a long period of time. The Persian Gulf War in 1991 and other confrontations in the Middle East were causes for concern in the United States regarding the possibility of chemical or biological warfare. While no incidents occurred, there remains a concern that such weapons could be involved in an accident or be used by terrorists.

More information on Bioterrorism preparedness and response is available online from the Department of Health and Human Services Center for Disease Control.

FACTS ABOUT TERRORISM (Prior to September 11, 2001)

- On February 29, 1993, a bombing in the parking garage of the World Trade Center in New York City resulted in the deaths of five people and thousands of injuries. The bomb left a crater 200 by 100 feet wide and five stories deep. The World Trade Center was the second largest building in the world and houses 100,000 workers and visitors each day.

- The Department of Defense estimates that as many as 26 nations may possess chemical agents and/or weapons and an additional 12 may be seeking to develop them.

- The Central Intelligence Agency reports that at least ten countries are believed to possess or be conducting research on biological agents for weaponization.

TERRORISM IN THE UNITED STATES

- In the United States, most terrorist incidents have involved small extremist groups who use terrorism to achieve a designated objective. Local, State and Federal law enforcement officials monitor suspected terrorist groups and try to prevent or protect against a suspected attack. Additionally, the U.S. government works with other countries to limit the sources of support for terrorism.

- A terrorist attack can take several forms, depending on the technological means available to the terrorist, the nature of the political issue motivating the attack, and the points of weakness of the terrorist's target. Bombings have been the most frequently used terrorist method in the United States. Other possibilities include an attack at transportation facilities, an attack against utilities or other public services or an incident involving chemical or biological agents.

- Terrorist incidents in this country prior to the September 11, 2001 attack have included bombings of the World Trade Center in New York City, the United States Capitol Building in Washington, D.C. and Mobil Oil corporate headquarters in New York City.

sample 7.2   bio

WILLIAM H. GATES, MICROSOFT CORPORATION

William (Bill) H. Gates is chairman and chief software architect of Microsoft Corporation, the worldwide leader in software, services and Internet technologies for personal and business computing. Microsoft had revenues of US$36.84 billion for the fiscal year ending June 2004, and employs more than 55,000 people in 85 countries and regions.

Born on Oct. 28, 1955, Gates grew up in Seattle with his two sisters. Their father, William H. Gates II, is a Seattle attorney. Their late mother, Mary Gates, was a schoolteacher, University of Washington regent, and chairwoman of United Way International.

Gates attended public elementary school and the private Lakeside School. There, he discovered his interest in software and began programming computers at age 13.

In 1973, Gates entered Harvard University as a freshman, where he lived down the hall from Steve Ballmer, now Microsoft's chief executive officer. While at Harvard, Gates developed a version of the programming language BASIC for the first microcomputer—the MITS Altair.

In his junior year, Gates left Harvard to devote his energies to Microsoft, a company he had begun in 1975 with his childhood friend Paul Allen. Guided by a belief that the computer would be a valuable tool on every office desktop and in every home, they began developing software for personal computers. Gates' foresight and his vision for personal computing have been central to the success of Microsoft and the software industry.

Under Gates' leadership, Microsoft's mission has been to continually advance and improve software technology, and to make it easier, more cost-effective and more enjoyable for people to use computers. The company is committed to a long-term view, reflected in its investment of approximately $6.2 billion on research and development in the 2005 fiscal year.

In 1999, Gates wrote *Business @ the Speed of Thought*, a book that shows how computer technology can solve business problems in fundamentally new ways. The book was published in 25 languages and is available in more than 60 countries. *Business @ the Speed of Thought* has received wide critical acclaim, and was listed on the best-seller lists of the *New York Times, USA Today*, the *Wall Street Journal* and Amazon.com. Gates' previous book, *The Road Ahead*, published in 1995, held the No. 1 spot on the *New York Times'* best-seller list for seven weeks.

Gates has donated the proceeds of both books to non-profit organizations that support the use of technology in education and skills development.

In addition to his love of computers and software, Gates is interested in biotechnology. He sits on the board of ICOS, a company that specializes in protein-based and small-molecule therapeutics, and he is an investor in a number of other biotechnology companies. Gates also founded Corbis, which is developing one of the world's largest resources of visual information—a comprehensive digital archive of art and photography from public and private collections around the globe.

Philanthropy is also important to Gates. He and his wife, Melinda, have endowed a foundation with more than $27 billion (as of March 2004) to support philanthropic initiatives in the areas of global health and learning, with the hope that in the 21st century, advances in these critical areas will be available for all people. The Bill and Melinda Gates Foundation has committed more than $3.2 billion to organizations working in global health; more than $2 billion to improve learning opportunities, including the Gates Library Initiative to bring computers, Internet Access and training to public libraries in low-income communities in the United States and Canada; more than $477 million to community projects in the Pacific Northwest; and more than $488 million to special projects and annual giving campaigns.

Gates was married on Jan. 1, 1994, to Melinda French Gates. They have three children. Gates is an avid reader, and enjoys playing golf and bridge.

sample 7.3   business letter

HIGHROAD PRODUCTS CORPORATION
3333 River Bend Blvd., Suite 101
Canyon Creek, U.S.A.

November 12, 20XX

Linda Riverworth
Account Executive
Public Relations, Inc.
222 Bosworth Rd.
Lincoln, U.S.A.

Dear Linda:

I look forward to working with you in what I'm sure will be a mutually rewarding and lasting relationship. I am confident that Highroad Products Corporation and Public Relations, Inc., working together, will develop a high-quality campaign. I want to take this opportunity to familiarize you with my expectations and philosophy regarding client–agency relationships.

I expect to have an open, honest, and respectful relationship with you and your agency during the project's term. Highroad Products is built on the belief that communication is the first and necessary step to organizational success. I believe that open client–agency communication is the key to satisfying results and a positive, enduring relationship between organizations.

As the client, I will provide the information and insight into the objectives needed to create an accurate, stimulating, and graphically sophisticated presentation of the product. In return, I expect that you will give the project your most thoughtful and dedicated efforts and will supervise and guide the project from beginning to end with your experience and expertise.

I look forward to meeting you and getting the project underway. I will be in touch, but, in the meantime, please feel free to call me if you have any questions or comments.

Sincerely,

Joanne Findersmith
Director, Public Relations, Inc.

U.S. DEPARTMENT OF LABOR

Fact Sheet

SUMMARY

Protection under OSHA's Hazard Communication Standard (HCS) includes all workers exposed to hazardous chemicals in all industrial sectors. This standard is based on a simple concept—that employees have both a need and a right to know the hazards and the identities of the chemicals they are exposed to when working. They also need to know what protective measures are available to prevent adverse effects from occurring.

SCOPE OF COVERAGE

More than 30 million workers are potentially exposed to one or more chemical hazards. There are an estimated 650,000 existing hazardous chemical products, and hundreds of new ones are being introduced annually. This poses a serious problem for exposed workers and their employers.

BENEFITS

The HCS covers both physical hazards (such as flammability or the potential for explosions), and health hazards (including both acute and chronic effects). By making information available to employers and employees about these hazards, and recommended precautions for safe use, proper implementation of the HCS will result in a reduction of illnesses and injuries caused by chemicals. Employers will have the information they need to design an appropriate protective program. Employees will be better able to participate in these programs effectively when they understand the hazards involved, and to take steps to protect themselves. Together, these employer and employee actions will prevent the occurrence of adverse effects caused by the use of chemicals in the workplace.

REQUIREMENTS

The HCS established uniform requirements to make sure that the hazards of all chemicals imported into, produced, or used in U.S. workplaces are evaluated and that this hazard information is transmitted to affected employers and exposed employees.

Chemical manufacturers and importers must convey the hazard information they learn from their evaluations to downstream employers by means of labels on containers and material safety data sheets (MSDS's). In addition, all covered employers must have a hazard communication program to get this information to their employees through labels on containers, MSDS's, and training.

This program ensures that all employers receive the information they need to inform and train their employees properly and to design and put in place employee protection programs. It also provides necessary hazard information to employees so they can participate in, and support, the protective measures in place at their workplaces.

All employers in addition to those in manufacturing and importing are responsible for informing and training workers about the hazards in their workplaces, retaining warning labels, and making available MSDS's with hazardous chemicals.

Some employees deal with chemicals in sealed containers under normal conditions of use (such as in the retail trades, warehousing and truck and marine cargo handling). Employers of these employees must assure that labels affixed to incoming containers of hazardous chemicals are kept in place. They must maintain and provide access to MSDS's received, or obtain MSDS's if requested by an employee. And they must train workers on what to do in the event of a spill or leak. However, written hazard communication programs will not be required for this type of operation.

All workplaces where employees are exposed to hazardous chemicals must have a written plan which describes how the standard will be implemented in that facility. The only work operations which do not have to comply with the written plan requirements are laboratories and work operations where employees only handle chemicals in sealed containers.

The written program must reflect what employees are doing in a particular workplace. For example, the written plan must list the chemicals present at the site, indicate who is responsible for the various aspects of the program in that facility and where written materials will be made available to employees.

The written program must describe how the requirements for labels and other forms of warning, material safety data sheets, and employee information and training are going to be met in the facility.

EFFECT ON STATE RIGHT-TO-KNOW LAWS

The HCS pre-empts all state (in states without OSHA-approved job safety and health programs) or local laws which relate to an issue covered by HCS without regard to whether the state law would conflict with, complement, or supplement the federal standard, and without regard to whether the state law appears to be "at least as effective as" the federal standard.

The only state worker right-to-know laws authorized would be those established in states and jurisdictions that have OSHA-approved state programs.

These states and jurisdictions include: Alaska, Arizona, California, Connecticut (state and municipal employees only), Hawaii, Indiana, Iowa, Kentucky, Maryland, Michigan, Minnesota, Nevada, New Mexico, New York (state and municipal employees only), North Carolina, Oregon, Puerto Rico, South Carolina, Tennessee, Utah, Vermont, Virgin Islands, Virginia, Washington, and Wyoming.

FEDERAL WORKERS

Under the hazard communication standard federal workers are covered by executive order.

sample 7.5   FAQs

QWEST COMMUNICATIONS

Investor FAQs (as they appeared October 2004)

What does Qwest "do"?

Qwest is a leading communications company providing a broad mix of products and services, including Internet-based data, voice and image communications, to millions of residential and business customers. Our employees follow our Spirit of Service™ commitment by providing world-class services that exceed customers' expectations for quality, value and reliability. We have combined one of the world's fastest networks with a strong local exchange business.

When was Qwest incorporated?

Qwest was incorporated in January 1996.

How many people does Qwest employ?

As of March 31, 2004, Qwest employed approximately 46,000 people worldwide.

How long has Qwest been in business?

In 1988, Southern Pacific Telecom was established as a subsidiary of Southern Pacific Railroad to lay telecom cable. The company began offering limited long-distance services in 1991, changed its name to Qwest Communications in 1995 and incorporated in 1996 when it began construction of its nationwide fiber optic network. Qwest became a publicly-held company with its successful initial public offering (IPO) in June 1997.

In June 2000, Qwest became a company rich in history that dates back more than 120 years when the company merged with U S West, one of the original regional bell operating companies (aka Baby Bells) that resulted from the divestiture of AT&T in 1984. The seven Baby Bells were formed from the 22 operating Bell telephone companies known as the Bell System, a system that dates back to the 19th century and the invention of the telephone.

What is the stock symbol and CUSIP number for Qwest?

Qwest is traded on the New York Stock Exchange (NYSE) under the symbol "Q". Its CUSIP number is 749121109.

Does Qwest pay a dividend?

The last dividend payout was on June 29, 2001, and no plans have been announced regarding future dividend payments.

Can I buy stock directly from Qwest?

At this time, Qwest does not have direct stock purchase and sale plan. To purchase Qwest stock you must use a broker to complete your transaction.

What is Direct Registration (i.e., book-entry ownership)?

Direct Registration is a certificate-less form of stock ownership. Instead of getting a paper stock certificate, your shares are held in your name and kept electronically on our records (through our transfer agent).

The benefits of Direct Registration are:

- You do not have to worry about keeping track of your physical stock certificates;
- You avoid the cost and inconvenience of replacing your stock certificates if they are lost, stolen or destroyed;
- Your shares are automatically updated or credited in the event of a corporate action, such as an ownership transfer or stock split.

How do I sell my Qwest shares if I hold them in direct registration (book entry) or certificate form?

If you hold your shares in book entry, contact our transfer agent, The Bank of New York, to either have your shares transferred electronically to your brokerage account or issued in certificate form. If you hold your shares in certificate form, they can be sold by taking them to a broker. You cannot sell stock through Qwest or through Qwest's transfer agent, The Bank of New York.

I hold my shares in direct registration/book entry. Will I receive a yearly statement regarding my account?

If there is activity with your account (i.e., change in the number of shares, dividends paid, address change), you will receive a statement regarding your account. You will not receive a yearly statement if there is no activity on your account, but you can view your statement online at www.stockbny.com. You are also welcome to contact The Bank of New York at 877-268-2263 to have a statement sent to you.

I still have U S West Communications stock certificates. What should I do with them?

You must exchange your U S West stock certificates for Qwest shares before you can receive any past dividend payments, annual meeting materials and other stockholder information. You must also exchange your certificates prior to selling your stock. Please contact our transfer agent, The Bank of New York, for further instructions or download the Exchange Instruction Booklet.

I still have U S West Media Group stock certificates. What should I do with them?

U S West Media Group became MediaOne, which was bought by AT&T Broadband and then sold to Comcast. To exchange your U S West Media Group shares, you need to contact Comcast's transfer agent, Equiserve, at 888-883-8903.

What if I lost my stock certificate?

If you lost your stock certificate, please notify our transfer agent immediately by calling them toll free at 877-268-2263. A "stop" will be placed on the certificate to prevent any unauthorized transactions. To replace the certificate, you will need to purchase a "surety bond," which is approximately 2 percent of the current market value of the shares.

How do I change the registration information (i.e., transfer) on my shares?

You may download the stock transfer forms from our transfer agent, The Bank of New York. You may also call them at 877-268-2263 if you have questions or need assistance with the transfer of your shares.

How do I calculate my tax/cost basis?

To calculate your tax/cost basis, you may use our online calculator, download the worksheet or have a copy of one sent to you by ordering off the Request Materials site.

Where can I find the stock price for Qwest on a certain date?

To find the stock price on a specific date from Qwest's first day of trading—June 24, 1997—use the Qwest Historical Stock Lookup tool.

Where can I find the stock price for U S West on a certain date?

To find the stock price on a specific date from 1984 to 2000, use our U S West Historical Stock Lookup tool.

Where can I find information about the Qwest-U S West merger (i.e., exchange rate, closing stock price)?

Information about the Qwest-U S West merger, as well as other historical corporate actions, can be found on our History of Qwest Stock section.

sample 7.6   legislative alert

NATIONAL PTA ACTION ALERT

Tell Congress to increase education funding NOW!

In the coming days, Congress will work to approve an education funding bill for fiscal year 2005. It is critical that Congress substantially increases our nation's fiscal commitment to America's students.

Congress and the president must not back away from promises they made about accountability for all schools and in the process, there must be financial resources provided to help schools succeed. Most states are experiencing severe budget crises, and schools are strapped for funds to carry out basic educational services. Yet new demands are being placed on schools to improve student achievement, without sufficient resources to hire teachers, expand compensatory education programs, upgrade technology, repair facilities, or address any of the other challenges they face.

Without a substantial increased federal investment in education, our students will not receive the knowledge and skills needed to succeed in the 21st century. Education investment is essential if we are to ensure our economic and national security. In uncertain times, increased education investment is our best defense.

Take Action

Call and/or email your U.S. Senators and Representative and urge them to support the Senate version of the Labor-HHS-Education Appropriations bill for fiscal year 2005. You can be connected with your Representative by calling the U.S. Capitol Switchboard at 202-224-3121 and you can email your Representative by following the link below. Our voices raised together can send a powerful message to Congress that this budget has the wrong priorities for our nations' children and families.

Talking Points

Urge your U.S. Senators and Representative to support the Senate version of the Labor-HHS-Education Appropriations bill for fiscal year 2005.

America's students struggle under current funding levels:

- These cuts come at an especially inopportune time, as state education budgets continue to shrink and schools are struggling to provide quality services to increased numbers of disadvantaged students and students with special needs, while also being required to implement accountability and testing mandated under NCLB and IDEA.

- America's 4.6 million low-income students remain inadequately equipped to meet the goals of the No Child Left Behind Act. This coming year, over half of the nation's school districts will receive less Title I funding than they did last year while the federal government is demanding more of them.

- America's 6.9 million students with disabilities across the nation are receiving less than half of the federal funding for special education promised to states and local governments when the law was passed.

America's Students will struggle if funding is not increased beyond what is included in the House bill. The House bill would:

- Eliminate over 20 vital proven education programs including dropout prevention, state grants for innovative education, parental assistance centers, arts in education, and community technology centers.

- Cut vital support services necessary for student success such as comprehensive school reform, educational technology state grants, and smaller learning communities.

- Level fund many essential support services for students such as elementary and secondary school counseling, magnet schools, school libraries, and after school learning centers.

Remind your Representative that:

- A December 2002 National PTA poll of citizens who voted in the 2002 mid-term elections found that 61 percent of American citizens feel federal spending for education must be increased to fulfill the commitments made in NCLB. Further, 74 percent felt the law would not be effective if Congress failed to provide the funding authorized in the law.

- 5 Cents Makes Sense: Increasing federal education funding from 2.7 cents to 5 cents would enable schools to provide universal preschool/early childhood education, recruit, hire, and train new, quality teachers to reduce class size and serve 2.4 million low income students with Title I services.

Your Message

This system requires that you provide your name and contact information. This information will not be used for any purpose other than to identify you to the recipient.

Subject:

Education Funding for 2005

Required text: This text will be included in your message.

As a concerned constituent and voter, I write to you on behalf of National PTA, an organization of 6 million parents, teachers, students, and child advocates. I urge you to support an education appropriations bill that substantially increases our nation's fiscal commitment to America's students. I urge you to support the Senate version of the Labor-HHS-Education Appropriations bill for fiscal year 2005.

The House version of the Labor-HHS-Education Appropriations bill for fiscal year 2005 provides the smallest increase for America's students in nearly a decade at a mere 3.6 percent increase. At the same time, the White House has proposed to cut education funding by $5 billion over the next five years, Congress must not allow this to occur. The Senate version of the education funding bill provides a $3.2 billion, or 5.7 percent, increase for education over fiscal year 2004. Additionally, the Senate version would restore most of the programs eliminated in the House bill and the President's proposed budget.

Congress and the president must not back away from promises they made about accountability for all schools and in the process, there must be financial resources provided to help schools succeed. Most states are experiencing severe budget crises, and schools are strapped for funds to carry out basic educational services. Yet new demands are being placed on schools to improve student achievement, without sufficient resources to hire teachers, expand compensatory education programs, upgrade technology, repair facilities, or address any of the other challenges they face.

Without a substantial increased federal investment in education, our students will not receive the knowledge and skills needed to succeed in the 21st century. Education investment is essential if we are to ensure our economic and national security. In uncertain times, increased education investment is our best defense. I urge you to support the Senate version of the Labor-HHS-Education Appropriations bill for fiscal year 2005.

Thank you for your consideration of my views.

LEGISLATIVE ALERT!
VALDOSTA-LOWNDES COUNTY CHAMBER MEMBERS
TAKE ACTION!

Civil Justice Reform Needs Immediate Action

Senate Bill 133: the Common Sense Civil Justice Reform Act, has passed from Senate Judiciary Committee and will be heard on the Senate floor *Thursday morning*, March 27. This bill is supported by the Chamber on the 2003 Legislative Agenda for Business. Georgia's healthcare industry, doctors, hospitals, and nursing homes, are struggling to pay unaffordable medical malpractice insurance premiums resulting from ever-rising jury awards. Passage of this agenda item with its original provisions will bring about a much needed balance in the system under which plaintiffs and defendants operate. The result for Georgia business: new companies will seek to do business here and existing business will expand, creating more jobs and more tax revenue for the state.

What YOU can do

1. **Please call or email Senators and ask them to vote YES on SB 133 and YES on all amendments listed:** Cap on non-economic damages in medical malpractice cases, joint and several liability, comparative negligence, expert witness rule, emergency room provision.

2. You will most likely reach their Capitol secretaries. Simply leave a message asking them for support as outlined above. Include your name and business name to lend further credibilty to your request.

3. Thank them for their support.

Senate Members (phone number and email address):

Senator David Adelman (Decatur), (404) 463-1376, dadelman@legis.state.ga.us
Senator Don Balfour (Snellville), (404) 656-0095, ss9balfour@aol.com
Senator Peg Blitch (Homerville), (404) 656-0053, pblitch@legis.state.ga.us
Senator Rooney Bowen (Cordele), (404) 656-7580, rbowen@legis.state.ga.us
Senator Robert Brown (Macon), (404) 656-5035, rbrown@legis.state.ga.us
Senator Joey Brush (Martinez), (404) 657-0406, jbrush@legis.state.ga.us
Senator John Bulloch (Ochlocknee), (404) 463-8056, jbulloch@rose.net
Senator Gloria Butler (Clarkston), (404) 656-0075, gbutler@legis.state.ga.us

Senator Casey Cagle (Gainesville), (404) 656-6578, kccagle@bellsouth.net

Senator Don Cheeks (Augusta), (404) 656-0045, dcheeks@legis.state.ga.us

Senator Chuck Clay (Marietta), (404) 463-1318, cclay@bcwr.com

Senator Ginger Collins (Smyrna), (404) 656-5114, gcollins10@cs.com

Senator Mike Crotts (Atlanta), (404) 656-0071, mcrotts@legis.state.ga.us

Senator Nathan Dean (Rockmart), (404) 656-5121, ndean@legis.state.ga.us

Senator Vincent Fort (Atlanta), (404) 656-5091, vfort@legis.state.ga.us

Senator Hugh Gillis (Soperton), (404) 656-5080, hgillis@legis.state.ga.us

Senator Tim Golden (Valdosta), (404) 656-0082, tgolden@legis.state.ga.us

Senator Randy Hall (Augusta), (404) 463-1363, rhall@huntermaclean.com

Senator Bill Hamrick (Douglasville), (404) 656-0036, bhamrick@legis.state.ga.us

Senator Ed Harbison (Columbus), (404) 656-0074, eharbison@legis.state.ga.us

Senator Seth Harp (Midland), (404) 463-3931, sethharp@aol.com

Senator Steve Henson (Tucker), (404) 463-1316, stevehenson@mindspring.com

Senator Jack Hill (Reidsville), (404) 656-5038, jhill@legis.state.ga.us

Senator George Hooks (Americus), (404) 656-0065, ghooks@legis.state.ga.us

Senator Ralph Hudgens (Comer), (404) 463-1361, ralphhudgens@aol.com

Senator Carol Jackson (Cleveland), (404) 656-0094, senatorjackson@alltel.net

Senator Eric Johnson (Savannah), (404) 656-5109, ejohnson@legis.state.ga.us

Senator René Kemp (Hinesville), (404) 656-0070, rkemp@legis.state.ga.us

Senator Brian Kemp (Athens), (404) 463-1366, bkemp@legis.state.ga.us

Senator Robert Lamutt (Marietta), (404) 656-5085, rlamutt@mindspring.com

Senator Dan Lee (LaGrange), (404) 651-7738, danlee@mindspring.com

Senator Liane Levetan (Atlanta), (404) 463-1374, llevetan@attbi.com

Senator Michael Meyer von Bremen (Albany), (404) 656-0037, mmeyer@legis
.state.ga.us

Senator Dan Moody (Alpharetta), (404) 463-8055, danmoody@bellsouth.net

Senator Jeff Mullis (Chickamauga), (404) 656-0057, jmullis@legis.state.ga.us

Senator Tom Price (Roswell), (404) 656-0040, tomprice@legis.state.ga.us

Senator Kasim Reed (Atlanta), (404) 463-1379, kreed@legis.state.ga.us

Senator Mitch Seabaugh (Sharpsburg), (404) 656-6446, gasenate28@aol.com

Senator Valencia Seay (College Park), (404) 656-5095, vseay@legis.state.ga.us

Senator David Shafer (Duluth), (404) 656-0048, dshafer@legis.state.ga.us

Senator Faye Smith (Milledgeville), (404) 656-0044, sensmith@accucomm.net

Senator Preston Smith (Rome), (404) 463-1369, pwsmith@legis.state.ga.us

Senator Mary Squires (Norcross), (404) 463-1378, senatorsquires@yahoo.com

Senator Terrell Starr (Jonesboro), (404) 656-7586, tstarr@legis.state.ga.us

Senator Bill Stephens (Canton), (404) 651-7738, bstephens@legis.state.ga.us

Senator Connie Stokes (Decatur), (404) 651-7741, cstokes@legis.state.ga.us

Senator Charlie Tanksley (Marietta), (404) 656-0150, charlie@browningtanksley.com

Senator Horacena Tate (Atlanta), (404) 463-8053, htate@legis.state.ga.us

Senator Regina Thomas (Savannah), (404) 463-7784, rthomas@legis.state.ga.us

Senator Nadine Thomas (Decatur), (404) 656-0078, nthomas@legis.state.ga.us

Senator Don Thomas (Dalton), (404) 656-6436, dthomas@legis.state.ga.us

Senator Steve Thompson (Powder Springs), (404) 656-0083, sthompson@legis
.state.ga.us

Senator Ross Tolleson (Perry), (404) 463-8056, rosstolleson@alltel.net

Senator Rene'e Unterman (Loganville), (404) 463-1368, reneeu@bellsouth.net

Senator Tommie Williams (Lyons), (404) 656-0089, tommie@tommiewilliams.com

Senator Sam Zamarripa (Atlanta), (404) 463-8054, sam@zamarripa.com

Please let us know of your contact with these senators! Contact Mary Bione at the Chamber (229) 247-8100 or email mbione@valdostachamber.com

sample 7.8   letter invitation

EYEWAVES, INC.
4444 Paveway Rd.
Mountain Meadow, U.S.A.

Rodney Hamperfeld
Chief Executive Officer

July 3, 20XX

Steve Penwriter
Editor
Traveling Traveler Magazine
4444 Rockbend Blvd.
Grand River, U.S.A.

Dear Mr. Penwriter:

I am inviting you to become part of entertainment history. You are invited to next month's world premiere of *Saturn Signals Life* and the introduction of our new product that promises to change the way viewers experience entertainment.

The world premiere will be like many other star-studded openings with one unique twist. Instead of watching *Saturn Signals Life* on the big screen, stars such as Tom Foot and Julia Hand will experience the movie on individually worn Eyewaves, a personal video monitor that is worn comfortably over a person's eyes and connects to DVD players. This device will give its users complete control over their entertainment options, a feature that is sure to appeal to travelers of planes, cars, and trains. You are being invited because of the prestige that your magazine has with distinguished business travelers.

The premiere will be held at the BZB Theater in Holywood at 8 P.M. on Thursday, July 15, 20XX. You will be seated in the theater with other distinguished professionals and will receive as a gift your own Eyewaves device. You are also invited to a reception following the movie to meet the cast of *Saturn Signals Life* to discuss what they think of our new product.

A formal invitation to this exciting event will arrive in several days along with a VIP parking pass, directions to the theater, and an RSVP card.

I look forward to having you join us.

Sincerely,

Rodney Hamperfeld

sample 7.9   letter to customers

THE CUSTOMER COMES FIRST WITH HUD

Customer Satisfaction Report, November 1996

U.S. Department of Housing and Urban Development

Table of Contents

An Open Letter to HUD Customers

During the past four years, I have concentrated on transforming HUD into a right-side up, "community first" Cabinet agency focused on customer service. To accomplish this, HUD has developed customer service standards and implemented new and more effective ways of communicating with you - our customers. We have also streamlined operations, eliminated or simplified regulations, and provided customer relations training to HUD staff.

But, most importantly, we listened to you. We listened to you on direct telephone calls, at forums, in focus groups, on the World Wide Web, and in numerous other ways. We listened and responded by changing the way we do business and by changing our programs to suit your needs.

President Clinton directed Federal agencies to undertake a "continual reform of the executive branch's management practices and operations to provide service to the public that matches or exceeds the best service available in the private sector." Further, the President directed Federal agencies to set customer service standards, obtain customer feedback, measure their performance against these standards, and use the results to change the way they do business.

In response to those directives, I am pleased to share HUD's first Customer Satisfaction Report, which lets you—our customers—know how well we are serving you.

Thank you. We could not have made these changes without your support.

Henry Cisneros

PRODUCTION RESOURCE GROUP

To Our Valued Customers:

It is indeed a pleasure for us to announce to you today that the merger between PRG and VLPS has been completed. We have met all required conditions, and the period of regulatory review has expired. As of July 9, 2004 we have become one company—the new PRG.

Our name has been officially changed to Production Resource Group, with operating divisions PRG Lighting, PRG Audio, PRG Scenic Technologies and Showpay.

As we move quickly to ensure that our integration is a seamless one, we anticipate no interruptions in our service to you. In fact, we expect there will be many positive changes:

- We are now able to offer you a much greater array of resources, with access to the best and most advanced production solutions on the market today.

- With our increased locations and larger inventories worldwide, you can now benefit from cost savings associated with greater efficiencies in distribution and economies of scale.

- Our research and development has become a top priority, so you will always have access to the most technologically advanced equipment available.

By now, you have been contacted personally by a member of our team to discuss the merger and its impact on you. We trust that we were able to answer all your questions adequately, given the limitations imposed on us at that time. Now, with the merger complete, we stand ready to address any other concerns you may have.

To those of you who currently work with representatives of both PRG and VLPS, we will institute changes only after close consultation with you.

This merger is an historic change for the entertainment industry, one that we believe will truly benefit you. We thank you for your business, and we look forward to continuing our work with you.

Sincerely,

Jere Harris   Rusty Brutsché
Chairman   *Vice Chairman*

Courtesy of Jeremiah J. Harris with assistance of RFBinder Partners.

sample 7.11   letter to government

CENTRAL MICHIGAN UNIVERSITY

Dear Friend of CMU:

Central Michigan University continues to need your help in Lansing. A $1.3 billion shortfall in the state's budget for the current fiscal year will lead to another round of budget cuts for our universities, including CMU. With demand for public higher education increasing and revenues decreasing, CMU faces a significant threat to its ability to remain accessible to deserving students.

Please write or e-mail our state's elected officials and express your support for CMU—and for Michigan public higher education. Your communication with Michigan's leaders can help influence decisions and preserve the quality of our state's public higher education. The advocacy talking points on this Web site provide information that will be useful in your correspondence.

With Michigan lagging behind the rest of the nation in terms of the number of citizens with undergraduate degrees, CMU and its peers are charged with helping change this situation for the better. However, cuts in state funding for higher education have made this increasingly difficult to achieve. Additional cuts to public higher education funding would have truly devastating effects on Michigan's ability to educate its residents.

It is my hope that you will take a moment to communicate your support for CMU and public higher education with the individuals who have the power to determine who and what will receive funding. Your involvement makes an important difference.

Sincerely,

Mike Rao
President

TECHNOLOGY TOOLS CORPORATION
55666 Circuit Drive
Highport, U.S.A.

George Tools
Chief Executive Officer

November 22, 20XX

John Johnson
Executive Director
Association of Businesses
Capital Highway
Rutherford, U.S.A.

Dear John:

The technology companies in this state are concerned about efforts in the current legislative session to impose a state tax on congeneric mergers. As you know, this state is home to hundreds of technology companies and mergers and acquisitions are a big part of the industry dynamic.

I am writing as a member of the association to ask that you discuss this matter with the board and hopefully vote to have the organization take a position against House Bill 9934.

If you like, I will be happy to make a full presentation on the ill-conceived proposal to you and your staff and also to the board. We are very concerned about getting this measure stopped dead in its tracks. It's not healthy for us or for the state.

Thanks. I will follow up with a call this week.

Sincerely,

George Tools

sample 7.13   letter to parents

VANCOUVER PUBLIC SCHOOLS
State of Washington

Dear Parents and Community Patrons:

With public schools across the nation facing federal and state mandates to increase student achievement, we are fortunate in Vancouver to have a solid school system and a history of parent and community support. We pledge to continue improving education and focusing on the needs of our children and youth.

I would like to share with you some developments that are shaping public education in America. Under state and federal legislation, schools are being held accountable to improve education for all students, and that's a positive direction. States and school districts are developing rigorous academic standards, and teachers are using data from tests and other sources to ensure that students are learning what they need to know and be able to do in the 21st century.

The Elementary and Secondary Education Act (ESEA), reauthorized in 1992 as "No Child Left Behind" (NCLB), was written with a good purpose—to raise expectations for all schools and all students. In Vancouver Public Schools, we have focused on what's most important—the learner. More than a decade before the enactment of NCLB, our board of directors already had engaged the community in creating vision, mission and long-range goal statements that affirmed our commitment to the success of each student.

Every Vancouver school has a school improvement plan that is evaluated annually and altered to capitalize on strengths and to address areas of weakness. We use a variety of assessments to evaluate how students are doing and to guide their education. When needs are identified at schools, we send support teams to those schools to work with teachers. Mentoring and tutoring programs are available to help struggling students. Throughout the district, we promote a strong foundation of literacy at all grade levels.

We serve a wonderfully diverse mix of students in Vancouver. The number of children who speak English as a second language is greater here than in most communities, and we act as a regional service center for many special education students. We offer advanced academic courses and several high school magnet programs, which allow students to build on their unique abilities, talents and interests. We provide a wide range of educational opportunities and school access to every young person in our community.

According to NCLB, all students must meet the same high proficiency levels in reading and mathematics by 2014. This unprecedented national goal presents a daunting challenge given the diversity and magnitude of student and family needs. Realistically, we know that not every child comes to school with the same advantages, and not every child will meet the standards in the same way or at the same time. We are committed to helping each student reach her or his full potential.

Under the new federal legislation, every school and school district has targets that must be met to achieve Adequate Yearly Progress (AYP). Progress is determined by the Washington Assessment of Student Learning (WASL) scores of 4th, 7th and 10th graders as well as other factors. Student achievement data for each school are analyzed in 37 different categories, including racial groups, children who have not yet learned English, students with all levels and kinds of disabilities, and economically disadvantaged students. To make AYP, a school or district must meet the same high standards for all student groups.

Please do not hesitate to contact the school district if you would like to receive more information about "No Child Left Behind" and its impact on our schools and community.

Sincerely,

John W. Erickson, Ph.D.
Superintendent
Vancouver Public Schools

sample 7.14   media advisory or alert

INTEL CORPORATION

Intel To Announce Server Technology Innovation During March 2 Web Cast With Thomson Financial

What: Intel will announce enhancements to its server processor family and discuss the benefits of deploying standards-based enterprise systems during a live web cast broadcast from Thomson Financial in New York. The web cast will include a 30-minute question and answer session.

When: Tuesday, March 2
11 A.M.–noon, EST

Who: Richard Dracott
General Manager, Enterprise Marketing & Planning Intel Corporation

Jeremy Lehman
Senior Vice President, Technology
Thomson Financial

Call-in: To listen to the call and participate in the question and answer session, dial:
Domestic dial-in number: (877) 396-7472
International dial-in number: (706) 679-6071

Website: To view the content for the briefing, go to: http://www.firstcallevents .com/service/aiwz401400155gfl2.html

Contact:

INTEL CORPORATION

'Prepare to be Entertained' with Intel at Digital Life 2004

Hear:
Shared will be details of the emerging digital home experience and new products that are revolutionizing the way people experience entertainment in the home.

'Prepare to be Entertained' keynote

Robert Crooke, vice president, Desktop Platforms Group and general manager, Desktop Marketing and Strategic Planning, Intel Corporation.
Thursday, Oct. 14, 2–3 P.M. EDT

Digital Life 2004 (Oct. 14-15)
Jacob K. Javits Convention Center, Special Events Hall, New York City

See:
Check out Intel's exhibit at Digital Life 2004 (Booth #1536) showcasing some of the latest digital technologies for the home, including the first Entertainment PCs available from major PC manufacturers in time for the holiday season. Designed to simply and easily interact with a television using a remote control, the Entertainment PC combines the functionality of a home's audio and video devices with the power of a high-performance multimedia computer. Attendees will also be able to see the latest notebooks designed for mobile entertainment and new portable media players that allow you to create, edit, store, manage and share digital content in and around the home and on-the-go.

Experience:
Taste the digital lifestyle by viewing digital home movies and photos, checking out high-definition movies and experiencing 10-foot wireless gaming on a large plasma screen in the Home Zone. Challenge others to a wireless gaming face-off using the latest high-performance desktop and mobile PCs. Scan the latest online surf report using the Intel@ Centrino™ mobile technology wireless surfboard.

Contact:

sample 7.15   media advisory

ALCOA MEDIA ADVISORY

WHO: Officials from AIRBUS and ALCOA, local, state and government officials, and hundreds of employees from Alcoa Mill Products' Davenport Works in Riverdale, IA.

WHAT: Celebrate production of the largest commercial airplane in the world (the Airbus A380) and its impact in supporting American jobs, including increases at Alcoa Mill Products' Davenport Works facility.

WHERE: Alcoa Mill Products - Davenport Works
        Learning Center
        4900 State Street
        Riverdale, Iowa
        United States

WHEN: Tuesday, June 29, 2004 at 11:00 A.M. (Central Time)

WHY: The Davenport Works celebration of the new Airbus A380, a 555-seat aircraft, is the second of three planned by Alcoa and Airbus (the first was held last month in Torrance, California) to hail the creation and retention of American jobs in the development of the A380.

STATEMENT

Bill Jeffery, L.LB., National Coordinator

Centre for Science in the Public Interest at Health Canada's
Media briefing on the final mandatory nutrition labelling rules

Room 0115C, Lower Level
Brooke-Claxton Building
Tunney's Pasture
Ottawa, Ontario

January 2, 2003

Good afternoon. My name is Bill Jeffery. I am the National Coordinator of the Centre for Science in the Public Interest.

The Centre for Science in the Public Interest (CSPI) is an independent consumer health advocacy organization with offices in Ottawa and Washington, D.C. CSPI is supported by over 100,000 Canadian subscribers to our *Nutrition Action Healthletter*. I am pleased to participate in this historic event on behalf of CSPI. We have advocated mandatory nutrition labelling since 1997 when we were joined in that effort by the Alliance for Food Label Reform—a coalition of nonprofit groups representing two million consumers, scientists, and health professionals.

This is a landmark event for health promotion in Canada. Preventable diet-related disease causes tens of thousands of premature deaths and costs the economy $5.3 billion each year. The new nutrition labels will help consumers improve their diets and reduce their risk of heart disease, cancer, and diabetes. Agriculture and Agri-food Canada estimates that the new labels will save Canadians more than $5 billion over the next two decades as a result of reduced health-care costs and improved productivity.

Under the old, market-driven system, nutrition labelling appeared on only about half of all food labels, was incomplete (often revealing the good news while concealing the bad news about the nutrient content of a food), was based on unrealistic serving sizes (over which manufacturers had discretion), and failed to inform consumers how much saturated fat, sodium, fibre, and other nutrients a food contributed to the amounts one should be eating daily to be healthy.

Mandatory labelling rules will ensure that nutrition information appears on practically all foods, is displayed in a format that is easy to read and interpret, and discloses amounts of most nutrients that are important to the public's health. The new labels will aid consumer choice and encourage manufacturers to improve the nutritional quality of their products.

Today the Government of Canada is taking a very important step in the direction advocated by the Romanow Commission, and helping to make our public health-care system a bit more sustainable as a result of improvements in health as consumers begin to use the new labels to improve their diets.

Health Canada officials, including Dr. Margaret Cheney, Mary Bush and Pat Steele among many others, and Ministers Anne McLellan and Allan Rock under whose watch these regulations were drafted all deserve to be commended. The federal government deserves special credit for sustaining the proposed method for disclosing amounts of *trans* fat (along with saturated fat) on nutrition labels. *Trans* fats—found in margarine and many baked and deep fried starchy foods that contain partially hydrogenated vegetable oils—promote high levels of LDL serum cholesterol which is an important risk factor in the development of cardiovascular disease. Many food companies lobbied hard to block, delay or water down trans fat labelling requirements in Canada, and food companies have stymied similar regulatory efforts in the United States for years.

I do not want to detract from our strong support for these new rules, but I would be remiss if I did not identify three areas for future improvement:

- First, mandatory nutrition labelling should apply to *all* fresh meat, poultry and seafood, not just ground beef and prepared meats.

- Second, health marketing claims should *not* be permitted on foods like whole (3.25%) milk or high-fat cheeses—which, though calcium-rich, are high in saturated fat. Such foods may decrease the risk of one disease (like osteoporosis), but increase the risk of another (like heart disease).

- Third, the amounts of "added sugars" (not just "total sugars") should be disclosed on labels. It is the added sugars that promote obesity, tooth decay, and dilute the nutritional quality of the diet.

CSPI will continue to advocate such changes and looks forward to working with many of you here today.

Also, we must now turn our attention to nutrition promotion and physical activity efforts that can lead to further improvements in public health. I look forward to working with ministries of health and legislators at all levels of government to help develop additional public policy changes that will help reduce the burden of preventable diet-related disease in Canada.

Thank-you.

MEMO

TUESDAY, NOVEMBER 12, 20XX

TO: MANAGEMENT STAFF
FROM: LEO LEONARD

SUBJECT: HEADQUARTERS RELOCATION

KingsRings has finalized plans to relocate headquarters to Portland, Oregon, in May 20XX. An announcement will be made to all employees at 3 PM today after which you may feel free to discuss the news with anyone. There will be a meeting tomorrow, November 19, at 8 AM, in the employee cafeteria to give everyone detailed background on the decision to move and to answer questions.

In recent years, we have experienced unprecedented sales growth, the majority of which comes from the Pacific Northwest. In addition, the company has outgrown its facility here due to greater product demand. After much thought and deliberation, it has been decided that relocation to Portland is the most suitable course of action for KingsRings to continue providing customers with the superior quality products they have come to expect while being geographically closer to our largest market.

We understand the troublesome implications of relocation. We wish to make the transition as easy and as stress-free as possible, and to assist in this process, a relocation committee has been established to provide assistance with transfer-related issues, as well as job-placement services.

Attached to this memo is a list of employees who are being offered the opportunity to relocate. I would like you to make sure that all employees are made aware of their status before the end of the workday. The move will be made at least sixty days after this announcement.

L.L.

sample 7.18   memo to employees

MEMO

Date: September 21, 2001

To: All Delta Employees Worldwide

From: Fred Reid, President and Chief Operating Officer

Subject: TOLERANCE

Dear Colleagues,

Last Tuesday's tragedy has affected us in ways that would have seemed inconceivable as little as two weeks ago. Unfortunately, we've seen some Americans become suspicious of people of other cultures—especially those of Mideast descent. And across the airline industry, we've heard stories of passengers being deplaned because of their skin color or the sound of their accents.

We cannot afford to follow this tragic behavior. It is exactly what our enemies are striving for: the end of our open, diverse, and tolerant way of life.

Delta's *Code of Ethics and Business Conduct* states that, "Delta has an uncompromising policy never to discriminate against customers on the basis of race, gender, age, national origin, disability, sexual orientation or similar classifications. The law mandates this policy—discrimination is not only illegal, it is wrong and will not be tolerated."

Safety is our first priority at Delta, and we will not compromise that. If a passenger behaves suspiciously or in a manner that suggests a possible security concern while in the airport or on board our aircraft, we should always take action to investigate the behavior. But our response must be based on the passenger's conduct, not on race or national origin.

Last Tuesday's events changed the way airlines do business from now on, not only in America, but throughout the world. Already, Delta has instituted strict security measures designed to make certain those intent on evil do not reach our airplanes. And our security measures continue to evolve and tighten.

Please continue to be observant and vigilant when enforcing security that protects our passengers and our people. But don't let last Tuesday's events change you into someone suspicious of people just because of the way they look—if you do that, then the terrorists will have won.

Thank you for the strength of character you've shown since the sad events last week. You make me proud to work with you.

MICROSOFT CORPORATION: MISSION AND VALUES

June 25, 2003

Over the last three decades, technology has transformed the way we work, play, and communicate. Today, we access information and people from around the world in an instant. Groundbreaking technologies have opened the door to innovations in every field of human endeavor, delivering new opportunity, convenience, and value to our lives.

Since its founding in 1975, Microsoft has been a leader in this transformation. As a reflection of that role—and to help us focus on the opportunities that lie ahead—we have established and embraced a new corporate mission.

Microsoft's mission: To enable people and businesses throughout the world to realize their full potential.

Delivering on Our Mission

The tenets central to accomplishing our mission stem from our core company values:

Broad Customer Connection

Connecting with customers, understanding their needs and how they use technology, and providing value through information and support to help them realize their potential.

A Global, Inclusive Approach

Thinking and acting globally, enabling a diverse workforce that generates innovative decision-making for a broad spectrum of customers and partners, innovating to lower the costs of technology, and showing leadership in supporting the communities in which we work and live.

Excellence

In everything we do.

Trustworthy Computing

Deepening customer trust through the quality of our products and services, our responsiveness and accountability, and our predictability in everything we do.

Great People with Great Values

Delivering on our mission requires great people who are bright, creative, and energetic, and who share the following values:

- Integrity and honesty.

- Passion for customers, partners, and technology.

- Open and respectful with others and dedicated to making them better.

- Willingness to take on big challenges and see them through.

- Self-critical, questioning, and committed to personal excellence and self-improvement.

- Accountable for commitments, results, and quality to customers, shareholders, partners, and employees.

Innovative and Responsible Platform Leadership

Expanding platform innovation, benefits, and opportunities for customers and partners; openness in discussing our future directions; getting feedback; and working with others to ensure that their products and our platforms work well together.

Enabling People to Do New Things

Broadening choices for customers by identifying new areas of business; incubating new products; integrating new customer scenarios into existing businesses; exploring acquisitions of key talent and experience; and integrating more deeply with new and existing partners.

At Microsoft, we're committed to our mission of helping our customers scale new heights and achieve goals they never thought possible.

AWB MISSION STATEMENT

The Association of Washington Business' purpose is to create an economic climate in which business and citizens can be successful. It accomplishes this purpose by providing leadership in Washington State public policy formation with the executive offices, legislature and regulatory agencies and by providing value-added member services.

—September 1999

AWB Vision Statement

The vision of the Association of Washington Business for the State of Washington is a rising standard of living and an improved quality of life for the state's citizens and the creation of economic resources for state and local government to provide essential public services.

This vision will be achieved through a framework of public policy—laws and regulations—that encourage the creation of private sector jobs, increased productivity, economic growth, private ownership of property, perpetuation of private entrepreneurship and initiative, and the continued profitability of the private sector.

—Adopted in 1990

sample 7.21   news release

ALCOA SELECTED TO COLLABORATE WITH FERRARI ON NEXT-GENERATION ALUMINUM SPACEFRAME

MODENA, Italy–(BUSINESS WIRE)–Jan. 5, 2004–Alcoa (NYSE:AA) Strategic Partner uses its Pan-European Resources to Provide Aluminum Structural Solutions for High-Performance Sports Car Maker's Latest Model: the 612 Scaglietti.

Alcoa Advanced Transportation Systems (AATS) announced today that it has been selected by Ferrari as the sole provider for the next-generation aluminum spaceframe for its new, 12-cylinder, front engine 2+2 sports car, the 612 Scaglietti. Full-series production begins this year.

"Alcoa is pleased to have been chosen to collaborate with Ferrari once again to help meet the design, interior space and performance challenges of what is destined to become one of the world's most exciting automobiles," said Rick Milner, President of Alcoa Automotive Transportation Systems. "The Ferrari 360 Modena has successfully demonstrated the capability of a highly-engineered aluminum structure to significantly increase interior space and occupant comfort while not only maintaining, but improving, driving performance. We also believe that the demonstrated safety performance of Alcoa's aluminum structures will be very important in helping Ferrari satisfy Europe's demanding safety requirements."

Alcoa's Pan-European Connections

Production of Ferrari spaceframe components illustrates Alcoa's pan-European manufacturing and supply capabilities. Cast, extruded and fabricated components are produced in Hungary, Germany and the Netherlands and shipped to Modena, Italy, where they are assembled into the finished spaceframe at an Alcoa facility inside Ferrari's Scaglietti Works.

Ferrari/Alcoa History

Ferrari and Alcoa first began working together in 1994, when the company was seeking a development partner for an aluminum-structured vehicle to replace its older models. In June of that year, Alcoa assumed the primary design and engineering role for the aluminum spaceframe body structure development, with full production beginning in 1998. To date, Alcoa has supplied more than 12,000 frames to Ferrari for its Modena model—a model recognized today as one of the best performing sports cars in the world.

Alcoa is the world's leading producer of primary aluminum, fabricated aluminum and alumina, and is active in all major aspects of the industry. Alcoa serves the aerospace, automotive, packaging, building and construction, commercial transportation and industrial markets, bringing design, engineering, production and other capabilities of Alcoa's businesses to customers.

In addition to aluminum products and components, Alcoa also markets consumer brands including Reynolds Wrap® foils and plastic wraps, Alcoa® wheels, and Baco® household wraps. Among its other businesses are vinyl siding, closures, precision castings, and electrical distribution systems for cars and trucks. The company has 127,000 employees in 41 countries. More information can be found at www.alcoa.com.

sample 7.22   news release

INTEL REVEALS FIRST ENTERTAINMENT PCs SIGNALING NEW ERA OF DIGITAL HOME ENTERTAINMENT

DIGITAL LIFE, New York, Oct. 14, 2004—In a keynote speech here today, Intel Corporation executive Robert Crooke outlined products and technology trends that will revolutionize the way people experience entertainment in their homes. The company also unveiled several of the first available Entertainment PCs.

Soaring sales of digital cameras, MP3 players, CD/DVD players, digital TVs, personal video recorders and a slew of other digital devices highlight the pervasiveness of digital entertainment. Consumers who want to enjoy this vast selection of digital content on their home TVs and stereos now have an easier way to do so due to a new category of PCs: the Entertainment PC.

The media "command center" of the digital home, Entertainment PCs are designed to sit on an entertainment rack and work with a television set with a remote control. The Entertainment PC combines the functionality of home audio and video devices with the power of a high-performance multimedia computer.

Easy to use, Entertainment PCs keep digital content in one convenient, central location, accessible via remote control or wireless keyboard. Entertainment PCs act as a combined CD/DVD player and recorder, FM stereo and music server, and personal video recorder. By adding a broadband connection, an Entertainment PC becomes an on-demand entertainment store, allowing users to download the latest movies, music, news and more.

"Entertainment PCs are an all-in-one digital film vault, music collection, photo gallery and game room," said Crooke, Intel general manager of Desktop Marketing and Strategic Planning. "With an Entertainment PC, you can experience cinematic quality entertainment at home without ever leaving your favorite chair."

Based on Intel® Pentium® 4 processors supporting Hyper-Threading Technology and the Intel® 915 Express Chipset, high performance Entertainment PCs have the power to simultaneously perform demanding tasks, such as watching a DVD while recording a live TV program or playing an interactive game while downloading a movie in the background.

Now available from a number of manufacturers, Entertainment PCs are just one of the hot items for the holiday season. Other new products include the latest Intel® Centrino™ mobile technology-based entertainment notebooks and Intel® XScale™ processor-based portable media players.

Consumers can see these and other innovative products at the Intel exhibit at Digital Life (Booth #1536). Attendees can experience the digital lifestyle, viewing digital home movies and photos, checking out high-definition movies and experiencing wireless gaming on a large plasma screen. They can challenge others to a PC gaming face-off using the latest high-performance desktop and mobile PCs. Or they can scan the latest online surf report using the Intel Centrino mobile technology wireless surfboard.

Intel, the world's largest chip maker, is also a leading manufacturer of computer, networking and communications products. Additional information about Intel is available at www.intel.com/pressroom.

Intel, the Intel logo, Pentium, Centrino and XScale are marks or registered trademarks of Intel Corporation in the United States and other countries.

*Other names and brands may be claimed as the property of others.

[1]Hyper-Threading Technology requires a computer system with an Intel? Pentium? 4 processor supporting Hyper-Threading Technology and an HT Technology enabled chipset, BIOS and operating system. Performance will vary depending on the specific hardware and software you use. See www.intel .com/info/hyperthreading/ for more information including details on which processors support HT Technology.

sample 7.23   news release

WASHINGTON ROUNDTABLE NAMES NEW PRESIDENT

SEATTLE—June 28, 2004—The Washington Roundtable, a public policy organization comprised of CEOs from Washington's 40 major employers, today named Stephen F. Mullin as president of the organization. Mullin previously served as the Roundtable's vice president for eight years.

"As Washington slowly emerges from recession, it is more important than ever that the business community stay highly engaged in advancing policy issues that are critical to making this state a better place to live and do business. Steve will serve the Roundtable well in this effort. He clearly understands the challenges facing our state and its employers. He brings a demonstrated record of success working with policymakers and leveraging the expertise and knowledge of the Roundtable board to accomplish its objectives," said William W. Krippaehne, Jr., president and CEO of Fisher Communications and Roundtable chair.

"I am honored to lead an organization comprised of such well-respected state business leaders and I am excited to continue the hard work the Roundtable has put into building a better Washington," Mullin said. "Our state is showing signs of economic recovery, but there is still much more work to be done to rebuild our economy. I look forward to this challenge and to continued close collaboration with policymakers, business and community leaders across our state."

Mullin is a native of Washington state and brings more than 20 years of public policy experience. Prior to joining the Roundtable as vice president in 1996, Mullin served as executive director of the Partnership for Learning, an independent organization focused on improving public awareness and understanding of state education reform. Before that, he served as a public policy consultant and was involved in a number of statewide referendum and political campaigns. He also served as an aide to U.S. Senator Slade Gorton early in his career.

Mullin serves as secretary/treasurer of the Partnership for Learning and a board member of the Alliance for Education. He is a member of the priority based budgeting guidance team in Snohomish County and the Community Development Roundtable. He holds a master's degree in public administration from the University of Washington and a bachelor of arts degree from Middlebury College.

About the Washington Roundtable

The Washington Roundtable is a nonprofit public policy organization comprised of 40 chief executives representing major private sector employers throughout Washington state. Since 1983, the Roundtable has worked to create positive change on critical policy issues that foster economic growth, generate jobs and improve quality of life for Washingtonians. Areas of focus include economic climate, state fiscal policy and public education.

sample 7.24   news release

NEWS

For Immediate Release

Contact: Carol Philips
Marketing and Public Relations Manager
Phone: (541) 682-8380
Fax: (541) 682-5426
carol.l.philips@ci.eugene.or.us

HULT CENTER PRESENTS
AMAZONES: The Women Master Drummers of Guinea

EUGENE, Ore.—August 24, 2004—The Hult Center presents the U.S. premiere performance of Amazones: The Women Master Drummers of Guinea on Thursday, Sept. 30 at 8 P.M. in Silva Concert Hall. Amazones is joined by the traditional male group, Les Percussions de Guinee, in a powerful display of West African song, dance and drumming.

The all-female Amazones ensemble plays the traditional Djembe drum, making both a musical and social statement. Historically, only men were allowed to play the Djembe in West Africa, using distinct rhythms to tell stories and recount historical events through music. Before Amazones, women were forbidden from even touching a Djembe because the act of playing it is part of a long-standing sacred brotherhood for men only.

Named after the valiant woman-warriors from the ancient kingdom of Dahomey (now known as the West African country of Benin), Amazones is comprised of women from the most difficult living conditions in West Africa. They often come from poverty stricken backgrounds of illiteracy, homelessness, and prostitution. Mamoudou Conde created Amazones in 1998. Inspired by both the art of the Djembe and the power and independence of women, he sees the Amazones as warriors of circumstance.

Mamoudou Conde said: "My goal was to help the people that had nothing. The women who really needed our help."

However, he struggled to gain government acceptance of the group because officials were fearful of the community's reaction to such enormous change in tradition. When Mamoudou received widespread approval from village elders, the government leaders of Guinea endorsed the group, acknowledging their efforts toward gender equality within their culture.

The national director of culture for the Republic of Guinea said the female master drummers have become experts of the Djembe and its art form.

In less than five years the group has gained worldwide recognition for their skilled performances with the Djembe.

Dr. Saidou Dioubate, national director of culture for the Republic of Guinea, said:

The Djembe originates from West Africa and is carved specially from redwood, sewing goatskin and an intricate system of laced cords that create a rich sound with sophisticated phrasing and sonorities.

Amazones will tour in 2004 throughout 23 cities in the United States and Canada. The performance features the world-renowned styling of the traditional Les Percussions de Guinee, a government sponsored troupe founded in 1987. The group includes 15 of the most respected musicians and dancers in West Africa. Including seven master drummers, an orchestra of flutes, balafons (African xylophones), koras (West African string instruments), and Guinea's traditional dancers.

Amazones continues to perform with the primary objectives of restoring the musical tradition of Guinea and improving the economic status of women through the rhythmic stories of the Djembe.

Visit Amazones' Web site at www.amazoneswomandrummers.com to find photographs, more details, and short clips of their astounding performances.

Summary:

THE HULT CENTER PRESENTS	
Who:	Amazones: The Women Master Drummers of Guinea
What:	A rhythmic storytelling performance by Amazones with the West African traditional Djembe drum, featuring world-renowned Les Percussions de Guinee
When:	Thursday, Sept. 30 at 8 P.M.
Where:	Silva Concert Hall
Tickets:	$18–28, students $14

Located at 7th Avenue and Willamette in downtown Eugene, the Hult Center for Performing Arts is owned and operated by the City of Eugene.

For show information, visit the Hult Center Web site at http://www.hultcenter. org.

Ticket Information:
Buy online anytime at www.hultcenter.org
Order by phone: (541) 682-5000
Visit Hult Center Box Office at 7th and Willamette in downtown Eugene
Or visit the ticket outlet at the University of Oregon ticket office in the EMU

sample 7.25   newsletter article

NHTSA ADMINISTRATOR PRESENTS SAFETY AWARDS TO WORLD'S TOP AUTO ENGINEERS AND ADVOCATES AT GLOBAL CONFERENCE

National Highway Traffic Safety Administrator Dr. Jeffrey Runge presented vehicle safety engineering and special appreciation awards to 12 international automotive engineers and safety proponents from six countries during the 19th International Technical Conference on the Enhanced Safety of Vehicles being held this week in Washington, D.C.

"We are recognizing these 12 automotive engineers, researchers and advocates for their unparalleled contributions to automotive safety throughout the world," Dr. Runge said. "Technical conferences like the ESV are essential for U.S. and international highway safety experts to share research and to advance the latest technologies enhancing vehicle and traffic safety on the world's roads," he added.

NHTSA awards for "Safety Engineering Excellence" went to the following individuals:

Dr. Jeff R. Crandall (United States, University of Virginia), for his expertise in the area of biomechanics, human injury causation and modeling of biosystems, including research activities in thoracic injuries in vehicle crashes, pediatric injuries and the effect of safety belt characteristics on injury to children.

Dr. Lotta Jakobsson (Sweden, Volvo Car Corporation), for her contributions to traffic injury research as an internationally renowned impact-trauma biomechanics expert involved in developing vehicle designs for safety.

Mr. Koichi Kamiji (Japan, Honda, R&D Co., Ltd.), for contributions to the development of intelligent airbag systems and improved body structures that enhance both pedestrian protection and crash compatibility.

Dr. Richard Lind (United States, Delphi Corporation), for his contributions in helping produce systems for monitoring driving performance and minimizing driver "workload". He has been instrumental in developing lane tracking systems and advanced vision/radar fusion technologies.

Mr. Jan Olsson (Sweden, Autoliv, Inc.), for his contributions to airbag technologies, including innovations in the fields of side impact airbags, inflatable curtains, anti-whiplash systems and rollover protection.

Dr. Peter E. Rieth (Germany, Continental Automotive Systems), for contributions to such key safety technologies as brake assist, electronic stability control, and steering control systems.

Professor Pete Thomas (United Kingdom, Vehicle Safety Research Centre), for his contributions to crash analysis and resulting improvements to vehicle safety as a world-wide authority on crash studies. His work contributed to research on frontal impact standards in 1990, and he has since identified many areas for additional safety improvements.

In addition to these safety engineering excellence awards, "special awards of appreciation" went to a number of individuals in recognition of their outstanding leadership and contributions in the field of motor vehicle safety:

Mr. Maurice Eaton (United Kingdom, EuroNCAP), for his management of Europe's New Car Assessment Program which has greatly accelerated the deployment of improved occupant protection systems throughout Europe.

Mr. Jean-Yves Foret-Bruno (France, PSA Peugeot-Citroen-Renault), for 30 years of research into "accidentology," which helped to improve the design of automotive structures, seat belts, air bags and load-limiting devices in today's passenger cars.

Professor Per Lövsund (Sweden, Chalmers University of Technology), for his significant contributions to impact biomechanics and traffic safety over the last 25 years, including the establishment of the Crash Safety Division at Chalmers University of Technology.

Mr. Brian O'Neill (United States, Insurance Institute for Highway Safety), for his work with IIHS in developing and communicating objective information about vehicle safety performance to the public, and enhancing automotive safety awareness among the motoring public, auto manufactures and the government.

Mr. Juichiro Takada (Japan, Takata Corporation), for his efforts in introducing safety belts, pre-tensioners and airbags in Japan, as well as for the development and commercialization of silicon coating of air bag fabrics; and for his work with the National Highway Traffic Safety Administration in the U.S. in the last major seat belt evaluation program using human volunteers.

The United States Department of Transportation, National Highway Traffic Safety Administration (NHTSA), Office of Vehicle Safety Research is the official government agency responsible for the implementation of the International Technical Conferences on the Enhanced Safety of Vehicles (ESV). The Conferences are held approximately every two years and hosted by participating Governments. Delegate and attendee participation includes worldwide governments, automotive industries, motor vehicle research engineers and scientists; medical, insurance, and legal professions; consumers; academia; private corporations; and international media.

The ESV Program originated in 1970 under the North Atlantic Treaty Organization (NATO) Committee on the Challenges of Modern Society, and was implemented through bilateral agreements between the governments of the United States, France, the Federal Republic of Germany, Italy, the United Kingdom, Japan, and Sweden. The participating nations agreed to develop experimental safety vehicles to advance the state-of-the-art technology in automotive engineering and to meet periodically to exchange information on their progress. Since its inception the number of international partners has grown to include the governments of Canada, Australia, the Netherlands, Hungary, Poland, and two international organizations—the European Enhanced Vehicle-safety Committee, and the European Commission. A representative from each country and organization serves as a Government Focal Point in support of the conference.

sample 7.26   newsletter, president's column

Washington Business Magazine

May/June 2004

PRESIDENT'S COLUMN: QUIT MONKEYING AROUND; GIVE CHARTER SCHOOLS A CHANCE

by Don C. Brunell, AWB President

The Washington Education Association (WEA) needs to quit monkeying with the new law that authorizes charter public schools. The law allows just 15 such schools over the next three years, most of which must focus on serving educationally disadvantaged students.

Instead of embracing this opportunity to improve learning for our children, the teachers' union has become anti-choice—at least when it comes to education. They want to deny giving a choice to parents who cannot afford to send their kids to private schools or move to better public schools in the suburbs.

If the union's Referendum 55 qualifies for the November ballot, all the work at the Superintendent of Public Instruction's Office to secure $5 million per year in federal charter school funding will come to a grinding halt. If the referendum passes, Washington will remain one of only 10 states in the nation without a charter public school law.

What a travesty! After all, isn't the goal of public education to teach our kids as effectively and efficiently as possible? Traditional and charter public schools can comfortably co-exist, and the traditional schools may even improve with a little healthy competition. What's wrong with that?

Forty other states have charter public schools and there are thousands of success stories of how learning improves when students, parents and teachers come together and form their own charter public schools.

Vaughn Next Century Learning Center is Charter School Success

Last spring at AWB's Annual Spring meeting in Spokane, Dr. Yvonne Chan, founder of the Vaughn Next Century Learning Center in Los Angeles, got a spontaneous standing ovation for her work and enthusiastic leadership in education. Dr. Chan and her school were transformed by the freedom they gained from California's 1992 charter school law.

Vaughn students live in poverty. More than two-thirds of its 1,500 elementary-age children are learning to speak English as their second language. Ninety-five percent of the students are Hispanic, and five percent are African-American.

Vaughn was a failing school for decades before Dr. Chan arrived and transformed it into a charter public school in 1993. Since then, student achievement has soared, attendance is near perfect and the founders have achieved goals other schools only dream of, including:

- Class size reduction to 20 in all grades.

- Universal preschool education.

- Accelerated English learning.

- Special education full inclusion.

- A school-based clinic, museum, family center and business co-op.

- A community library and university professional development center.

- A school-wide teacher peer-review system.

- A performance pay plan for all staff.

This year, Washington state lawmakers finally passed legislation that will allow parents and teachers to create charter public schools to help turn around persistently low-performing traditional schools. Gov. Locke signed the bill, saying that charter public schools will help disadvantaged students and struggling public schools.

That being the case, why is the WEA trying to kill charter public schools before they have a chance to get started? After all, if they don't work, parents will return to traditional public schools. And if they do work, children will get a better education.

Just what is the WEA afraid of?

sample 7.27   op-ed article

The Register-Guard—Wednesday, March 10, 2004

OPINION

GUEST VIEWPOINT

FREE SPEECH IS OUR STRENGTH IN TIMES OF CRISIS

by Kyu Ho Youm

Which country has the freest press in the world?

"The United States," many of us Americans will answer.

Our response may be correct if we think about our pre-Sept. 11, 2001 news media. But our intuitive perception of our press freedom in the past $2\frac{1}{2}$ years is clearly off base.

The United States is not among the top 13 "free" press nations, according to the 2003 survey of Freedom House in New York. Reporters Without Borders, an international organization that advocates press freedom, ranked the United States 31st in its October report on 166 nations.

The poor rankings should serve as a lesson in our political rights and civil liberties since Sept. 11—particularly this week, as we mark the 40th anniversary of the landmark New York Times vs. Sullivan U.S. Supreme Court case.

On March 9, 1964, the Supreme Court held that a public official cannot recover damages for a defamatory falsehood relating to his official conduct unless he proves that the libel was published with knowledge of its falsity or with reckless disregard for its truth.

Our participatory democracy, declared Justice William Brennan, who wrote the majority opinion, is based on our "national commitment to the principle that debate on public issues should be uninhibited, robust, and wide-open, and . . . may well include vehement, caustic, and sometimes unpleasantly sharp attacks on government and public officials."

The Sullivan decision brought about a constitutional revolution in America. It did not affect the news media alone. The case was about the "citizen critic" of government—that is, every citizen's right to criticize the government and its officials under the First Amendment. Since Sullivan, Americans have been increasingly unrestrained in speaking out on their government.

In many ways, the Sullivan case has made freedom of expression a religious tenet rather than a legal concept. Burning the flag in a political protest is protected, as is hate speech, in the United States—which stands in sharp contrast with the rest of the world.

Since the Sept. 11 terrorist attacks, however, freedom of speech has been noticeably constrained in the United States. Balancing national security with freedom of expression has taken on a heightened urgency. Nonetheless, our 200-plus years of experience with free speech and press as a fundamental right cautions us against going too far and too fast in weighing national (and political) security interests over essential First Amendment freedoms.

Instead of starting from the often ill-informed premise that freedom and security are antithetical during critical times, we should ask: What has made our country the envy of the world? The undisputed answer should be that we have deliberately risked adopting the free exchange of ideas as the modus operandi of our polity since our nation's founding.

In this light, the USA Patriot Act and other measures that purport to enhance national security are likely to undermine our proven strength and resiliency as an open democracy.

The paternalistic and sometimes dismissive attitude of the federal government toward an inquisitive press and an engaged citizenry is repugnant to the central meaning of the Sullivan case: Criticism of the government is not a crime, but a right under the First Amendment.

Indeed, the Sullivan case arose during a time of crisis. The Supreme Court's ringing rejection of seditious libel as a notion in our law suggests that the First Amendment is designed to prepare our society for the worst of times. Freedom of expression is most fragile when security is perceived to be at stake, but that's when it should be most consciously and vigorously protected.

Journalists in many emerging democracies emulate American news media as the model of a free, independent press. Thus, the continuing retrenchment in freedom of expression as a democratic value in the United States should not be considered solely as a matter of domestic concern. As former President Mary Robinson of Ireland observed at her University of Oregon lecture last week, "Other countries use the erosion of human rights in the United States to justify their own abuses."

While celebrating the 40th anniversary of Sullivan, we're being questioned, with good reason, whether our country is the dependable standard bearer of human rights at home and abroad. This compels us to be eternally vigilant in the defense of Sullivan's legacy as the defining symbol of our stated commitment to a liberal democracy.

Kyu Ho Youm is the Jonathan Marshall First Amendment Chair at the University of Oregon School of Journalism and Communication.

sample 7.28   photo news release

NEWS PHOTO

Sailors work to load bags of mail into a C-2 Greyhound aircraft

U.S. Navy sailors work to load bags of mail into a C-2 Greyhound aircraft on the flight deck of the USS John C. Stennis (CVN 74) on Aug. 27, 2004. Stennis and her embarked Carrier Air Wing 14 are conducting exercises at sea on a regularly scheduled deployment. The Greyhound, from Fleet Logistic Support Squadron 30, is responsible for the delivery of passengers, cargo and mail to the ship in support of the strike group. DoD photo by Petty Officer 3rd class Mark J. Rebilas, U.S. Navy. (Released)

040827-N-6213R-002
http://www.defenselink.mil/photos/Aug 2004/040827-N-6213R-002.html

PRODUCTS ALL AROUND, INC.
5555 Kensington Road
Sisterville, U.S.A.

March 2, 20XX

John Starter, Life Editor
Morning News Star
P.O. Box 10
Austin, Texas 77666

Dear Mr. Starter:

Your lighthearted and informative article about Valley Pedometers last week made me think your readers would like to know about another public demonstration of a product with health benefits.

Because Austin has been identified by the Asthma and Allergy Society (AAS) as the very worst city for spring allergies in 20XX, we will have more than one hundred Airtop air purifiers at the Big Steer Mall next month as allergy season kicks in to full gear. Our air purifiers are endorsed by AAS and can really help folks who suffer from allergies.

We will be giving away an Airtop air purifier and we will have a great visual display of all the pollen and pollution the air purifiers are taking out of the air. You will want to bring a photographer to take pictures of the huge towers of air purifiers at the doors into Big Steer Mall.

The best time to reach me is from 8 AM to 2 PM weekdays at Products All Around at 123–456–7891. You can also call me on my cell phone at 123–321–9876. I will call you in a few days to check in and ask if you need any other information.

Regards,

Ellen Biggs Insurance
Director, Public Relations

sample 7.30   pocket point card

COMMUNICATING IN A CRISIS

Crisis Communication Checklist

- Follow business unit emergency operating procedures.

- Notify John Smith, director of public affairs: work: 404–846–4642 home: 770-664-7581 cell phone: 404–550–7522

Gather the facts—Prepare a statement:

- The statement should be cleared by corporate headquarters' Public Affairs and Law departments and issued by the local facility or PR manager.

- Reassure that appropriate authorities are taking control. State that the company is stepping up to its responsibilities. State that top management is apprised and is providing support.

- Acknowledge publicly the assistance police, fire departments, and others give during the crisis.

- Tell as much as you can about the situation and get it out quickly.

DO NOT SPECULATE ON:

- dollar estimate of damage;

- time estimated for resuming production;

- possible causes of the accident;

- original cost estimates of the equipment;

- estimates of insurance coverage; and

- identities or medical conditions of injured or missing persons.

DO NOT use negative words, technical terms or jargon. Once the following information has been cleared, it CAN BE GIVEN to the media in the statement:

- what happened;

- where it happened;

- when it happened;

- how it happened;

- to whom it happened (once the immediate family has been notified);

- number of injured/affected;

- where the injured/affected were taken for treatment; and

- what equipment was damaged.

Work with the media:

- Have media calls logged—assure reporters that their calls will be returned promptly and that there will be frequent updates as information becomes available.

- Designate an emergency press room/briefing area—with phone and fax lines if possible.

- Meet reporters upon their arrival. If they arrive on the scene before the PR manager or spokesperson, the reporter should be told that a spokesperson will soon provide the facts.

- Identify yourself as the spokesperson.

- Provide frequent reports, even if only to repeat information. Keep media restricted to the briefing area and provide company escorts for media when they leave the area.

- Allow pictures only in the media briefing area.

- Ask media to respect the privacy of employees and not to attempt interviews at the accident site.

- Escort media with cameras to view an accident site only after receiving prior approval from corporate headquarters.

- Convey new information to the media as soon as it becomes available.

- Be calm during media interviews and/or briefings—look for your friends and family in the camera and speak to them rather than the lens.

- Show concern for every question asked—even if you don't have an answer, let the press know you are actively seeking an explanation.

- Provide a fact sheet describing your facility to the media. Monitor first editions of newspapers and radio and TV news reports for content, and immediately correct erroneous information with reporters.

Ensure that:

- the needs of all groups are addressed—victims and their families, indirect victims, ALL employees and their families, community residents, etc.

- hospitalized persons or survivors receive proper care.

- phone calls from the general public are handled politely and appropriately.

MEMORANDUM

FROM: Bharat Mathur
           Acting Regional Administrator

TO: All Region 5 employees

SUBJECT: Working with the Press

EPA's policy is to be responsive and open in providing the public with access to information. An informed public is key to EPA's mission of protecting human health and the environment. Open communication fosters a better understanding of EPA actions and how people can protect their environment and families.

One of our challenges is shaping consistent messages and working as a team to communicate the Agency's policies and priorities. I want to ensure that the Region puts its best face forward—that we speak with a consistent voice and that we're effective in spreading the word about our work.

The Office of Public Affairs press team will work with Region 5 staff to ensure that reporters' requests are responded to appropriately. This will ensure that reporters receive information that accurately reflects EPA actions and policies, and will prevent EPA management from being surprised by news coverage. Please follow these procedures.

Here are the specifics:

- If you receive any request for information or an interview from a member of the media, you should refer the caller to OPA (see the list of contacts at the end). Please refrain from answering such inquiries directly. OPA will determine the appropriate response—and who should respond—after consultation with program staff, and if necessary, after elevating issues for senior-level attention. Often, OPA will coordinate direct interviews between program staff experts and the media.

- If you receive any request for written information from a member of the media, please refer the caller to OPA. Occasionally, media sources are instructed to request Agency documents under the Freedom of Information Act. OPA will coordinate the response to these media requests after consultation with appropriate FOIA office staff, and if necessary, after elevating the request for senior-level attention.

- On a case-by-case basis, some employees may be authorized to work directly with the media. For instance, on-scene coordinators, remedial project managers and community involvement staff are sometimes approached by the media while in the field. They are authorized, in these situations, to speak directly to the press about their sites without prior approval, but should report their conversation to Public Affairs after the fact. If you need similar authorization, please contact one of the OPA contacts listed below.

- Any request for EPA to provide an article for publication should be referred to OPA. OPA will consult with the lead program and senior management before making any commitments to the media. (Articles for scientific journals should go through the Region's peer review process. Contact Gilberto Alvarez, OSEA, for more information.)

- OPA is responsible for initiating contact with the media. This includes making phone calls and sending news releases, letters to the editors and op-eds. If you think you have a good story that you'd like to publicize, please work with OPA. OPA staff is responsible for working with the media to set up interviews, press conferences, editorial boards and briefings. Also, please consult with OPA prior to attending such events set up by other organizations.

When you are called by a reporter—or have news you want to get out—these are the people to call:

Press Team
Phillippa Cannon, 353-6218 Team Leader, Water, Great Lakes National Program Office, Office of Strategic Environmental Analysis
Bill Omohundro, 353-8254 Air and Radiation
Karen Thompson, 353-8547 Waste, Pesticides and Toxics
Mick Hans, 353-5050 Superfund
Jeff Kelley, 353-1159 Chief, Public Information and Education Section
Elissa Speizman, 353-2073 Director, Office of Public Affairs

Social Responsibility

WORLDWIDE ENVIRONMENTAL POLICY

OUR CREDO COMMITMENT

We are responsible to the communities in which we live and work and to the world community as well. . . . We must maintain in good order the property we are privileged to use, protecting the environment and natural resources.

POLICY STATEMENT

Johnson & Johnson is committed to environmental leadership, instilling the highest environmental values in all employees, utilizing the best environmental practices in all we do, and focusing on sustainable growth.

Johnson & Johnson is committed to:

OPERATING BEYOND COMPLIANCE with all applicable laws and regulations by uniformly meeting Johnson & Johnson global environmental policies and standards, ISO 14001 environmental management system standards, and other voluntary principles to which we subscribe.

MAINTAINING A STRUCTURE at the corporate and operating companies that assures proper oversight, using environmental accountability as a measure for management performance.

INTEGRATING ENVIRONMENTAL GOALS into our business strategies and plans while publicly reporting on our progress.

STRIVING FOR ZERO WASTE, 100% resource efficiency, and enhancement of the environment.

UTILIZING INNOVATIVE TECHNOLOGIES and leveraging best practices globally for the greatest environmental gain and continuous improvement.

FOSTERING AN ENVIRONMENTAL ETHIC among our management, employees, stockholders, customers, suppliers and communities worldwide.

BUILDING RELATIONSHIPS with regulatory agencies, interest groups, thought leaders, and communities to engender collaboration, cooperation, and mutual understanding.

ENHANCING CORPORATE SOCIAL RESPONSIBILITY by supporting environmental health and education, conservation and community-based programs worldwide.

sample 7.33   position

ALCOA POSITIONS

Biodiversity

Definition of Biodiversity

Biodiversity refers to the diversity of living organisms and the ecosystems and processes of which they are part. It includes animals, plants, fungi, algae, protozoa, bacteria and viruses. It is most often used in the context of flora and fauna and those organisms required to sustain the ecosystems necessary for these higher life forms.

Biodiversity is usually considered at three different levels: genetic diversity, species diversity and ecosystem diversity.

Genetic diversity is the sum total of genetic information contained in the genes of the individual animals, plants, and microorganisms that inhabit the earth.

Species diversity refers to the variety of living organisms on earth. Globally, a total of about 1.5 million species has been described. Estimates of the total number of species vary between 5 and 50 million with a figure of 10 million being generally accepted.

Ecosystem diversity relates to the variety of habitats, biotic communities and ecological processes that occur on earth. Ecosystem diversity is easier to measure and is often used as the basis of land management and conservation.

Variability of Biodiversity

The level of biodiversity on a worldwide basis is highly variable. The greatest diversity occurs in tropical forests. Although these areas cover only about 7% of the earth's land surface, they account for more than half the world's species (some estimates place the number as high as 70% to 90%). Other habitats that are particularly rich in diversity include areas with Mediterranean-like climates, islands, coral reefs, and some lakes.

While areas especially rich in species or endemic species (those with limited ranges) occur most often in the tropics, scientists caution that preservation of other less diverse areas, such as arid zones, is also critical to maintaining the world's biodiversity.

Biodiversity as a Worldwide Issue

Although humans have inhabited this planet for many thousands of years, our population has been low (less than half a billion) and sparse until relatively recent times. In 1950 the world's human population was 2.6 billion. It grew to 5 billion by 1989. In 2025 the population is projected to reach 8.5 billion. This population growth causes increasing pressure for more space, food, energy and natural resources. The ecosystem destruction resulting from meeting the needs of the growing population has led to a loss of biodiversity.

Loss of habitat is considered the greatest current threat to biodiversity. However, other important factors include competition from or predation by introduced plants and animals, and susceptibility to introduced pathogens. Introduced species of birds, insects, animals, plants, and bacteria have had significant ecological impacts in many parts of the world.

Although the actual numbers can never be known, extinction of plant and animal species is occurring at a high rate. Extinction rate estimates ranging from thousands to tens of thousands of species per year have been published in the scientific literature. Some extinction is a normal part of the evolutionary process, but it is generally accepted by the scientific community that the high rate that is currently being experienced cannot be sustained without serious implications.

Ecosystem losses are also occurring. Globally, half of all marshes and wetlands have been filled or drained. In North America, 99% of tall grass prairies have been lost. Estimates are that Latin America loses 1.3% of its remaining forest each year. Such ecosystem losses are clearly not a natural part of the evolutionary process.

As an expression of the growing worldwide concern, representatives of more than 150 countries signed an international Convention for the Conservation of Biological Diversity at the U.N. Conference on Environment and Development held in Rio de Janeiro in June 1992. The Convention came into force in December 1993.

Values of Biodiversity

Maintenance of the diversity of biological resources helps ensure the continued viability and balance of life by sustaining ecosystems, many of which are highly interdependent. While the values of biological resources may not always be quantifiable, or represent a direct benefit to humans, they are nonetheless significant. They include the range of resources which are the basis of survival by providing a food source, shelter or warmth.

Some values can be measured in monetary terms, for example, products that are harvested by humans and exchanged in formal markets. National income accounts typically identify values for harvesting of fuelwood, timber, game, fish, skins, medicinal plants, honey, fibers and so forth. Overexploitation for human use, e.g., fish stocks, can be a significant threat to biodiversity in itself.

It is not possible to place a monetary value on resources and processes that are of major benefit but are not directly consumed by humanity. Maintenance of water cycles, prevention of erosion, production of soil, provision of recreational, scientific and aesthetic values are illustrations of these very important resources and processes. A broad gene pool is essential for the development and maintenance of a stable ecosystem.

There are other less tangible values of biodiversity such as potential future values of medicinal, genetic, chemical and economic resources. A good example is that of communal animals.

Ants, termites, wasps etc. have developed contagious disease resistance systems through millions of years of communal evolution. The solutions to some human disease problems may be found through the careful scientific study of these kinds of organisms.

Although factors such as cultural background and economic well-being influence people's perceptions differently, the conservation of plant and animal species is widely seen in many countries as an important ethical issue.

Alcoa's Position on Conservation of Biodiversity

Consistent with Alcoa's environmental policy and its published position on sustainable development, the company actively endorses the concept of conservation of biodiversity by operating worldwide in a manner which minimizes impacts on natural habitats and biological resources.

Alcoa's operations can play a positive role in conserving biodiversity by adopting appropriate land management practices (reference position paper on Land Management) and rehabilitating land disturbed by the operations in an appropriate manner (reference Bauxite Mine Rehabilitation Standards and Guidelines).

New or expanding operations should document the level of ecosystem and species diversity within their area of influence by applying techniques, procedures, and information generally accepted by the international scientific community. Measures to minimize adverse impacts on ecologically significant ecosystems or species should be adopted. Particular attention should be paid to the conservation of rare biological communities and rare, endangered or threatened species.

Where relatively extensive operations such as bauxite mining are carried out in natural habitats, rehabilitation of the disturbed land should in most circumstances favor the return of the pre-existing vegetation and fauna communities. Such rehabilitation should aim to re-establish the broadest practicable genetic base using local genetic material and provenances wherever possible.

STATEMENT BY THE PRESS SECRETARY

Today the Department of State, the Central Intelligence Agency, the Department of Defense, the Federal Bureau of Investigation, the National Archives and Records Administration, and the Department of Justice are releasing newly declassified and other documents related to events in Chile from 1968–91. These documents are part of a discretionary review of U.S. government files related to human rights abuses, terrorism, and other acts of political violence prior to and during the Pinochet era in Chile. National Security Council staff coordinated this interagency effort on behalf of the President.

Agencies made an initial release of approximately 5,800 documents on June 30, 1999, concentrating on the period from 1973–78, which corresponds to the period of the most flagrant human rights abuses in Chile. A second release of over 1,100 documents concentrating on the years 1968–73 followed on October 8, 1999. While the focus for this final release was on documents dated from 1978–91, additional documents from the earlier periods also are being released today.

This third and final release consists of more than 16,000 documents, including approximately 13,050 from the Department of State, 1,550 from the CIA, 620 from the Federal Bureau of Investigation, 370 from the Department of Defense, 310 from the National Archives, 110 from the National Security Council, and 50 from the Department of Justice. Information has been withheld from some of the released documents to protect the privacy of individuals, sensitive law enforcement information, and intelligence sources and methods; or to prevent serious harm to ongoing diplomatic activities of the United States.

One goal of the project is to put original documents before the public so that it may judge for itself the extent to which U.S. actions undercut the cause of democracy and human rights in Chile. Actions approved by the U.S. government during this period aggravated political polarization and affected Chile's long tradition of democratic elections and respect for the constitutional order and the rule of law.

The Chilean people deserve our praise and respect for courageously reclaiming their proud history as one of the world's oldest democracies. Healing the painful wounds of the past, Chileans from across the political spectrum have rededicated themselves to rebuilding representative institutions and the rule of law. The United States will continue to work closely with the people of Chile—as their friend and partner—to strengthen the cause of democracy in Latin America and around the world.

A complete set of the released documents is available for public review at the National Archives in College Park, Maryland. They also are being released simultaneously in Chile. Copies of the documents will be available on the Internet. Also available at this website are copies of the September 2000 Hinchey Report on "CIA Activities in Chile" and the relevant 1975 Church Committee reports on Chile.

PRESS STATEMENT ON FDA ADVISORY ON ANTIDEPRESSANT USE IN CHILDREN BY CARDEN JOHNSTON, MD, AAP PRESIDENT

"The American Academy of Pediatrics encourages the manufacturers of 10 antidepressant drugs to swiftly adopt the label changes as requested today by the Food and Drug Administration. Stronger cautions and warnings will better inform pediatricians, psychiatrists, family physicians and other clinicians who prescribe these drugs to their patients.

"Today's action by the FDA is yet another step in an ongoing process to ensure that all the drugs prescribed to children are safe and effective. The AAP supports two federal laws that are increasing the testing of medicines prescribed to children: The Best Pharmaceuticals for Children Act and the Pediatric Research Equity Act, also known as the Pediatric Rule. Getting medication properly studied and having labels changed to reflect new safety, efficacy and dosing information as soon as possible is a critical goal in pediatric treatment. In this particular case, the FDA reviewed the current data and determined that a prominent label warning was warranted given concerns, but no concrete evidence, about the drugs contributing to suicides or suicidal thoughts.

"The American Academy of Pediatrics appreciates the FDA's work, and will notify its membership of the need to closely monitor children with depression on this medication."

The American Academy of Pediatrics is an organization of 57,000 primary care pediatricians, pediatric medical subspecialists and pediatric surgical specialists dedicated to the health, safety and well being of infants, children, adolescents and young adults.

American Academy of Pediatrics
Department of Federal Affairs
601 13th Street, NW
Suite 400 North
Washington, DC 20005
202/347-8600

sample 7.36   press statement

TALKING POINTS: U.S. DEPARTMENT OF LABOR OCCUPATIONAL SAFETY & HEALTH ADMINISTRATION

Talking Points for Paula White
VPP Workshop for Airline Industry Alliance
Atlanta, GA June 4, 2003
10:45–11:00 am

Good morning. I am delighted to join you for this daylong look at OSHA's Voluntary Protection Programs.

The March 2002 VPP approval of Delta's Technical Operations Base Maintenance here in Atlanta was a groundbreaking event. Delta can be proud, as we in OSHA are, of its pioneering efforts to strengthen worker safety and health in the airline industry. By committing to VPP, Delta managers and workers are betting that labor-management-government cooperation, and the establishment of effective safety and health management systems, are feasible and worthwhile goals.

I think that's a safe bet, given that the VPP process has a 20-year proven track record at saving lives and preventing workplace injuries and illnesses. Yes, VPP is a process, (not a flavor of the month program) that works for all worksites (small, large, union, non-union, public, and private sector). The VPP process works at a variety of industries also. In fact there are over 200 different industry types participating.

VPP is not for every company, however. It is designed for companies and worksites with a culture that values the safety and health of their employees on equal footing with production, quality, and profits.

Once the VPP process is adopted by a company, very few companies drop out. Also, the VPP compliments many other quality improvement programs such as ISO and Malcolm Baldridge.

As the value of VPP becomes more widely understood within the airline industry, I'm looking forward to seeing other airlines, and additional Delta worksites, on VPP's roster of worksite excellence.

WHY PURSUE VPP?

Why pursue VPP? While some believe that the VPP requirements are too tough to meet, and require too much paperwork, most find that benefits far outweigh the effort.

VPP participants are OSHA's advocates and role models, proving that safety and health add value to your business, to your workplace, and to your life.

The value for business is clear: Focusing on safety and health management systems is the right thing to do; it saves money and adds value to the organization. Safety Pays: Since it's inception in 1982, VPP sites have saved over a billion dollars, and on average, their injury and illness rates at 54% below the national averages for their industries.

Safety and health add value to the workplace as well. VPP companies have shown that the benefits include increased productivity, higher quality, improved morale and reduced turnover.

And clearly, safety and health add value to your life. Anyone who has had an on-the-job injury can tell you that getting hurt or sick is not just physically painful. On-the-job injuries and illnesses can significantly reduce income, increase stress and impact your family life. But at VPP sites, the chances of getting hurt are greatly reduced.

In 2001, by having injury and illness rates roughly 54% below the national averages, VPP sites avoided approximately 6,000 lost workday cases. Think about it: That's 6,000 people who went home to their families healthy and unharmed!

ALL OF OUR EFFORTS ARE PAYING OFF

VPP companies are helping OSHA achieve its mission. Overall, there has been a 62% reduction in workplace fatalities and a 40% decline in injury and illness rates over the last 30 years. In addition, injuries and illnesses in 2001 were the lowest in 9 years! So all of our efforts are paying off.

I am often asked . . . what is the key to VPP' s success? I think a case could be made that VPP's extraordinary experience rests on a simple but radical concept: labor, management, and government can work together with amazing results. Positive, lasting relationships are possible and are well worth the effort.

It is this successful relationship with VPP that has paved the way to expand OSHA's menu of cooperative programs.

In fact, improving voluntary programs and partnerships as well as expanding outreach, education and compliance assistance efforts through alliances are at the top of Assistant Secretary Henshaw's priority list.

Because of this OSHA is building strategic partnerships, alliances, and new compliance assistance strategies to reach a broader range of industries and locales, as you can attest.

NEW COMPLIANCE ASSISTANCE TOOLS

To assist employers and employees in these new cooperative ventures, we are improving existing and developing new compliance assistance tools to help identify workplace hazards and develop systems of prevention and control.

These include an improved web page and e-tools; availability of compliance assistance specialists in every area office and hosting our second annual compliance assistance conference in June of this year.

WHAT WE NEED TO DO

VPP has an important role to play in this effort. So let's talk about what VPP has accomplished and what we need to do now.

We are fast approaching the end of our yearlong celebration of VPP's 20th anniversary. We've taken the time to look back and see just how far we've come. VPP has grown from only 11 participants in 1982 to 951 current participants in both federal and state plan VPP.

In addition, VPP participants cover 208 different industries and almost 600,000 employees.

VPP will reach 1,000 participants within the next few months!

But OSHA covers 7 million sites so VPP's 951 sites represent a tiny fraction of the whole, not even 1%, only 1/100th of 1%. We need many, many more sites turning onto the road to excellence.

So OSHA challenges the airline industry: As part of our alliance, help us make a quantum leap from fewer than 1,000 participants to 8,000, and also expand the VPP into the airline industry.

Many of you may have heard Assistant Secretary John Henshaw announce this vision. And I can tell you that if you convince even one company to strive for VPP, Mr. Henshaw will be grateful.

STEPS WE ARE TAKING TO MEET THE CHALLENGE

Let me tell you about steps OSHA is taking to meet this VPP challenge and provide you with the tools you need to help us.

We are committed to expanding the Special Government Employees (SGE) program. This is a unique program where OSHA trains personnel from approved VPP companies. They then volunteer to assist OSHA on VPP onsite evaluations of other VPP applicants or participants. This is a way that our VPP companies give back to us. Currently there are 306 trained SGEs nationally. We trained just over 100 new SGE's last year, and plan on doing the same this year.

Tools are also available through the Voluntary Protection Programs' Participants' Association (VPPPA) including free mentoring, and other products, workshops, and conferences. In fact their national conference is being held in Washington, DC the week of September 12th. I encourage you to attend.

We want to see more small businesses in VPP. We're nearing completion on a small business kit jointly developed by OSHA and the Association. We're almost ready to publish.

We've greatly improved the VPP tools that are available to the public including a new VPP web page. From this web page you can download the new VPP Policies and Procedures Manual, Application Brochure, and Report Format.

In addition, OSHA VPP Managers are available in every OSHA Regional Office. They are available to give VPP presentations to appropriate persons within your company to help sell the VPP idea.

As we look at ways to expand VPP, we are exploring opportunities for an entry-level program to assist companies who want to be on the road to excellence but need extra help or a road map to get going. Perhaps some of you would be interested in piloting this new program. In addition we are exploring new strategies for corporations and construction.

I am confident that through this alliance, we can spread the word throughout the airline industry: Positive labor-management-government relationships make a difference. We have seen how these relationships lead to safety and health excellence. We are saving lives, and preventing injuries and illnesses at across the nation.

So please seriously consider VPP as a process to improve safety and health in your workplace. Become part of the VPP family and be recognized by OSHA for being a leader in safety and health. With VPP recognition comes prestige, a competitive advantage, opportunity to networking with the best, and an improved relationship with OSHA. Shouldn't the airline industry be able to take advantage of these benefits? I sure think so!

Thank you for your commitment, your enthusiasm, your continual striving for excellence, and your model relationship with OSHA. I look forward to continuing to work with you through this alliance and expand VPP through out the airline industry.

The Airline Industry Alliance addresses ergonomic issues associated with the handling of passenger checked baggage. It explores ways to promote communication, outreach, training, education and a national dialogue to reduce ergonomic-related injuries. This agreement also focuses on a number of goals including:

Training and Education

- Develop a biomechanics training module for employees handling checked baggage and make it available free-of-charge to all airlines and OSHA.

Outreach and Communication

- Review and provide input on ways to improve OSHA's eTool.
  Conduct a one-day seminar for participating airlines, as well as any other interested aviation participants, on OSHA's VPP process.
  Conduct a one-day seminar with airline and OSHA personnel to address ergonomic issues associated with passenger checked baggage.

Promoting the National Dialogue on Workplace Safety and Health

- Educate and solicit ideas from interested parties for improving the ergonomic process related to the handling of baggage during a national safety conference.

Signatories are:

Air Canada	Jetblue Airways
Airtran Airways	Midwest Express Airlines
Alaska Airlines	Southwest Airlines
American Airlines	United Airlines
American Trans Air	U.S. Airways
America West Airlines	National Safety Council, Interna-
Continental Airlines	tional Air Transport Section
Delta Air Lines	

SPEAKING NOTES

Bill Jeffery, L.L.B., National Coordinator

Centre for Science in the Public Interest at Health Canada's
Media briefing on the final mandatory nutrition labelling rules

Room 0115C, Lower Level
Brooke-Claxton Building
Tunney's Pasture
Ottawa, Ontario

January 2, 2003

Good afternoon.

I am pleased to participate in Health Canada's landmark announcement on behalf of the Centre for Science in the Public Interest.

CSPI has advocated mandatory nutrition labelling for nearly six years with the assistance of the Alliance for Food Label Reform—a coalition of nonprofit groups representing two million Canadian consumers, scientists, and health professionals.

The new nutrition labels will help Canadians reduce their risk of heart disease, cancer, and diabetes by

- helping consumers select more nutritious foods and

- encouraging manufacturers to improve the nutritional quality of their products.

Agriculture and Agri-food Canada estimates that the new labels will save Canadians more than $5 billion over the next two decades as a result of reduced health-care costs and improved productivity.

Mandatory labelling rules will ensure that nutrition information

- appears on practically all foods,

- is displayed in a format that is easy to read and interpret, and

- discloses amounts of most nutrients that are important to public health.

I do not want to detract from our strong support for these new rules, but I would be remiss if I did not identify areas for future improvement:

- Mandatory nutrition labelling should apply to all fresh meat, poultry and seafood, not just ground and prepared meats.

- Health marketing claims should not be permitted on foods like whole (3.25%) milk or high-fat cheeses—which, though calcium-rich, are high in saturated fat. These types of foods may decrease the risk of one disease (like osteoporosis), but increase the risk of another (like heart disease).

As the Romanow Commission report stressed—

- all levels of government now need to direct their attention and energies to additional public policy improvements that can enhance public health by promoting improved nutrition and physical activity.

Today's announcement is an excellent first step.

Thank-you.

HORMEL FOODS CORPORATE PROFILE

Hormel Foods Corporation is a multinational manufacturer and marketer of consumer-branded meat and food products, many of which are among the best known and trusted in the food industry. The company enjoys a strong reputation among consumers, retail grocers, and foodservice and industrial customers for products highly regarded for quality, taste, nutrition, convenience, and value.

Products manufactured by the corporation include hams, bacon, sausages, franks, canned luncheon meats, stews, chilies, hash, meat spreads, shelf-stable microwaveable entrees, salsas and frozen processed foods. These selections are sold to retail, foodservice and wholesale operations under many well-established trademarks that include ALWAYS TENDER, BLACK LABEL, CARAPELLI, CURE 81, CUREMASTER, DI LUSSO, DINTY MOORE, DUBUQUE, FAST 'N EASY, HERDEZ, HOMELAND, HORMEL, HOUSE OF TSANG, JENNIE-O TURKEY STORE®, KID'S KITCHEN, LAYOUT, LIGHT & LEAN, LITTLE SIZZLERS, MARY KITCHEN, OLD SMOKEHOUSE, PATAK'S, PELOPONNESE, RANGE BRAND, ROSA GRANDE, SANDWICH MAKER, SPAM, and WRANGLERS.

Hormel Foods sells products in all 50 states through a direct sales force assigned to offices in major cities throughout the United States. Their efforts are supported by sales brokers and distributors.

The headquarters for Hormel Foods is in Austin, Minnesota, along with its research and development division and flagship plant. Company facilities that manufacture meat and food products are located in Algona, Knoxville, and Osceola, Iowa; Atlanta, Georgia; Aurora and Rochelle, Illinois; Beloit, Wisconsin; Fremont, Nebraska; Stockton, California; and Wichita, Kansas. Custom manufacturing of selected Hormel Foods products is performed by various companies that adhere to stringent corporate guidelines and quality standards.

The Fremont plant also has a pork slaughtering operation that provides the company with additional raw material through its pork slaughtering operation. Jennie-O Turkey Store, a wholly owned subsidiary based in Willmar, Minnesota, is the nation's number one producer of whole and processed turkey products sold to retail and foodservice outlets.

Another wholly owned subsidiary, Dan's Prize, Inc., headquartered in Gainesville, Georgia, operates manufacturing plants in Long Prairie and Browerville Minnesota, that produces roast beef, corned beef, prime rib, pastrami, and other cooked meats for foodservice and deli operators.

Hormel Foods International Corporation (HFIC), a wholly owned subsidiary in Austin, has established numerous joint venture and license agreements internationally that include Australia, China, Denmark, England, Japan, Korea, Mexico, Panama, the Philippines, Spain, and other nations. HFIC exports products to more than forty countries.

With more than 15,600 employees, Hormel Foods is owned by approximately 11,200 shareholders of record. Hormel Foods common stock is listed on the New York Stock Exchange under the ticker symbol HRL.

Sally Robins

IT'S SALLY WHO 'SAVES THE DAY'

Sally Robins loves her job, mostly because it gives her time to spend with her family. On the other hand, the job enables her to help other families get settled or set new directions. Either way, she gets to become part of other people's lives, which means a lot to this successful real estate agent.

Because she's good with detail, task-oriented, and highly organized, she finds it easy to come to the rescue of others. The bottom starts falling out of a deal and it's Sally who saves the day.

Five-foot six, about 135 pounds, and strawberry blonde, Sally enjoys getting the best out of every day, usually by doing something for someone else. She's a talented arbiter. The goal is always to help each side win something and feel good about the negotiation.

At age forty-two, with eight years of experience, Sally has become the most successful agent in the county. In some ways she's like a walking computer holding an enormous amount of detail upstairs. Imagine dealing daily with buyers, sellers, appraisers, bankers, inspectors, and, of course, lawyers.

She has a special sense about the business. She seems to know how a house will show and what people will like and dislike.

More recently, Sally has wanted to have more to do with the big picture. She's been thinking about giving back to the community that has enabled her to become so successful. That has caused her to look ahead much more than ever before. She is getting more philosophical in her outlook.

Her boss, Arnold Hut, says that she's a sensitive young woman. But, he quickly adds that a little praise and expression of appreciation are all that's required to keep her spirits up and coming to the rescue for others.

sample 7.40   progress report

ALCOA ACTS ON CLIMATE CHANGE ISSUE

Based on available evidence, Alcoa has concluded that greenhouse gas emissions from human activities affect climate. The company also recognizes that the risk of significant climate change is an issue of vital importance that requires action.

Alcoa has committed to a 25% reduction in its worldwide directly controlled greenhouse gas emissions by 2010 from a base year of 1990. A 50% reduction by 2010 may also be possible if major technological improvements, such as inert anode technology, prove successful.

In 2003, Alcoa achieved the 25% reduction and is now working to maintain that reduction as the company expands. In addition, Alcoa adopted a specific goal to reduce perfluorinated carbon (PFC) emissions 27% by 2005 from the levels achieved in 2000. The implementation, in 2004, of a more comprehensive system to manage Alcoa's greenhouse gas emissions on a worldwide basis will further advance Alcoa's greenhouse gas measurement and reporting capabilities and drive continued reductions.

Alcoa remains committed to improving energy efficiency in all operations through appropriate combinations of best practice technologies to further reduce greenhouse gas emissions. Through the Alcoa Energy Efficiency Network, the company has identified significant energy savings opportunities (currently more than US$59 million) and has captured over US$16 million per year in these energy savings to date. More than US$50 million in annual energy cost reductions are expected by 2007 due to efficiency upgrades.

Alcoa's commitment to help customers be successful within their markets promotes the development and use of transportation products that will contribute to substantial life-cycle greenhouse gas reductions and an increase in the use of recycled metal. For example, Alcoa is working with its aerospace customers to develop new technologies and integrated solutions that are focused on making aircraft more efficient, reliable, and cost-effective to operate over the increasingly extended life cycle of an aircraft. The capabilities Alcoa is developing continue to reduce the cost and weight of airframe structures *and* deliver increased engine efficiencies—key requirements to delivering the next generation commercial and military aircraft.

In ground transportation, Alcoa's unique ability to integrate materials, structural engineering, and advanced manufacturing techniques helps manufacturers design and build vehicles that deliver improved performance, safety, fuel efficiency, and environmental performance. In terms of greenhouse emissions, a kilogram (2.2 pounds) of aluminum used in a typical automobile will reduce the greenhouse gas generation by that car over its lifetime by 20 kilograms (44 pounds) more than the greenhouse gases that were produced in the manufacture of the aluminum and the aluminum parts used in the car. Greenhouse gas savings in excess of 40 kilograms (88 pounds) can be achieved in trucks and up to 200 kilograms (440 pounds) in trains by the use of a kilogram of aluminum.[1]

Alcoa also participates in a range of voluntary programs with governments around the world to abate greenhouse gas emissions. The programs include the Voluntary Aluminum Industrial Partnership (VAIP) with the U.S. Environmental Protection Agency; the U.S. Climate Leaders and Climate Vision programs; the voluntary reduction agreement with the Government of Quebec; the Greenhouse Challenge program in Australia; the World Resources Institute Green Power Market Development Program (Alcoa is a founding member); and the World Economic Forum's Global Greenhouse Gas Register.

[1] International Aluminium Institute

sample 7.41   Q & A

CENTER FOR DISEASE CONTROL

Q & A: West Nile Virus Poliomyelitis

Q. What is the "acute flaccid paralysis" that sometimes occurs with WNV infection?

A. In addition to West Nile fever, meningitis, or encephalitis, some people who become infected with WNV can develop "acute flaccid paralysis"—a sudden onset of weakness in the limbs and/or breathing muscles. In most persons, acute flaccid paralysis is due to the development of West Nile poliomyelitis—an inflammation of the spinal cord that causes a syndrome similar to that caused by the poliovirus. West Nile poliomyelitis was first widely recognized in the United States in 2002. Persons with West Nile poliomyelitis may develop sudden or rapidly progressing weakness. The weakness tends to affect one side of the body more than the other, and may involve only one limb. The weakness is generally not associated with any numbness or loss of sensation, but may be associated with severe pain. In very severe cases, the nerves going to the muscles that control breathing may be affected, resulting in rapid onset of respiratory failure. It is important to recognize that this weakness may occur in the absence of meningitis, encephalitis, or even fever or headache—there may be few other clues that the weakness is due to WNV infection.

Q. How often does West Nile poliomyelitis occur?

A. We don't know for sure how often West Nile poliomyelitis occurs, but it does occur less frequently than meningitis or encephalitis. Scientists are continuing to monitor persons with West Nile poliomyelitis to get a better understanding of how often, and in whom, it occurs.

Q. Are there other types of weakness or "acute flaccid paralysis" caused by WNV infection?

A. The vast majority of persons with WNV "acute flaccid paralysis" suffer from West Nile poliomyelitis (an inflammation of the spinal cord). Some persons with WNV infection may instead develop an illness similar to Guillain-Barré syndrome, which is a disease of the peripheral nerves and not the spinal cord. Weakness of the facial muscles may also develop in persons with WNV infection. While many persons with WNV infection experience fatigue and feel weak all over, this is not the same as "acute flaccid paralysis".

Q. Who tends to be affected by West Nile poliomyelitis?

A. People of any age can be affected by West Nile poliomyelitis. While persons over the age of 65 are at highest risk for all forms of WNV neuroinvasive disease, including poliomyelitis, persons of younger age groups (e.g., in their 30's and 40's) can also develop West Nile poliomyelitis. West Nile poliomyelitis may affect people who are otherwise healthy and without prior medical conditions.

Q. What is the likelihood that people who experience weakness due to West Nile poliomyelitis will recover?

A. It is not yet clear the extent to which people who develop weakness due to West Nile poliomyelitis will recover. Some people do recover completely, others recover partially, and there are still others who have not shown significant recovery in over one year. Researchers continue to monitor patients who have been affected in order to better understand the long-term outcome of West Nile poliomyelitis and to determine whether there are any treatments that are beneficial.

sample 7.42   remarks in handout form

REMARKS by Director of Central Intelligence George J. Tenet to Employees of the Central Intelligence Agency and the U.S. Intelligence Community

For the past nine years, I have been privileged to be part of a great American family—the family of American Intelligence. I have lived in the heart of the CIA family. In that long and eventful time, we have shared moments of success and disappointment, of happiness and sorrow.

Today, I share with you news that I gave the President last evening. I have decided to step down as Director of Central Intelligence, effective July 11th, the seventh anniversary of my being sworn in as DCI.

I did not make this decision quickly or easily. But I know in my heart that the time is right to move on to the next phase of our lives.

In an organization as vital as this one there is never a good time to leave. There will always be critical work to be done, threats to be dealt with, and challenges that demand every ounce of energy that a DCI can muster.

We have thrown our hearts into rebuilding our Intelligence Community and I have been richly rewarded with the gratification of working with the finest group of men and women our nation can produce.

I want to say a word of special thanks to President Bush. On entering office he immediately recognized the importance of rebuilding our intelligence capabilities. He spends time with us almost every day. He has shown great care for our officers. He is a great champion for the men and women of US Intelligence and a constant source of support.

It has been an honor for me to serve as his Director of Central Intelligence.

And I am especially proud of the leadership team that we have assembled in the Intelligence Community and which will continue fighting the good fight long after I have taken my leave.

I want to thank Mike Hayden, and Jim Clapper, Jake Jacoby, Pete Teets, John Russack and Tom Fingar for their friendship and support.

As I look back on how the Intelligence Community has evolved over the past decade, there is much to be proud of.

First as Deputy Director of Central Intelligence, and then as Director, I have had the chance to be part of a massive transformation of our intelligence capabilities. That revolution may not make headlines, but it will continue to benefit our country for years to come.

American Intelligence has, after the drought of the post-Cold War years, begun to receive the investments—in people and dollars and attention—that we need to meet the security challenges of a new century and a new world.

You, the men and women of American Intelligence, have put those investments to powerful use. And I believe the American people will continue to demand that this great community of patriots receive the funding and support that you so richly deserve.

At CIA, we have made good progress in rebuilding the Clandestine Service. We have expanded and empowered our corps of analysts. We have restructured and streamlined our support operations. We have developed and acquired the technologies on which intelligence and espionage depend. With new schools and training facilities, we have sharpened instruction for each of our core professions. We are recruiting the finest men and women in our history in record numbers.

These initiatives—and I can talk of only a few—complement those of other intelligence agencies, and our enduring efforts to build what we call ourselves, what I believe us to be: a true community, working more closely than ever with our partners in the military and in law enforcement, and overseas.

We have done these things together—not out of some bureaucratic imperative, but to be better at our mission of protecting American families and the freedoms that make America worth protecting.

For many years now, we have been at war with a deadly threat to the United States and its values: the threat of terrorism. Like other wars, it has been a struggle of battles won and, tragically, battles lost. You have acted with focus and courage through it all, before and after 9/11.

What you have achieved in this fight against a clever, fanatical enemy, around the world—the cells destroyed, the conspiracies defeated, the innocent lives saved—will for most Americans be forever unknown and uncounted. But for those privileged to observe these often hidden successes, they will be an unforgettable testament to your dedication and your valor.

On other issues, too, you have done magnificent work. Outstanding support to American forces—not only in Iraq and Afghanistan, but around the world. Remarkable successes against weapons proliferators and drug traffickers. Unique insights into the full range of dangers and opportunities that face the United States beyond its borders.

In short: each day, here and abroad, from diverse backgrounds, with varied skills, you come together for a single purpose: to give our country an essential advantage—in its understanding of the conditions in the world, and in its ability to change those conditions for the better.

To be sure, there is much yet to do. But there is a strong foundation of talents and resources on which to build.

This I say with exceptional pride: The Central Intelligence Agency and the American Intelligence Community are stronger now than they were when I became DCI seven years ago, and they will be stronger tomorrow than they are today.

That is not my legacy. It is yours.

You have done the hard work, turning new ideas into actions, and new recruits into seasoned officers. You have taken bold risks analytically, operationally, and with powerful technology.

As I often tell younger and older officers—we have put this Agency and our Community on an irreversible course. Directors are stewards of a great institution for very limited periods of time. You are the owners of the institution and in your hands we have placed enormous confidence and trust. I want you to always believe in yourselves and the power that you have—each and every one of you—to ensure that we stay on course—ensure that our families are taken care of—young officers are nourished—and our mission come first always.

Our record is not without flaws. The world of Intelligence is a uniquely human endeavor and as in all human endeavors we all understand the need to always do better. We are not perfect but one of our best kept secrets is that we are very, very, very good.

Whatever our shortcomings, the American people know that we constantly evaluate our performance, always strive to do better, and always tell the truth. These are our values as professional intelligence officers. We get up every day with only one purpose—to protect this country and its families. And I believe to the depth of my soul that Americans are proud of each and every one of you. They have said thank you to me in Peoria, Illinois, in Norman, Oklahoma, in College Station, Texas, in Rochester, New York—everywhere I have ever had a chance to speak about speak about the wonderful men and women that work here.

When I tell people being Director of Central Intelligence is the best job in government—and the best job I will ever have—I say it because of you. Because of your passion, your creativity, your spirit and everything you do every day in taking risks and meeting perils around the world.

Here at CIA, I have had the greatest of colleagues, starting with John McLaughlin—a man of magical warmth, wit—you know his nickname is Merlin—wisdom, and decency, the finest deputy and friend I could ever have and he will be a great acting director.

This is the most difficult decision I have ever had to make. And while Washington and the media will put many different faces on the decision—it was a personal decision—and had only one basis in fact—the well being of my wonderful family. Nothing more and nothing less.

Nine years ago when I became the deputy director, a wonderful young man sitting in the front row was in the second grade. He came right up to my belt—I just saw a picture of the day Judge Freeh swore me in—and he's grown up to be . . .

Anyway, the point is, John Michael is going to be a senior next year. I'm going to be a senior with him in high school.

We're going to go to class together. We're going to party together. I'm going to learn how to instant message his friends—that would be an achievement!

You've just been a great son, and I'm now going to be a great dad. Thank God you took like your mother. You're damned good looking.

The most important woman in my life, who I refer to as the home minister . . . look, if I could tell you the number of times I get an elbow in the middle of the night about what I've forgot to do for families at the CIA and our spouses and for our kids . . . honey, you'll be the best first lady this institution has ever had, and I love you. You are terrific.

You have all given us so much warmth, so much support and encouragement. The most difficult part of this decision was knowing that I would not be here with you every day—in our offices, the cafeteria, conference rooms or the gym—but I do hope I have earned a lifetime membership.

It is difficult in knowing that I will not be as directly connected to the thousands of men and women overseas who along with their families sacrifice so much to protect our country.

But there is also great joy in knowing that I will never be far away in heart and spirit from all of you. You will have no greater advocate wherever I may be for you and your families.

So, I wanted to see you all today—to tell you personally about all of this. Fully recognizing that we will have more time over the next few weeks to be together in your workspaces so that we can thank you for what you have done for us.

And so, as I tell you about my plans to depart—with sadness, but with my head held very, very high, as yours should always be because what you do is critical to everything our nation stands for—its goodness, its decency and its courage.

I want to thank you for the support you have given me and my family. For being colleagues and friends. You will always be in our thoughts and prayers. It has been an honor for us—for Stephanie, for John Michael—to be by your side.

It has been the greatest privilege of my life to be your Director.

May God always bless you and bless your families.

As Dick Helms used to say, let's get on with it and get back to work.

sample 7.43   remarks in speaker's format

Some of you may be environmentalists who are actively involved and emotionally committed to the protection of the Arctic National Wildlife Refuge.

Some of you may be against oil drilling in the refuge, but do not feel driven to action.

Some of you may be industrialists who support oil drilling in the Arctic, while some of you may not be aware of the issue at all.

This morning, I am going to talk about the Arctic National Wildlife Refuge, and why allowing oil exploration and development in its coastal plain would cause irreversible ruin to one of this country's most astounding wildernesses.

I will highlight the attributes that make the refuge so rare and incredible, the reasons why it is worth saving, and the ways in which that should be done.

By experiencing the environmental wonders that exist in Alaska's arctic, you will be committed to preserving and protecting the pristine wilderness.

What are the environmental wonders in Alaska's arctic that make it so special and unique?

One thing that makes the Arctic Refuge so incredible is the dynamic spectrum of ecosystems that converge there to form the most complex, diverse refuge in North America.

U.S. SURGEON GENERAL: RESEARCH CONCLUSIONS

Scientists have identified a number of personal characteristics and environmental conditions that put children and adolescents at risk of violent behavior and some that seem to protect them from the effects of risk. These risk and protective factors can be found in every area of life, they exert different effects at different stages of development, they tend to appear in clusters, and they appear to gain strength in numbers. The public health approach to youth violence involves identifying risk and protective factors, determining when in the life course they typically come into play, designing preventive programs that can be put in place at just the right time to be most effective, and making the public aware of these findings.

Many years of research have yielded valuable insights into the risk factors involved in the onset and developmental course of violence. Less work has been done on protective factors, but that situation is changing. Some basic principles have emerged from these studies:

- Risk and protective factors exist in every area of life—individual, family, school, peer group, and community. Individual characteristics interact in complex ways with a child's or adolescent's environment to produce violent behavior.

- Risk and protective factors vary in predictive power depending on when in the course of human development they occur. As children move from infancy to early adulthood, some risk factors will become more important and others less important. Substance use, for example, is a far more powerful risk factor at age 9 than it is at age 14.

- Risk factors do not operate in isolation—the more risk factors a child or young person is exposed to, the greater the likelihood that he or she will become violent. Risk factors can be buffered by protective factors, however. An adolescent with an intolerant attitude toward violence is unlikely to engage in violence, even if he or she is associating with delinquent peers, a major risk factor for violence at that age.

- Risk factors increase the likelihood that a young person will become violent, but they may not actually cause a young person to become violent. Scientists view them as reliable predictors or even as probable causes of youth violence. They are useful for identifying vulnerable populations that may be amenable to intervention efforts.

- Risk markers such as race or ethnicity are frequently confused with risk factors; risk markers have no causal relation to violence.

- No single risk factor or combination of factors can predict violence with unerring accuracy. Few young people exposed to a single risk factor will become involved in violent behavior; similarly, most young people exposed to multiple risks will not become violent. By the same token, protective factors cannot guarantee that a child exposed to risk will not become violent.

- Researchers have identified at least two onset trajectories for youth violence: a childhood trajectory that begins before puberty and an adolescent one that begins after puberty. Violence peaks during the second decade of life. The small group of offenders who began their violent behavior in childhood commits more violent offenses, and the larger group of adolescent offenders begins to become involved in violence.

- Early risk factors for violence in adolescence include involvement in serious (but not necessarily violent) criminal acts and substance use before puberty, being male, aggressiveness, low family socioeconomic status/poverty, and antisocial parents. All of these early risks stem from a child's individual characteristics and interaction with his or her family. The influence of family is largely supplanted in adolescence by peer influences; thus, risk factors with the largest predictive effects in adolescence include weak social ties to conventional peers, ties to antisocial or delinquent peers, and belonging to a gang. Committing serious (but not necessarily violent) criminal offenses is also an important risk factor in adolescence. Drug selling is a risk factor, but its effect size has not been established.

- Identifying and understanding how protective factors operate is potentially as important to preventing and stopping violence as identifying and understanding risk factors. Several protective factors have been proposed, but to date only two have been found to buffer the risk of violence—an intolerant attitude toward deviance and commitment to school. Protective factors warrant more research attention.

- Violence prevention and intervention efforts hinge on identifying risk and protective factors and determining when in the course of development they emerge. More research in these areas is needed, particularly concerning why violence stops or continues in childhood and adolescence. Nonetheless, the research carried out to date provides a solid foundation for programs aimed at reducing risk factors and promoting protective ones—and thereby preventing violence, the subject of Chapter 5.

STATEMENT: SUCCESSES OF AND CHALLENGES FACING U.S. PUBLIC DIPLOMACY

Tré Evers, Commissioner, United States Advisory Commission on Public Diplomacy

Statement before the House Committee on Government Reform Subcommittee on National Security, Emerging Threats and International Relations
Washington, DC
August 23, 2004

Chairman Shays and distinguished members of this subcommittee: I want to thank you on behalf of our Chairman Barbara Barrett and the five other members of the bipartisan U.S. Advisory Commission on Public Diplomacy for this opportunity to share my thoughts on the successes achieved by and the challenges facing U.S. public diplomacy.

The members of my commission are currently preparing the final version of our annual report for its release on September 28th. The report reviews areas of public diplomacy previously identified as challenges, recent progress, and areas that still need to be addressed. Today, I hope to present some of these challenges and advances and address the recommendations presented in the 9/11 Commission report. Specifically, I will focus on five areas: broadcasting, exchanges and libraries, international youth opportunity fund, coordination of America's message, and how to measure success.

Broadcasting

The 9/11 Commission report made the following recommendation on international broadcasting: "Recognizing that Arab and Muslim audiences rely on satellite television and radio, the government has begun some promising initiatives in television and radio broadcasting to the Arab world, Iran, and Afghanistan. These efforts are beginning to reach large audiences. The Broadcasting Board of Governors has asked for much larger resources. It should get them."

Bringing accurate and objective news and information to audiences in the Middle East is vital to counter myths about the United States and provide alternatives to Islamic extremism in the region. The U.S. held no effective presence in Middle Eastern media until recently. Broadcasting in the region was largely unprofitable for the private sector and undervalued by government agencies. Thus, media organizations with attitudes unfavorable to U.S. policies largely dominated the public sphere in countries where such sentiments were already widespread.

My friend Ken Tomlinson will certainly address the important issues in international broadcasting for you. I will simply highlight a few areas where the Commission has noted progress and challenges.

Radio Sawa was launched in March 2002. Recent surveys have shown that the percentage of adults listening to Sawa on a weekly basis are: 73% in Morocco, 42% in Kuwait, 35% in UAE, 27% in Jordan, 11% in Egypt, and 41% in Qatar.[1] In addition, Alhurra, the new Middle East satellite network, is a great advancement. Despite accusations that American broadcasting in the region was unlikely to succeed, initial surveys regarding the network are promising.

Satellite broadcasting has changed the international media landscape. Satellite technology now allows broadcasters to instantly reach audiences all over the globe even in areas that lack terrestrial broadcast infrastructures. Satellite broadcasting has seen exponential growth in the Middle East. Nilesat, the most popular satellite distributor in the Middle East, doubled its household reach from 2003 to 2004. Where appropriate, these technologies should be further developed and employed.

Broadcasting English language programs establishes a mutually beneficial relationship with audiences that few other public diplomacy programs can match. Learning American English through programs like VOA's Special English builds psychological bonds and deeper cultural understanding while giving listeners tools they need to succeed in the world.

Yet these programs, despite being popular and efficient, are restricted by budget constraints. Despite increases in programming from 20 hours to 23.5 hours a week from FY2003 to FY2004, their budget increased only marginally.

Highly efficient initiatives, like Radio Sawa, Alhurra, and VOA English programs, should certainly receive adequate funding.

Exchanges and Libraries

The 9/11 Commission report has also remarked on the sad state of our exchange and library programs, noting, "The United States should rebuild the scholarship, exchange, and library programs that reach out to young people and offer them knowledge and hope."

American exchange and library programs, though they may not show results for years, are essential to fostering support for the United States. Exchanges seek to establish the trust, confidence, and international cooperation with other countries that sustain and advance the full range of American national interests. Prominent alumni of these programs, such as Tony Blair and Hamid Karzai, are a testimony to the programs' importance.

There is an increased perception that U.S. borders are no longer open to friendly students and visitors. Populations overseas believe that waiting time for visas has increased while in reality they have decreased. Last year, the wait time for students and scholars who require special clearances averaged two months. Now, 80 percent of these visas are issued within three weeks. The U.S. needs to streamline procedures while communicating the "secure borders, open doors" message.

Physical, face-to-face exchange is also conducted through five types of American information centers: American Corners, Virtual Presence Posts, Information Resource Centers, American Presence Posts, and a few remaining American Centers or Libraries.

The remaining American Centers or Libraries are slated for closure due to heightened security concerns. In Mexico City and Casablanca, these centers see tremendous success by hosting English language programs, American films and Internet access. By reaching out to non-elite youth populations, these centers have been transformed from mere libraries into truly modern day "American dialogue centers."

Physical public diplomacy outposts staffed and owned by the United States present prime targets for terrorists throughout the globe. The Pallazzo Corpi, a former American Consulate and Library in Istanbul, Turkey, located in the city center, was targeted at least six times by terrorists until it closed last year.

Newer programs—American Corners, Virtual Presence Posts, Information Resource Centers, and American Presence Posts—provide similar functions while addressing security concerns. Over the past year, the Department of State has significantly ramped up its investment in American Corners and Virtual Presence Posts. There are now 143 American Corners in Africa, South Asia, East Asia, Eastern Europe and the Middle East and plans to open another 130 in 2004.

Each of these programs is the result of entrepreneurship of different State Department offices. The e-Diplomacy office administers the Virtual Presence Posts while the bureau of International Information Programs administers American Corners. American Presence Posts are designated by individual missions and must receive approval from Congress. To direct these programs with maximum effectiveness, they should be assembled under one cohesive and comprehensive task force and cumbersome procedures such as Congressional approval should be streamlined.

International Youth Opportunity Fund

The 9/11 Commission also recommended that "The U.S. government should offer to join with other nations in generously supporting a new International Youth Opportunity Fund. Funds will be spent directly for building and operating primary and secondary schools in those Muslim states that commit to sensibly investing their own money in public education."

Education in the Middle East is a tremendous challenge. Lack of teacher training, high pupil/teacher ratio, and lack of access all contribute to the widespread illiteracy in the region. Deficiencies in skills and education can lead to large numbers of unemployed and unemployable, which, in turn, can lead to unstable situations that breed hate and terrorism.

USAID is the primary U.S. Government agency that funds schools and teacher training. Because an American presence is not welcomed or presents too great a security risk, USAID only provides educational support in Iraq, Egypt, Yemen, Morocco, and Afghanistan. The international youth opportunity fund could overcome these challenges and may well present a great opportunity for America to work with other nations to improve educational opportunities in the Middle East.

Coordination and Message

In this global, 24-hour communications environment, messages from the U.S. Government to the world are not all communicated by the State Department. Messages emanate from the White House, the Department of Defense, the CIA, the FBI, the Department of Homeland Security, and even Congress. Without co-ordination of these communications, the U.S. Government misses the magnifying effect that a unified message could have on overseas publics, or worse, shows inconsistencies that cost credibility.

No comprehensive inventory across agencies of all government public diplo-macy programs and activities has ever been conducted. The sum of the public diplomacy budgets of these various agencies is probably in the billions of dollars. Such an evaluation might show where efforts should be expanded, combined, or eliminated, particularly useful in an environment of scarce resources.

Several initiatives have attempted to better coordinate public diplomacy ef-forts. International Public Information Core Group, better known as the Fusion Team, provides information sharing capabilities for the varied government agencies involved in public diplomacy through [email subscription services] and weekly meetings. Another coordinating body, the Office of Global Communica-tions, or OGC, was established in January 2003 within the White House to coordinate strategic daily messages for distribution abroad, with the long-term goal of developing a National Communications Strategy. The OGC works with several hundred foreign journalists in Washington, providing them with access to White House events and briefings as well as interviews with the president and other top officials.

The public diplomacy Policy Coordination Committee, or PCC, was estab-lished in September of 2002 and is co-chaired by the National Security Council and the State Department. It ensures that all agencies work together to develop and disseminate America's messages across the globe. These two groups work together on strategic communications activities such as outreach to the Muslim world.

The creation of these mechanisms is not enough. They must also be more fully utilized and developed through an interagency strategic communications plan that clearly identifies messages, priorities, and target audiences.

Measurement

One of the most important recommendations from the 9/11 Commission is their observations on the need for measurement in public diplomacy. "Agencies need to be able to measure success. Targets should be specific enough so that reasonable observers—in the White House, Congress, the media, or the general public—can judge whether or not the objectives have been obtained."

Understanding audiences and their views through measurement is essential to crafting effective messages. According to the Council on Foreign Relations, the U.S. Government spends only a tiny fraction of what the private sector does on public opinion polling: $5 million compared to $6 billion.

One way to assess program effectiveness might be through an evaluation of a test region. The selected region would receive increased funding for a variety of public diplomacy programs structured around a cohesive strategy and funded through supplemental funding from Congress. Using standard polling procedures as well as qualitative analysis, public perceptions would be measured at regular intervals and at the beginning and end of the initiative. If perceptions moved in a positive trajectory, the approach could be replicated in other areas and eventually expanded globally.

Conclusion

As numerous reports, including the 9/11 report, have attested, public diplomacy needs to be a national security priority. International public opinion is influential in the success of foreign policy objectives, and adequate resource allocation for public diplomacy will determine success in the areas I've mentioned today. The Commission is pleased to see this concept being recognized and looks forward to working with the Administration and Congress toward achieving a better American dialogue with the world.

Thank you, and I am now pleased to answer any of your questions.

sample 7.46   tip sheet

Note to Editor: Please feel free to reprint the tip sheet as long as the contact information below is included.

SIX SHORTCUTS TO A SPEEDY MORNING
A Guide for Moms on the Go

1

Take 10 minutes the night before to set out what you and your children will wear. This will save a lot of arguing and stress in the morning.

2

Set out a list of school lunches at the beginning of the week. This way you won't have to think of a new creative meal each day and you will be able to do all of the grocery shopping at one time.

3

Have some sort of daily planner that you keep updated. This will help you manage your time and know exactly what needs to get done in that day.

4

Make sure to have specific places where you religiously put your most valued things such as car keys and cell phone. If you get in the habit of putting something in the same place, it is not as easy to lose.

5

Time your shower and make sure you are not spending more than 15 minuets indulging yourself. The longer you stay in, the more relaxed you get and the harder it is to get out. This slows down your morning by not giving you the motivation to get things done. Save the relaxing for the bath after work!

6

Do not press the snooze button on your alarm. Set the clock for the latest possible time you can get up and then get up on the fist ring. The longer you stay in bed the more groggy you will be for the day.

CONTACT: Sally Smith, ss@outoforbit.com, www.products.com

Index